Contents

Editor's Foreword

As an archaeologist working with the preservation of our historic monuments, I have come to the firm conclusion that one of the best methods of conservation is to awaken in people an awareness of the unique contribution that ancient sites make, enriching our landscape by their quiet presence. With that aim in mind, this series of four regional guides was conceived, covering, in turn: Dyfed; Glamorgan and Gwent; Gwynedd; and Clwyd and Powys. Each volume describes 150 well preserved monuments which are accessible to the public. The volume on Clwyd and Powys covers the area roughly equivalent to the old counties of Flint, Denbigh, and part of Merioneth (Clwyd) and Montgomery, Radnor and Brecon (Powys).

The time-span covered by the volumes is from the first appearance of early humans in the Old Stone Age to the 16th century AD. The 16th century heralded many changes which suggested it as an appropriate termination point for a guide devoted to ancient monuments rather than to townscapes and general landscapes. Speaking somewhat casually, it marked the end of serious use of the castle in Wales, the end of the monasteries and, with the Act of Union in 1536, the political merging of Wales with England.

Inevitably there are many omissions from the book, sometimes made very reluctantly. Churches in use are not included as, despite their obvious interest and appeal, they are neither ruins nor monuments, and their very number is such that they need a guide of their own. The remains of industrial sites are a particular casualty of the cut-off date, as the vast majority of the more spectacular date from later than the 15th century. There are other sites of which the very fragility of the archaeological remains, or the wildlife within them, render visits inadvisable. Yet more sites were left out because they were remote and difficult of access. The main omissions, however, were the many monuments which lie inaccessible to the public on private land, many of which are very fine. For this reason, an appendix has been added, listing well preserved sites for the majority of which special permission must be obtained before visiting.

Ancient sites are a tangible link with our past; they are our only link with the remotest past before literacy gave us a written history. And for the events of that written history, later sites are the stage, scenery and backdrop to the action that took place. To see these monuments makes our past come alive, if we can only clothe their stones and earthworks, battlemented walls and traceried windows with our imaginations. If this book helps the visitor to do this, its main objective will have been achieved.

Sian E Rees
Series Editor

How to Use the Book

The introduction to the book gives an outline of the physical characteristics of Clwyd and Powys. The main gazetteer is then ordered into period-based chapters, so that monuments of a class fall together, and each chapter is preceded by a brief description of the history and monuments of that period in Clwyd and Powys. Each site is given a number to aid its identification on the location maps.

Location

The monuments are ordered numerically in the gazetteer, and each is given the name by which it is normally known, which generally, but by no means invariably, is that found on the Ordnance Survey 1:50,000 maps. The nearest readily identifiable town or village is also given, although the access directions usually begin from larger centres. The site type, a rough indication of its date, the Ordnance Survey 1:50,000 map number and the site's six-figure national grid reference are also given. It is hoped that the directions alone will enable those without the 1:50,000 map to find the sites, but road and path signs, house names and the position of lay-bys change so rapidly that it is always safer to have the relevant map, if at all possible. The 1:250,000 Travelmaster sheet 7 is an economical alternative, although inevitably less detailed; it is also worth checking public libraries for 1:50,000 sheets.

To locate a site on an Ordnance Survey map, first get the appropriate 1:50,000 map, the number of which is given on each entry (e.g., OS 148). Then look at the grid reference for the site, which consists of two letters and six figures (e.g., SO 210783). The letters at the beginning of the reference can usually be ignored as long as the correct map is being used, as they are a large-scale reference for the appropriate 100km grid square. Then take the first three numbers, which refer to the numbers on the top or bottom of the map; the first two of these will indicate the western line of the 1km square in which the site lies. The third will measure in tenths how far eastward within that square the site lies. Repeat the procedure with the second group of three numbers, which refer to the numbers on the right or left side of the map and increase in value northwards. Although this may sound complicated, after doing a few trial searches there should be no problem with easily locating any given site.

Accessibility

A guide to the accessibility of each site is given by the following:

U Unrestricted, i.e., access at any reasonable time free of charge.

R Restricted, i.e., without full public access or limited by opening hours and/or entry charge. If this symbol is used, an explanation is usually given at the end of the access direction.

Cadw standard hours

Many monuments maintained by Cadw are unrestricted, while the opening hours of the few with admission charges do vary slightly from site to site and according to the time of year. It is safe to assume, however, that where 'Cadw standard hours' is indicated, a monument will be open from Monday to Saturday and often part of Sunday during main daylight hours, except for Christmas Eve, Christmas Day, Boxing Day and New Year's Day. Full details of opening hours may be obtained from Cadw on request.

Of the remaining three monuments with charges, two, belonging to the National Trust, are not open full-time (Chirk Castle, no. 113 and Powis Castle, no.115); full details of dates and hours may be obtained from their north Wales office or from the sites themselves. St Winifred's Well (no. 140) is open daily.

At a number of sites on private land, owners have requested that visitors should ask at the farm or make special arrangements before visiting. This is indicated in the access directions and should be respected.

Disabled visitors

An attempt has been made to estimate how accessible each monument may be for disabled visitors. The entries are rated 1 to 4, this number appearing directly after the U or R at the head of each entry.

1 Easy access for all, including wheelchairs.

2 Reasonable access for pedestrians but limited access for wheelchairs.

3 Restricted access for disabled, but view of site from road or car park.

4 Access for able-bodied only.

A few monuments tend to get covered with bracken in summer (June to October inclusive) and become difficult to appreciate. This has been indicated.

Abbreviations

These occur especially in the access directions:

BBNP	Brecon Beacons National Park
bc	uncalibrated radiocarbon date
km	kilometre
L, LHS	left, left hand side
m	metre
ml	mile
NT	National Trust
OS	Ordnance Survey
R, RHS	right, right hand side
tel	telephone
WT	The Woodland Trust

Welsh Place-Names

Any visitor to Wales will soon realise that the spelling of Welsh place-names can vary considerably, different versions of the same name being found on maps, road signs and in publications. Many Welsh place-names are compounded of two or more elements which are sometimes written as separate words and sometimes run into one. This series has attempted to use the most commonly found version of place-names, though the use of hyphens has been avoided wherever possible.

Safety

Anyone who makes periodic visits to ancient monuments will be aware of the hazards which different sorts of sites present to the unwary. Every visitor to sites in category 4 should have sensible footwear and clothing; in exposed areas, or even on country paths, sudden rain can make a walk a flounder, and mists equally suddenly can make familiar terrain look strange and baffling. A pocket compass is always a good idea. Best of all, tell someone where you are going and when you expect to return.

Ruins that are officially open to the public, however hard their proprietors try, may still be hazardous, especially for children, who should be supervised on higher areas of monuments and warned of the dangers of climbing on walls. Most monuments in categories 1, 2 and 3 are perfectly suitable for children of all ages as long as parents are aware of the hazards and avoid them. Many category 4 sites, though requiring longer walks, will also be quite suitable for older children, probably depending more on the temperament of the child than on age or physique.

Country Code

It is, of course, most important to observe the Country Code when visiting the majority of the monuments in the book, which are situated on public footpaths through private land. Keep dogs on leads, always shut gates securely and open and shut them (lifting works wonders!) rather than climbing over. Keep to paths, do not drop litter and avoid any action that could start a fire. If you keep to these rules, monuments in private hands will continue to be cherished and visitors welcomed.

Further Information and Useful Addresses

A number of the monuments described in the gazetteer are owned or maintained by Cadw: Welsh Historic Monuments, a body with the statutory responsibility for protecting, conserving and presenting the 'built heritage' of Wales on behalf of the Secretary of State. Many more of the sites listed in the book have been 'scheduled', or given statutory protection by the Secretary of State. Lists and maps of scheduled ancient monuments are produced by Cadw and a series of guidebooks provide detailed descriptions of the monuments it maintains. Further information can be obtained by contacting Cadw at: Brunel House, 2 Fitzalan Road, Cardiff CF2 1UY, tel. 01222 500200.

The Brecon Beacons National Park Authority covers not only the Beacons, but the Black Mountain to the west and the Black Mountains to the east. It maintains footpaths and works to increase public access in the area, as well as preserving its character by enforcing strict planning controls. Its management work includes the purchase of substantial areas of land. The park is also involved in the maintenance of a number of ancient monuments, either in its own right or in partnership with other bodies. It can be contacted at: 7 Glamorgan Street, Brecon LD3 7DP, tel. 01874 624437.

The National Trust has substantial holdings in areas of natural beauty, including a number of ancient monuments, which are carefully managed to preserve both their natural and cultural interest. Its major attractions in Clwyd and Powys, Chirk Castle, Powis Castle and Erddig, all lie within the area of its north Wales office, at: Trinity Square, Llandudno, Gwynedd LL30 2DE, tel. 01492 860123, but the southern part of Powys comes under the purview of their south Wales office, at: The King's Head, Bridge Street, Llandeilo, Dyfed SA19 6BB, tel. 01558 822800.

The Clwyd–Powys Archaeological Trust is the body responsible for maintaining a Sites and Monuments Record, a list of all known monuments in Clwyd and Powys. It carries out rescue excavation and survey work on sites which are threatened with development or erosion. The trust may be contacted at: 7a Church Street, Welshpool, Powys SY21 7DL, tel. 01938 553670.

The Offa's Dyke Association, based in Knighton, helps to maintain the Offa's Dyke Centre in the town and provides practical information and guides for those walking the long distance path (see Bibliography). Much of this material is available at the centre, which is also the base for the footpath officer, jointly funded by Powys County Council and the Countryside Council for Wales. The association and the footpath officer can be contacted at: The Offa's Dyke Centre, West Street, Knighton, Powys LD7 1EN, tel. 01547 528753.

The following museums have material from ancient sites in Clwyd or Powys:

National Museum & Gallery, Cathays Park, Cardiff.

Brecknock Museum, Captain's Walk, Brecon.

Llandrindod Wells Museum, Temple Street, Llandrindod Wells.

Old Market Hall, Llanidloes (enquiries to Llandrindod Wells Museum).

The Bell, Montgomery.

Powysland Museum, Canal Wharf, Welshpool.

Wrexham Maelor Heritage Centre, 47–49 King Street, Wrexham.

While all possible attempts have been made to ensure that the accessibility of monuments is as described, unforeseen circumstances can alter access quite suddenly; monuments may sometimes have to be closed for short periods for repair work, and sadly, footpaths, even well-established ones, do disappear from time to time. Discretion must therefore be exercised during visits and no liability can be accepted for errors in the information supplied.

Introduction

While the modern counties of Clwyd and Powys, covering eastern and north-eastern Wales, are a recent administrative creation, they contain within them a variety of more traditional regional identities, both geographical and political. The geographical regions range from the uplands of the Denbigh moors and the Cambrian mountains on the west to the Cheshire basin and the Severn and Wye valleys on the east and the Usk valley to the south; the political entities include the pre-1974 counties (Flint, Denbigh and part of Merioneth in Clwyd; Montgomery, Radnor and Brecon in Powys), some of which still have strong individual personalities, and reflect the identities of their predecessors, the Marcher lordships and Welsh princedoms which dominated the area during the medieval period. This combination of geographical constraints and historical influences is reflected in many aspects of the present landscape, as well as in the distribution of archaeological sites.

The Cambrian mountains, to the west, rise to heights of 500–750m, with poor acid soils and high rainfall; population is sparse today, as in much of the past. Most of the area is pasture for sheep, some of it very poor, while forestry is widespread. The few available routes westward tend to follow the main river valleys, where many of the major settlements have grown up: those along the Alwen, Dee (Llangollen, Corwen), Banwy (Llanfair Caereinion), Garno, Severn (Welshpool, Montgomery, Newtown, Llanidloes), Wye (Hay, Builth, Rhayader), Irfon and Usk (Crickhowell, Brecon) are still in use today. Also important is the northern coastal route through St Asaph, Abergele and Colwyn Bay.

The western political boundary of much of the two modern counties runs along the mountains, apart from in northern Powys, where Montgomeryshire extends westwards to the Dyfi estuary near Machynlleth. This gives the otherwise land-locked area of ancient Powys access to the sea at a point on the boundary between the heartland of medieval Gwynedd in north-west Wales and the kingdoms of the south. In southern Clwyd the Berwyn mountains, an easterly branch of the main massif, form the boundary between Clwyd and Powys.

Much of Powys is upland, the northern and central parts being built, like the Cambrian mountains, from Ordovician and Silurian shales and mudstones, dissected by the major valleys of the Severn and Wye, with their low-lying meadows. The hills, particularly in central Powys, are more gently rolling and more fertile than the mountains to the west, and enjoy a much lower rainfall. Some more easterly parts, such as the Walton basin, near New Radnor, and the Welshpool area are sufficiently dry and warm to support arable crops; these pockets of better land were clearly also prized in the past, although variations in climate and population pressure have occasionally seen more marginal areas pressed into cultivation. These eastern pockets have many similarities to neighbouring parts of England, with which they have at times shared traditions; the present boundary largely reflects political compromises made during the long and sometimes bloody history of the medieval Marches.

South of Builth, the land rises again in a series of mountain ranges, dissected by the broad valleys of the Wye and Usk, formed by the tilting of thick bands of Old Red Sandstone. This gives Mynydd Eppynt, Mynydd Ddu (the Black Mountain), the Brecon Beacons and the Black Mountains a distinctive profile with a steep scarp to the north and a gently sloping tail to the south, and means that communications through much of the area focus on the valleys, most of which run north-west to south-east. The southernmost parts of the area are of limestone, which forms the northern edge of the basin containing the south Wales coalfield.

Clwyd is a rather more complex region geologically than Powys. While to the south and west of the county, the Berwyns and the Denbigh moors are made up of the same Ordovician and Silurian shales and mudstones as the Cambrian mountains, with similar altitude and rainfall, the remainder of the county consists of rocks associated with the coal measures which attracted heavy industry to the area between Prestatyn, Wrexham and Oswestry in the 19th and early 20th centuries. The basic sequence tilts from west to east, consisting of limestones overlying the shales, with millstone grits and coal measures in turn above them, and Triassic New Red Sandstone at the top. Erosion over millions of years, including grinding down by ice during the Ice Ages, now means that the respective layers come to the surface roughly in order from west to east, each running north–south, although faulting to the east of the Vale of Clwyd, where the modern towns of Rhuddlan, St Asaph, Denbigh and Ruthin lie, breaks this sequence into two. The bottom of the Vale preserves the more fertile upper layers of New Red Sandstone, which otherwise only come to prominence on the east of the county where it adjoins the Cheshire plain, while on its upthrust eastern side, the underlying shales are once again visible forming the ridge of the Clwydian Hills, the western edge of the main sequence.

The geology of Clwyd and Powys provides a number of different building stones. While the Ordovician and Silurian shales and mudstones flake if exposed to frost, surviving well only if rendered, the limestones of Clwyd and the Old Red Sandstone and limestone of southern Powys are much more durable, and the millstone grit of Clwyd is also used. Many eastern areas shared a tradition of timber building with their English neighbours; bricks, for which Wrexham became a notable manufacturing centre, gradually replaced wattled panels between the main timbers, and ultimately took over as the chief building material in these areas, particularly in the 19th and early 20th centuries. Halkyn Mountain near Flint and the Plynlimon area north-west of Llanidloes are important sources of metal ores, chiefly lead, but also copper. While most workings date from the 17th to the early 20th century, Roman lead production in Flintshire is well-attested, and mining in both areas probably originated as early as the Bronze Age.

Farming throughout Clwyd and Powys is predominantly pastoral, concentrating perforce on sheep in the uplands, with only very limited pockets of arable. Wherever the climate allows (and local climatic conditions can vary from valley to valley in mid-Wales), cattle are also bred, for both milk and meat, and are still taken into England to fatten, although nowadays they go by lorry rather than on foot with the drovers, as in the medieval and early modern period. Many of the drovers' roads, away from the main routes, still survive to provide good hill walking.

While this book looks at individual sites, it is important to remember that these sites formed part of past landscapes. Landscapes of the recent past can often be reconstructed, using evidence from field boundaries and old maps; further back, environmental evidence can at least give us an idea of what sort of plants and animals were in an area. Some parts of the uplands preserve patterns of prehistoric or medieval ritual monuments or settlement which are probably virtually undisturbed, apart from the passage of time, while in the lowlands, and particularly in the industrial belt of north-eastern Clwyd, even relatively recent features have lost their contemporary landscape context. Most of the gazetteer entries describe the siting of the feature discussed, in the hope that this may help you to imagine it in its original place in the landscape.

1
The Story Begins

The earliest period of prehistory is the Palaeolithic, or Old Stone Age. The Lower, Middle and Upper Palaeolithic between them cover the two to three million years of human development from the first tool-making hominids in Africa to the sophisticated hunters of the last Ice Age. Throughout this period the main tools we find are of stone, although other materials, which do not survive so well, such as bone, antler and wood, would also have been used.

The first evidence for humans in Wales, at Pontnewydd Cave (no. 1), dates back to about 220,000 BC, late in the Lower Palaeolithic. The people here were of Early Neanderthal type; already highly evolved, although shorter and stockier than ourselves and with rather larger faces. They would have lived by hunting, using spears and traps, and by gathering plant material (roots, nuts and berries). They made a variety of stone tools, including hand-axes (pear-shaped stones sharpened around the edges), scrapers, knives and points, using the effective, if rather uneconomical, 'Levallois' technique to produce flake tools with a single blow from a carefully prepared core. They probably lived in small groups, following the movement of game, sometimes over long distances. Evidence from Europe, the Middle East and Asia shows that later Neanderthals could take pains to bury their dead, suggesting spiritual beliefs; they probably had some means of communication, although probably not a developed language in the fully modern sense. They lived in and at the mouth of caves, and also built shelters in the open.

The Ice Ages were not entirely cold, but ebbed and flowed over thousands of years, with ice covering much of Wales and England at times during the main cold phases (glacials) and receding to leave a climate much like today's, if not warmer, for relatively short intervals in between (interglacials). Even within the glacials, periods of milder climate known as interstadials could occur. Indeed, it is only some 17,000 years or so since the ice last began to recede, and it is a matter of lively debate among scientists when it will next advance.

The amount of water frozen in the large ice sheets during the main glacials would have left the sea level much lower than it is today. South-east England was joined to the Continent, and much of the Irish Sea was dry land. The land around the ice sheets would have been tundra, bare grassy plains with relatively few larger plants, supporting mammoth, bison, woolly rhinoceros and hyaena. In the warmer periods, woodland probably developed, and animals such as wolf, bear, narrow-

Reconstruction drawing of a settlement, 70,000 BC

nosed rhinoceros, large cats, deer and hippopotamus flourished. Animal bones found in caves can help to date the different layers to warmer or colder periods, while the application of scientific methods to stalagmite and burnt flint can provide rough calendar dates.

The scouring action of later ice sheets has left only chance survivals from the earlier periods, and humans were probably present in Wales only very occasionally during the Ice Ages. The Neanderthals seem to have died out by about 26,000 BC, during the last glaciation, to be replaced by fully modern humans with a more advanced stone and bone tool technology, generally classed as Upper Palaeolithic.

These people are known from a number of sites in Wales, chiefly in the south, including Hoyle's Mouth and Paviland Cave. Cae Gwyn and Ffynnon Beuno (no. 2) preserve traces of their tools, although these were found in much later debris flows. They worked stone (chiefly flint or chert) to produce blades (long flakes with a sharp edge on both sides) from a roughly cylindrical core, which could be worked until it became too small to manage, producing a great many blades very economically. Blades themselves were highly versatile, and could be trimmed and shaped into a large number of different types of tool, some of which were probably hafted. These people were responsible for the great cave art of France and Spain, and clearly had complex religious and social practices.

The end of the last Ice Age brought great changes. Maturing soils allowed the growth of birch, pine and hazel forests, probably reflected in the pronounced change in tool types about 10,000 BC, which ushered in the Mesolithic, or Middle

Stone Age. The stone tools became much smaller ('microlithic'), and many of them were clearly intended to be hafted in other materials, to make harpoons or barbed arrows; the bow and arrow seems to have come into use at this time. Axes designed for cutting down trees also appear, while traditional tools such as knives and scrapers continue in use.

The marshlands of the present Irish Sea and North Sea would have been rich sources of wildfowl, fish and shellfish before their final inundation about 6000 BC, while inland, cattle, red and roe deer and wild pig would gradually have moved into the developing forests; these changed to oak, ash, elm, lime and alder, while the high uplands became moorland. People were probably beginning to 'manage' the wild animals to ensure their continuity and their availability as food; Mesolithic woodland clearance by burning has been recorded in the Berwyns. The population in Wales seems to have risen considerably, especially in the warmer areas around the southern coasts. The people were still partially nomadic, perhaps moving seasonally, and their shelters remained fairly flimsy.

Most evidence for these Mesolithic hunter-gatherers has been found by accident during excavations of sites of other periods. Rhuddlan (no. 99), in the north of Clwyd, and Gwernvale (no. 8), in the south of Powys, have produced evidence of settlement in the form of stone tools, but traces from this period are widespread throughout the region.

The next major change, to the Neolithic or New Stone Age, came with the arrival of agriculture in the 4th millennium BC. The extent of immigration is uncertain, but many of the crops (emmer and einkorn wheat, and barley) and domestic animals (cattle, sheep and goats) which appear at this time came ultimately from the Middle East and must have been imported into Britain; pottery manufacture too was introduced. The more settled agricultural lifestyle brought with it a population explosion with important social consequences, since additional children were easily fed and could share the work, and would later move on beyond the settled belt to found new farms of their own.

The tools available for cultivation were generally simple, which probably confined grain cultivation to lighter fertile soils in coastal areas and on valley sides. In Clwyd and Powys, few settlement sites are known; these, like the Mesolithic sites, left little trace above ground and tend to be chance discoveries, such as the possible isolated house found during excavation of the Iron Age hillfort of Moel y Gaer, Rhosesmor (no. 48). In contrast, the more readily visible ritual monuments of the period, together with scattered finds, may give more clues to the main areas of settlement.

The ritual monuments seem to fall into two phases, running from 4300 BC–3200 BC and from 3200 BC–2400 BC respectively. In the earlier Neolithic, the characteristic monument was the chambered long cairn, although these are very unevenly distributed in Clwyd and Powys, with only two in the north, Tyddyn Bleiddyn

Reconstruction drawing of an early farming settlement

(SJ 007724), near Bontnewydd and Tan y Coed (appendix), in the upper Dee valley. By contrast in southern Powys there is a concentration around the Black Mountains east of Brecon, including nos 5, 6, 7 and 8 (see also appendix). These are of the 'Severn-Cotswold' type, found also in south-west England, consisting of a long wedge-shaped mound with one or more burial chambers built into the broad end and/or sides; bodies appear to have been placed into these when already partly decayed, and the insertion of new burials resulted in the apparently unceremonious sweeping aside of earlier remains. Many of these sites were apparently finally sealed in the period around 3200 BC. Possible chambered round cairns, similar to Irish examples dating to the later Neolithic, are found at Branas Uchaf in the north (no. 4) and Carn Goch, Llangattock in the south (no. 9). Not all the known areas of occupation have chambered cairns nearby, and it is possible that other types of burial monument, possibly of wood, not now visible above ground, were in use elsewhere.

Later in the Neolithic, the growing population started to move into the uplands; the variety of ritual monuments increases greatly. After about 3200 BC, summers were warmer and winters more severe than today; the weather was becoming drier but cooler. The highest concentration of Neolithic settlement (perhaps reflecting the fieldwork earlier this century of Ellis Davies, based at Whitford!) appears to be in north-east Clwyd, around the great artificial mound of The Gop Cairn (no. 3); another focus in the Severn valley saw settlements at The Breiddin (no. 58) and Ffridd Faldwyn (no. 59), while important, if relatively late, complexes of ritual monuments lay between Llanymynech Hill and Four Crosses, and south of Welshpool. Further south, there are tantalising suggestions in the cropmarks of the Walton basin, and in finds from the Wye valley around Hay, while occupation probably continued in the Black Mountains even after the long cairns went out of use.

The Severn valley and Walton basin cropmarks suggest a highly diverse and complex ritual life, and include pit alignments and a cursus, which probably belongs relatively late in the Neolithic, together with ring-ditches, probably the remains of Bronze Age barrows, and a pit circle, Sarn y Bryn Caled, which gave an early Bronze Age date when excavated in 1990–1. In Clwyd, some caves such as The Gop Cave were reused for burial in the later Neolithic.

The finds from the period also suggest considerable social complexity. Several faceted maceheads, bored stones cut and polished with a complex surface pattern, are known from Clwyd. They represent a considerable investment of time, effort and skill, and are probably status symbols suggesting a prosperous society which could support craft specialists. One of the most important Neolithic artefacts found throughout Britain is the polished stone axe, their workmanship again representing a considerable investment of time and energy. Suitable stone from a relatively small number of sources was traded widely, and one of the main quarries was at Graig Lwyd, Penmaenmawr, on the coast just beyond Clwyd's north-western corner. The people of northern Clwyd may have been able to profit as intermediaries in the trade of this stone, and may also have been involved in the finishing process. Further south, axes from Pembrokeshire are also known, while stone from Cwm Mawr, east of Montgomery, was used late in the period for battle-axes and axe-hammers.

It was into this populous, relatively complex society that metallurgy was introduced in the period after about 2400 BC. The changes which followed in its wake ultimately heralded the Bronze Age.

1
Pontnewydd Cave

Old Stone Age cave

220,000 BC

OS 116   SJ 015711   R3

From Denbigh, take A525 towards St Asaph. At Trefnant (3.4ml, 5.5km), take B5428 L. After 2.1ml (3.4km), take lane on R at LH bend. Park at Bontnewydd (1.6ml, 2.5km). From village, walk across bridge and up road round bend to R (prickly footpath cuts off corner). Site is above road on L c.200m from bend. View from road only, no public access

Aldhouse Green 1991

Pontnewydd Cave lies within limestone cliffs on a south-westerly facing slope high on the side of the Elwy valley. The entrance to the cave has been walled up, with a doorway which is kept locked for security reasons. Excavations by the National Museum of Wales have shown it to be a very important site, yielding both tools and human remains (teeth and bone fragments from several individuals) representing the earliest known occupation in Wales; it is, indeed, one of the three earliest finds of human remains in Britain.

The human occupation here probably belongs to the end of a warmer period during the Ice Ages, or perhaps to the beginning of the succeeding cold phase; the animal remains from the two successive layers with

Inside Pontnewydd cave during excavation

human traces, the Intermediate Complex and the Lower Breccia, suggest a difference in climate between them. The cave was apparently used intermittently by hibernating bears at the same period. These layers were dated using the known rate of radioactive decay of minerals in the covering stalagmite layer, which would have formed when water flowed through the cave again in the next warm phase.

The dramatic effects of advancing and receding ice sheets during the Ice Ages will have served to change the landscape considerably since the cave was occupied, removing other traces of human activity but, by chance, leaving Pontnewydd intact. Excavation suggests that the cliff face where the cave is situated has weathered back considerably since the period of occupation, removing the original cave mouth and the area around it, where the early people most probably camped. The archaeological remains were carried into the surviving part of the cave in mud flows, and contained no trace of either hearths or living areas. The cave itself was probably used only for storage and protection in severe weather.

Debris was found from both the maintenance and the manufacture of stone tools, including distinctive prepared 'tortoise' cores from which single-flake tools had been removed using the 'Levallois' technique; some flint suitable for working occurs naturally in the deposits underlying the occupation levels. The tools themselves included spear-points for hunting, hand-axes and Levallois flakes for cutting up the meat, and scrapers for defleshing the skins.

The human remains appear to be of early Neanderthal type; these people are found in association with stone tools of this type over most of Europe, although Pontnewydd is the most north-westerly known site of this date. It would have been well placed for hunters to watch animals in the valley below, and its south-westerly aspect would have given some protection from cold northerly and north-easterly winds, while catching the sun on fine days.

2
Cae Gwyn and Ffynnon Beuno Caves, Tremeirchion

Old Stone Age caves

36,000–16,000 BC

OS 116 SJ 085724 R3

From Denbigh, take A543/A541 towards Mold. After 4.3ml (6.9km), take B5429 L at Bodfari. After 1.9ml (3km), park on R in lay-by at Ffynnon Beuno. Take footpath signposted through garden up to lane (0.1ml, 0.2km) and continue for c.*100m; site visible from across valley only. Alternatively, turn car and drive up lane on L,* c.*0.4ml (0.6km)*

Aldhouse Green 1991

Cae Gwyn and Ffynnon Beuno Caves are situated close together in the south-facing limestone cliffs overlooking a small valley, on the east of the Vale of Clwyd. The small entrance to Cae Gwyn Cave lies high on the hillside, at the inner end of a passage which may represent a collapsed part of the cave, while the larger and more impressive entrance to Ffynnon Beuno Cave is further down the limestone cliff, below it and slightly to the east. The cave mouths have probably altered through time; parts of the interior

Cae Gwyn and Ffynnon Beuno caves

have certainly been affected by more recent mining trials, as shown by the shaft inside the corner of the fence to the east of Cae Gwyn Cave.

The two caves, although close together, do not interconnect, although the sequence of deposits in each is similar. Excavations in 1885 revealed animal bones and a few stone tools from a broad time-span, mixed together in a probable debris flow. A radiocarbon date of *c.*16,000 BC from a mammoth bone in the Ffynnon Beuno deposit suggests that the material was deposited by meltwater near the end of the last Ice Age, at or soon after this time. The earliest of the tools, an Aurignacian leaf point, dates to perhaps 36,000 BC, and the others to *c.*28,000–26,000 BC, indicating human activity somewhere nearby at these periods. A preponderance of hyaena bones from both caves, together with traces of gnawing on other bones in the deposit, suggests that they were the main occupants.

Despite the limited archaeological evidence, these caves might well have proved attractive to the human population, if only as temporary shelter. The basic way of life continued to rely on hunting and collecting, although tools and equipment, and probably social and religious practices, would have developed considerably since the period of Pontnewydd Cave (no. 1).

3
The Gop, Trelawnyd

Neolithic cairn and caves

4th–early 3rd millennium BC

OS 116 SJ 086802, SJ 086801 U4

From Rhuddlan, take A5151 through Dyserth to Trelawnyd (4.7ml, 7.6km). Turn L here towards Llanasa; parking on R after 100m. Walk up road to lane on L near RH bend; follow footpath along it and head up hill beyond stile. Caves visible just below upper boundary, beyond tank; kissing gate leads to cairn. Optional return along path through woods to E, passing small Bronze Age barrow on L at SJ 088802. At end of woods, turn R over stile, cross second stile, continue along wall to road; return to R

Boyd Dawkins 1901

The Gop caves, a short distance down the slope from the great cairn, consist of a rock shelter and cave in a low cliff face in the natural limestone. They had been completely hidden until their accidental discovery and subsequent excavation in 1886–7; the inner cave behind the western entrance was found even later. The lower layers in the rock shelter contained redeposited traces of hyaena

The Gop caves, with the cairn behind

activity from before the end of the last Ice Age, but above these a square enclosure surrounded by rubble walls had been built against the rear rock face, enclosing the remains of at least 14 people, buried at different times within the Neolithic period. To the west of this was found an area of intense burning, perhaps a hearth used in the burial ritual; burials apparently continued across this once the main chamber was full, and, later still, were cut into the debris from successive rituals on the cave floor. Six more burials, this time disturbed, were found in the inner cave.

The Gop cairn occupies a prominent hilltop with wide views in most directions except the immediate north, where another range of hills blocks the view to the sea. The second largest artificial mound in Britain, it is an oval, *c.*101m north-west to south-east by *c.*78m, built apparently of roughly piled limestone blocks, although a disturbance on the south-east has revealed traces of a kerb of drystone walling around it near its base. It is 14m high, although excavations in the centre in 1886–7, which revealed only a few bones of domestic animals and no structure, encountered natural rock 8m down. The top has been damaged by possible stone-robbing and by the excavations; its original shape is uncertain. It was used as a beacon in the 17th century.

The cairn has traditionally been regarded as Bronze Age, but it may well be Neolithic. It lies in an area with numerous Neolithic finds, including settlement sites, and may well have formed part of a sacred complex with the burials in the cave. Similar cairns of Neolithic date are known from Ireland, although they usually cover burials and none was found here, while other large mounds, notably Silbury Hill in Wessex, are also apparently Neolithic. Whatever its date, a considerable concentration of Bronze Age barrows, some of which are visible on the ridge to the north-west, surrounds the cairn, which remains a prominent local landmark.

4
Branas Uchaf, Llandrillo

Neolithic chambered round cairn

4th–early 3rd millennium BC

OS 125 SJ 011375 R3

From Llangollen, take A5 to Corwen. Beyond village (11.3ml, 18.2km from Llangollen), take B4401 L towards Cynwyd and Llandrillo. Beyond Llandrillo turn R (5.8ml, 9.3km from Corwen), crossing bridge after short distance; at T junction beyond (0.6ml, 1km), turn L. Site visible in field on L after 0.6ml (1km); parking in lay-by. No public access

Bowen and Gresham 1967

The chambered round cairn at Branas Uchaf is one of a number in the area. It occupies a low-lying spur position in the Dee valley, fairly close to a steep wooded slope on the north-west.

The site consists of a mound of soil and stones, originally about 28m across and 1.5m high. In its centre, large slabs forming a chamber, presumably for burials, are now exposed. Two uprights from the sides of the chamber survive on the south-west, and another, leaning slightly, on the north-east. A number of other stones on the mound may include a further fallen upright. Some of the remainder have been said to form a circle around the central chamber, but this is not

Branas Uchaf chambered round cairn

convincing. Further stones from the chamber, including probably the capstone(s), must have been removed; some may have been reused nearby as gateposts. The mound may well have been dug into by early excavators, but no record of this survives.

5
Pen y wyrlod, Hay on Wye

Neolithic chambered long cairn

4th–early 3rd millennium BC

OS 161 SO 224398 U4

From B4350 in Hay, take minor road SE for Craswall and Capel y ffin; after 0.6ml (1km), turn R; after another 0.5ml (0.8km), turn R past farm. 0.9ml (1.4km) further on, site lies c.*150m along footpath signposted over stile on R from LH bend. Parking* c.*80m further on along lane*

Morgan and Marshall 1921; Corcoran 1969

This site, one of the Black Mountains group of long cairns (see also nos 6, 7 and 8), lies immediately left of the footpath, just before a field corner. It consists of an irregular turfed mound, 18m long by 9m wide, with its tail to the left (south-west), at right angles to the path, which has slightly damaged its north-east end. A well preserved four-sided chamber sits at its summit, while a further chamber, possibly part of a secondary extension, can be traced among the loose stones of the tail. A flat stone to the north-west may be the displaced capstone of one of the chambers. The site sits on the slope of the hill, overlooking lower-lying land to the west.

Excavation in 1920 showed that the mound was a stone cairn, although failing to establish its outline. Work concentrated on the main chamber, which yielded remains, mostly fragmentary, of at least a dozen different individuals of all ages and both sexes. Some pottery, including Beaker fragments, was also found, together with a pig's tooth and the bones of a dog and a small ox or pony.

The main chamber of Pen y wyrlod, Hay on Wye

6
Ty Illtud, Llanhamlach

Neolithic chambered tomb/ early Christian carvings

4th–early 3rd millennium BC/ 7th–10th century AD

OS 161 SO 098264 R4

From Brecon bypass, take A40 towards Abergavenny. After 2.1ml (3.4km), just beyond Llanhamlach, turn L for Pennorth. Park at Manest Court on RHS 0.4ml (0.6km) further on; site near top of hill opposite. Old clothing advisable, torch useful. Please ask at house before visiting

Grinsell 1981

Ty Illtud, one of the Black Mountains group of long cairns (see also nos 5, 7 and 8), sits near the summit of the hill and enjoys wonderful views westwards across the Usk valley. The single stone chamber, which retains its capstone, lies within the remains of an unexcavated mound running north–south, measuring 23m by 15.5m. The entrance of the chamber gives on to a forecourt facing north (uphill); the additional stone to the north-east of the chamber probably marks one side of this. The general plan is probably of the

Ty Illtud, looking into the forecourt

Severn-Cotswold type (cf. no. 8), with a front entrance.

Of particular interest are the unusual incised carvings on the internal faces of all the uprights of the chamber. These consist almost entirely of small crosses, some of them enclosed by diamonds and some with crosslets across the ends of their arms. On the stone at the rear of the chamber is what appears to be a lyre of Roman type. The carvings may be prehistoric, but some of the crosses are of 7th- to 10th-century AD type, which would fit well with the tradition that the site was used by the 5th–6th century St Illtud, and had become a place of pilgrimage (the name means 'Illtud's house'). There are other 'Illtud' place-names in the vicinity, although the saint, who appears to have Breton connections, and possibly studied under St Germanus in Paris, is chiefly noted for his important monastic foundation on the Glamorgan coast at Llanilltud Fawr (Llantwit Major).

The accommodation is extremely cramped today (1.6m long by 0.9m, and 0.6m high), and indeed one needs to crawl inside to see the carvings properly (a torch can be useful). The floor level has, however, risen appreciably over the years; as recently as the end of the 17th century the chamber was said to be 4ft (1.2m) high, while it was down to 3ft (0.9m) by 1809. Given a ceiling clearance of 5–6ft (1.5–1.8m), short-term usage for shelter by a hermit might have been feasible.

Further carvings on the stones outside the chamber are now very difficult to make out. On the long stone north-east of the chamber is the date mccccxi(i?) (1311 or 1312), while the stone west of the chamber entrance has the date 15110, probably meant for 1510. These may perhaps refer to boundary perambulations of one of the parishes which meet at the site. Some of the crosses may also have been carved on such occasions.

7
Mynydd Troed Long Cairn, Llangorse

Neolithic chambered long cairn

4th–early 3rd millennium BC

OS 161 SO 161284 U2

From Crickhowell, take A40 towards Brecon. After 1.8ml (2.9km), fork R on A479. 5.3ml (8.5km) further on, turn L at Waunfach Forge. Park on saddle by gates after 2.1ml (3.4km). Site is to R of RH track, c.*100m from road. Walk S from here can include nos 39 and 40 if desired (see map for these entries)*

Crampton and Webley 1966

Mynydd Troed long cairn

This long cairn, one of the Black Mountains group (see also nos 5, 6 and 8), is one of several hereabouts in upland positions. It sits just above the base of a saddle, almost alongside a well-worn ridgeway route, and commands impressive views towards the south-east and the west, including the natural Llangorse lake.

The mound is 20m long and 16m wide, although its precise edges are not clear. It is oriented north-north-east to south-south-west, up and down the local slope. Fragments of stone sticking out of the undulating surface appear to be the remains of orthostats forming chambers; it is not clear how many chambers there were, although the plan suggests two or possibly three.

Two small trenches dug in the mid-1960s, one into either side of the mound, aimed to investigate the buried soil beneath the cairn for evidence of the environment at the time of its construction. The trench on the west was not easily related to the structure of the cairn, while that on the east encountered a carefully dumped deposit of stone apparently placed against the 0.45m-high outer revetment wall of the cairn proper, suggesting that the cairn was 'decommissioned' at the end of its life, as at Gwernvale (no. 8).

Environmental evidence from beneath the dumped stone and the outer revetment indicated that the area was heathland and open woodland and the soil less acid in the Neolithic (although alkaline leaching from the limestone orthostats may have affected the results). The original turf had not been stripped before work began. Charcoal immediately beneath the cairn suggested that wood was burnt on the site before its construction; whether this represents woodland clearance or ritual is not clear. Fragments of pottery confirmed that the site was Neolithic.

There are two boundary stones, and a hole for a possible third, close to the road at the top of the saddle. One of these is inscribed 'Mrs Macnamara 1821'; there is a similarly inscribed boundary stone at the parking place described for no. 39.

8
Gwernvale Long Cairn, Crickhowell

Mesolithic to Neolithic occupation/ Neolithic chambered long cairn

12,000–3000 BC

OS 161 SO 211192 U1 Cadw

From Crickhowell, take A40 towards Brecon. Just beyond end of speed limit, park in entrance to drive on RHS. Site on verge beyond, 0.8ml (1.3km) from town centre

Britnell and Savory 1984

The Gwernvale long cairn, one of the Black Mountains group (see also nos 5, 6 and 7), lies on a low terrace on the north side of the Usk valley, a little above the valley bottom. It was excavated in 1977 and 1978, before the A40 was moved from the north to the south of the site. The surviving remains are displayed for visitors.

The excavations showed that the cairn was only the most recent in a long sequence of prehistoric activity on the site. Tools used by hunter-gatherers as early as *c.*12,000 BC were recovered, and hunters seem to have returned to the site intermittently over a long period thereafter. A relatively intensive occupation by a farming population in the earlier part of the Neolithic, radiocarbon dated to 3100 bc (*c.*3900 BC), was suggested by the remains of pits and pottery and traces of one, or possibly two, rectangular buildings.

These buildings lay on the same east–west alignment as the cairn itself, and may have immediately preceded it. Six post-holes lay in two parallel rows in the area which later became the cairn's forecourt, while to their north, later buried beneath the cairn's northern horn, trenches marked the position of walling; this part of the structure at least must have been demolished before the cairn was built.

Considerable information was obtained about the cairn itself, even though much of it had underlain the pre-1978 road. The remains

Gwernvale long cairn during excavation, with forecourt to bottom left

were totally obliterated only at the far western end, where an 18th-century hollow way preceding the old road had cut through them. Most of the cairn's outline was recovered; it was at least 45m long, and trapezoidal, narrowing symmetrically from nearly 17m wide near the forecourt to just 6.5m at its surviving western limit; analogy with similar cairns suggests that only a little of the original length had actually been lost. The forecourt was an open space *c*.5m long between two rounded 'horns'; at its inner end stood a large orthostat, giving the appearance of an entrance door, but, typically for this sub-group of the Severn-Cotswold type, this was for show only.

The chambers themselves were distributed within the fabric of the cairn, each with its own separate entrance. The nearest chamber to the entrance faced south. Unusually, this chamber was polygonal rather than rectangular, and there was a bend in its entrance passage. It was the only feature clearly visible before the recent excavations began, and had been excavated in 1804 by Colt Hoare, a prolific Wessex barrow-digger, together with three Welsh antiquarians, Fenton, Jones and Payne. None of them had ever tackled such a site previously, but, having destroyed the capstone which had thus far survived, they were destined to disappointment, recovering only a little charcoal and a few bones. These were insufficient to confirm that the chamber was used for burial, although the excavators were intrigued to note the drystone walling filling the spaces between the orthostats.

The modern excavations identified two more chambers, roughly halfway along the cairn, one on each side. These were of more conventional rectangular shape, with straight entrance passages. At the extreme western end, very ruined traces suggested a further chamber, although no orthostats survived and the complete plan could not be recovered. The first chamber and the positions of the central two are still visible. The probable heights of the chambers, and comparison with similar sites, suggest that the mound also tapered in profile, from about 2m at the eastern facade to *c*.0.5m at the western end.

Construction of the cairn probably began with the inner core, built in at least three sections from east to west. The first of these apparently extended to just short of the two central chambers, while the second included them and the third formed the remainder of the mound. A makeshift revetment wall was provided around the sides. Once the core was complete, and the capstones had been placed on the chambers, a much neater drystone outer revetment wall was provided all the way round to finish off the monument. This varied in thickness from *c*.1.5m near the western end to *c*.2m at the east, probably reflecting the height to which it rose at the respective ends; nowhere was it bonded into the core of the mound. This outer wall was apparently carried right across the entrances to the chambers, although faces were provided within it on either side of them; the portions in front of the entrances were subsequently dismantled and carefully replaced on several occasions, presumably to allow burials. This process may perhaps have expressed the transition from the world of the living to that of the dead. Puzzlingly few bones were found, however, by comparison with other similar sites, where, as each successive inhumation was added to the chambers, mourners pushed the decayed remains of previous interments out of the way, leaving a mixture of articulated and disarticulated remains.

At Gwernvale, the tomb was apparently systematically 'decommissioned' after 600–700 years, probably around 2500 bc (*c.*3200 BC), judging from the radiocarbon dates; this presumably included the removal of most of the bones. At this time too, the entrances to the chambers were crudely blocked, with additional stone heaped up in front of the openings. Shortly afterwards, probably during the same process, some parts of the outer revetment were pulled down and stone was added in front of others and in the forecourt; this must have reduced the monument to a featureless mound. Pottery from the chambers suggests that this was probably done at a time when such tombs were generally ceasing to be built; there are relatively few finds from the period during which the cairn was in use.

9
Carn Goch, Llangattock

Neolithic chambered round cairn

4th–early 3rd millennium BC

OS 161 SO 212177 U2

In Crickhowell, take A4077 towards Gilwern. After crossing bridge, turn L and immediately R into Llangattock; turn L down Park Drive after 0.3ml (0.5km). Parking on road; site in playing field to L near roadside fence

Carn Goch

Carn Goch is an irregular, slightly oval earthen mound, now turf-covered. It contains a single stone cist, the capstone of which can be seen lying on the side of the mound. Its location, on the valley bottom, is compararable with similar sites such as Branas Uchaf (no. 4). The nearby chambered tomb at Gwernvale (no. 8) occupies a similar position, although it is of a completely different type. Some commentators have argued that this mound may be Bronze Age, because of its relatively rounded shape and apparently single cist. It was excavated in 1854, when it yielded an adult male inhumation burial with traces of charcoal.

2
The First Metallurgists

Copper technology seems to have reached Britain in about 2400 BC as part of a package of new ideas visible to archaeology as a new burial tradition. These burials, rare in Wales, were of single individuals, and are usually fully articulated, unlike those of the Neolithic. For the first time, we find grave goods with the corpse, including the distinctive red pottery beakers, probably intended to look like copper, from which the Beaker period takes its name. Other items found include copper daggers, jet buttons and small rectangular plates thought to be archers' wristguards.

It is not clear how many actual immigrants came with this Beaker material, which probably reached Britain from the Rhineland. Skilled specialists at least must have been involved, possibly even at the request of existing elites. Many features of Neolithic life in Wales apparently continued; the henges and cursus remained in use, and the earlier tradition of communal burial persisted in parts of Clwyd and Gwynedd. Traces of Beaker occupation have been found under later remains at Brenig (no. 14) and in the Severn valley. The burial rite soon changed, and cremations in pots known as food vessels, under small individual mounds, dating to *c.*2100 BC, have been excavated at Trelystan, south-east of Welshpool.

During the Beaker period and the earlier part of the Bronze Age, a drier, more continental climate meant that the uplands were warmer in summer, giving a good growing season, even if the winters were somewhat harder. The population expanded up the mountains, and probably also into some of the valley bottoms which had hitherto been too wet, although some of the areas worked in the Neolithic may have become exhausted. In Clwyd, the Bronze Age population in the far north, still apparently numerous as in the Neolithic, seems to have concentrated further up the inland hills. Stock rearing may have been more important in the uplands, although pollen evidence indicates that crops were also grown.

Bronze Age settlements generally left few obvious traces and, like earlier sites, are largely recovered by accident, although their broad distribution can be deduced from casual finds and the pattern of funerary and ritual monuments. Present distribution maps, however, reflect patchy investigation and further upland fieldwork will probably reveal more widespread remains. Some of the stone hut circles and enclosures already known in the uplands may be of Bronze Age origin.

After about 1900 BC, the henges apparently went out of use. Stone circles, standing stones, stone rows and avenues, and the many variants of barrows and cairns, took their place as the main public monuments. Differing local traditions were already developing; the people of north-eastern Clwyd favoured single standing stones, while to the west and south of the county, groupings of cairns with a variety of differing characteristics, as at Brenig (no. 14) or on the Eglwysegs (no. 19) were preferred. Stone circles are rare in Clwyd, but several are known in Powys, concentrating around the Cwm Mawr stone source on the border east of Montgomery, and around the headwaters of the Usk and the Tawe (Mynydd Bach Trecastell no. 33; Nant Tarw no. 35; Cerrig Duon no. 36), while the standing stone at Cwrt y gollen (no. 43) is representative of a group of such monuments in the Usk valley.

Earthen barrows and (more usually) stone cairns, often containing a cremation in an urn, and frequently a number of secondary cremations, are almost ubiquitous, occupying, among other positions, most mid-Wales hilltops. Several examples are included in this book, but many more can be visited if you are fit and have an adequate map. Barrows and cairns probably served in various ways as territorial or direction markers as well as for burials; stone cairns may also reflect clearance for cultivation.

During this period, metal-working technology progressed, with bronze (in reality a variety of copper alloys) soon being introduced as a harder alternative to copper.

The gold-covered shoulder-cape from Mold

The early Irish flat axes, a hoard of which was found at Moel Arthur (no. 50), cast in an open mould, were superseded after about 1700 BC by palstaves, a type of tool which provided a much firmer seating for the haft but needed a two-piece mould. A hoard from Acton Park, Wrexham, shows that local bronzesmiths were in the vanguard of development, using copper and lead from nearby Halkyn Mountain.

Bronze objects: flat axe, socketed axe, palstave, gouge and dagger

This industry or its immediate precursors may have brought the area the prosperity suggested by the impressive gold-covered shoulder-cape from a burial at Mold, now in the British Museum.

Later in the Bronze Age, falling average temperatures produced a more maritime climate, wetter and windier with much cooler upland summers. Widespread peat formation began over soils nearing exhaustion, and the growing season became too short to ripen crops at altitude. Settlement was forced to contract, and agriculture apparently intensified; the emphasis on stock may have increased.

The period around 1300 BC was one of upheaval throughout Europe, and Wales was no exception. The public monuments seem to have fallen into disuse, and ritual activity is reflected in increasing deposits of metalwork, including gold torcs, some at least in wet locations. While suggesting an understandable need to propitiate the forces responsible for the increasing rainfall, these deposits probably also helped to maintain the social status of those with sufficient surplus wealth to sacrifice. Some hoards contain scrap, perhaps intended for recovery. A gold-covered model shale boat discovered in a bog at Caergwrle probably dates to this period.

The main later Bronze Age metalwork innovation was the socketed axe, although swords, spearheads, gouges and other tools continued to be developed. The socketed axe required a two-piece mould with an extra core to form the socket into which the haft fitted. This type was not universally adopted in Wales, the people of north-western Clwyd and Gwynedd preferring to keep to variants of the palstave. The bronze industry of north-east Clwyd apparently lost momentum, and many of the socketed axes found there come from elsewhere in Britain. In mid-Wales, the Severn valley seems to have had links with the area now over the border to its east; a hoard from Guilsfield contains material otherwise unknown in Wales. In south Wales, as far north as Builth, a local type of socketed axe was current. These different metalwork preferences coincide roughly with the known tribal areas of the later Iron Age and Roman periods.

A few hillforts such as The Breiddin (no. 58) and possibly Ffridd Faldwyn (no. 59) were first defended for a short period around 1000 BC, although some time then elapsed before their main Iron Age fortification. Pressure on land was probably causing friction between neighbouring groups, which could no longer reliably be dissipated by diplomacy. By the time iron was introduced in the 7th century BC, many of the main social and economic features of the Iron Age were already in place.

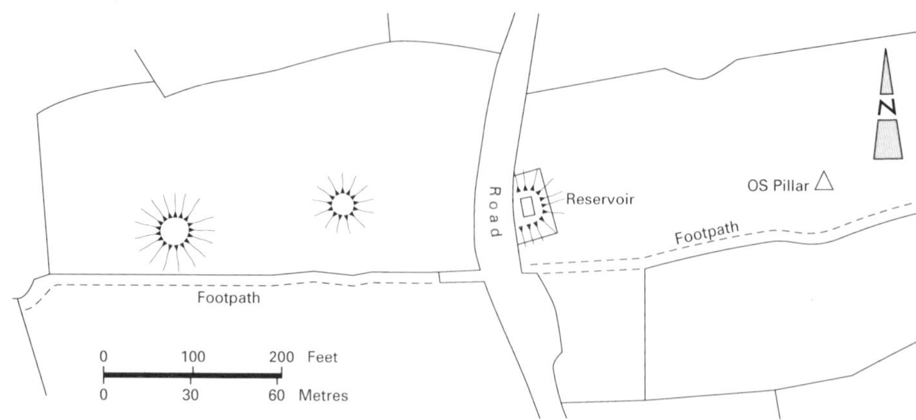

Axton Barrows

10
Axton Barrows, Trelawnyd

Round barrows

2nd millennium BC

OS 116 SJ 104803 R3

From Rhuddlan, take A5151 E through Dyserth and Trelawnyd for 5.2ml (8.4km). After Trelawnyd, take second turn of pair on L. After 0.6ml (1km), turn L in Axton; parking on R near cattle grid by barrows 0.3ml (0.5km) further on. View from viewpoint (see text) only

A group of barrows, probably burial mounds, lies along the prominent east–west ridge here, forming part of a concentration around The Gop Cairn (no. 3) about a mile to the west. From the viewpoint on top of the reservoir to the right (east) of the road, the two best preserved barrows are visible just to the west; these are *c.*20–25m in diameter and 1.5m high, slightly flattened by ploughing. Construction of the reservoir in 1929 largely destroyed a further barrow, reportedly revealing a cist containing a pot. No trace now survives of two further mounds recorded to the east.

11
The Ysceifiog Circle and Barrow

Earth circle and barrow

Late 3rd millennium BC

OS 116 SJ 152752 R3

From Holywell, take A5026 towards St Asaph. After 2.3ml (3.7km), turn L for Gorsedd. Continue straight through village and over A55; site in field beyond farm on R, 1ml (1.6km) from turn. View from road only

Fox 1926

The Ysceifiog Circle, a rare survival of an interesting complex ritual monument, is an oval enclosure, possibly a henge, 100–110m across, with a low bank and external ditch, containing a burial mound situated slightly off-centre towards the south. Running north-west and south-east from the circle are linear earthworks, each consisting of a bank with a ditch to either side; these have been claimed as part of Offa's Dyke, but more probably relate to the circle. The circle, although damaged, survives well on the side facing the

The Ysceifiog circle and barrow, with the associated ditches

road, while the linear banks were previously somewhat more extensive.

Excavation in 1925 failed to date the circle and banks, while a single inhumation was found within a pit beneath the barrow, almost totally decayed ('like porridge'). This pit had an access ramp to the north-west, and is described as being large enough to contain five standing people around the body. It was surrounded by a 1m-deep ditch, also subsequently buried, with a probable access ramp on the north. The excavator, Cyril Fox, assumed that all these features were used in the burial ritual, of which he provides an imaginative reconstruction.

Flints sealed beneath the mound dated the original burial to the very early Bronze Age. Three later Bronze Age cremations were inserted in and around the mound, reflecting changing traditions.

12
Parc y Prysau Barrows, Pentre Halkyn

Round barrows

2nd millennium BC

OS 116 SJ 183725, SJ 185723 U4

From Holywell, take B5121 towards Brynford and Nannerch. After 2.2ml (3.5km), turn L at crossroads for Pentre Halkyn. Footpath to barrows begins by Parc y Prysau farm on R 0.7ml (1.1km) further on. First barrow in middle of first field; second in rough patch near fence beside common beyond (see map, p24)

The first of these two burial mounds, in a not particularly commanding position, is grass-covered, 23m across and 1.5m high, with no visible ditch. The second, 25m across and up to 3.4m high, has wider views to the east, but has been disturbed by the mine workings, mainly for lead, on this part of Halkyn Mountain. The cemented piles of stones nearby cover disused shafts, and the existing landscape is cluttered with remains from different periods of mining activity. This somewhat disguises the fact that there is a concentration of Bronze Age barrows in the area, demonstrating its importance in early prehistory.

13
Boncyn Crwn, Llansannan

Round barrow

2nd millennium BC

OS 116 SH 919622 U1

From Denbigh, take A543 towards Pentrefoelas. After 10.6ml (17.1km) turn R for Llyn Aled. Barrow on LHS after 4.4ml (7.1km), on rise just before forestry. Parking in lay-bys to N and S

Boncyn Crwn is reached after an impressive drive past Llyn Aled and Llyn Aled Isaf. It is a large, grass-covered burial mound 22m across and 1.8m high, with a slight central hollow, presumably from an old excavation. It occupies a high point on a moorland ridge running north-east to south-west, with splendid views across the Denbigh moors, and is intervisible with other hilltop barrows.

On the skyline to the south-east stands Gwylfa Hiraethog. This shooting lodge, built

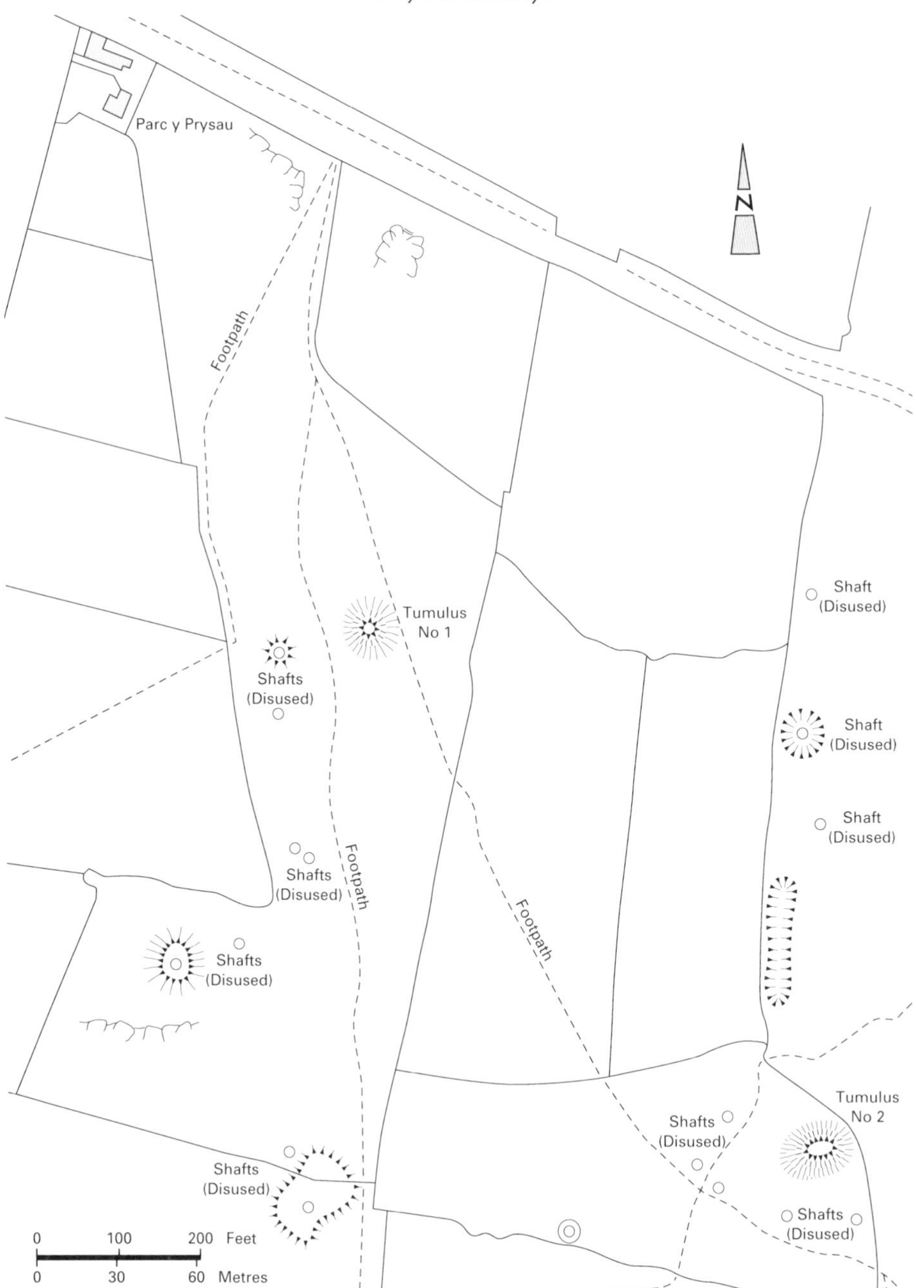

Parc y Prysau barrows

by Lord Devonport in 1908, was briefly the highest occupied building in Britain, although used for only two months of the summer. Improving communications rendered overnight lodging unnecessary, and by his lordship's death in 1934 the house was little used, although some staff remained. Since they left in the 1950s, it has become a ruin.

14
Brenig Archaeological Trail

Mostly Bronze Age antiquities
Mainly 2nd millennium BC
OS 116   start SH 983574   U4

From Denbigh, take B4501 towards Cerrigydrudion. After 7.2ml (11.6km), turn L along lane signposted for Archaeological Trail. Car park (toilets) after 1.1ml (1.8km). Trail starts from stile beyond, L of information board. Waymarkers clearest going clockwise. Shorter walk to hafotai *returns straight to ring cairn and Boncyn Arian. Boots advisable*

Lynch 1993

This walk covers an upland landscape with remains of various dates. The main focus of interest is the wide range of Bronze Age cairns, barrows and ritual monuments, forming a cemetery occupying much of the upper reaches of the valley containing Llyn Brenig. Most of these were excavated in the 1970s before the reservoir's construction (a higher level Stage 2 was originally planned), and have been reconstructed, *in situ* where possible.

Radiocarbon dating of the various structures making up the Bronze Age cemetery suggested that, while it appears to have remained in use for a period of about 500 years, it saw three main phases of intensive activity, the first around 1700–1600 bc (*c.*2000 BC), the second between 1600 and 1400 bc (*c.*1900–1700 BC), and the third between 1450 and 1200 bc (*c.*1700–1500 BC). The ring cairn (see p27) is the only monument to see use through all three phases, although Boncyn Arian, alongside it, seems to have been built in the first phase, and to have had an outer palisade added or repaired in the last. Other monuments, where dated, seem to have remained in active use for rather shorter periods.

To start the walk, cross the bridge and follow the stream uphill to the *hafotai* (SH 986574), near the forestry. These are the remains of small rectangular stone buildings of *c.*AD 1550, probably with heather or rush roofs, scattered along either side of the stream, with related enclosure banks. They were used only during the summer, while cattle and sheep grazed the upland pastures; butter and cheese would be made, and wool spun. Internally they housed a hearth, stone benches and small items of equipment; some probably included space for animals. The information board shows how they might have looked. The ring of wooden posts outlines a probably Iron Age building, 4m in diameter with a central hearth.

400m further south, the reconstructed cairn north of Hafoty Sion Llwyd (SH 986569) is visible down to the right, just before the path starts downhill. This small cairn, about 7m along its longer north–south axis, surrounded by a kerb, had been disturbed several times before 1974, although one burial near its edge had survived; it occupies a classic spur position overlooking the valley.

Across the valley and up the shoulder of the hill, the reconstructed platform cairn (SH 989566) lies just down to the right (north of Hen Ddinbych). This too occupies a classic spur location, with wide views over the valley; traces of earlier, Beaker period, occupation were found beneath it. An information board shows how the cairn, which was built in two stages, might originally have looked. The first cairn, which has been reconstructed, consisted of a broad ring, 22m across and 7m wide, of medium to large stones packed tightly together and finished flat on top; slightly larger stones supported the outer edge. In its centre was an open area about 8m across, the inner edge of the ring around it

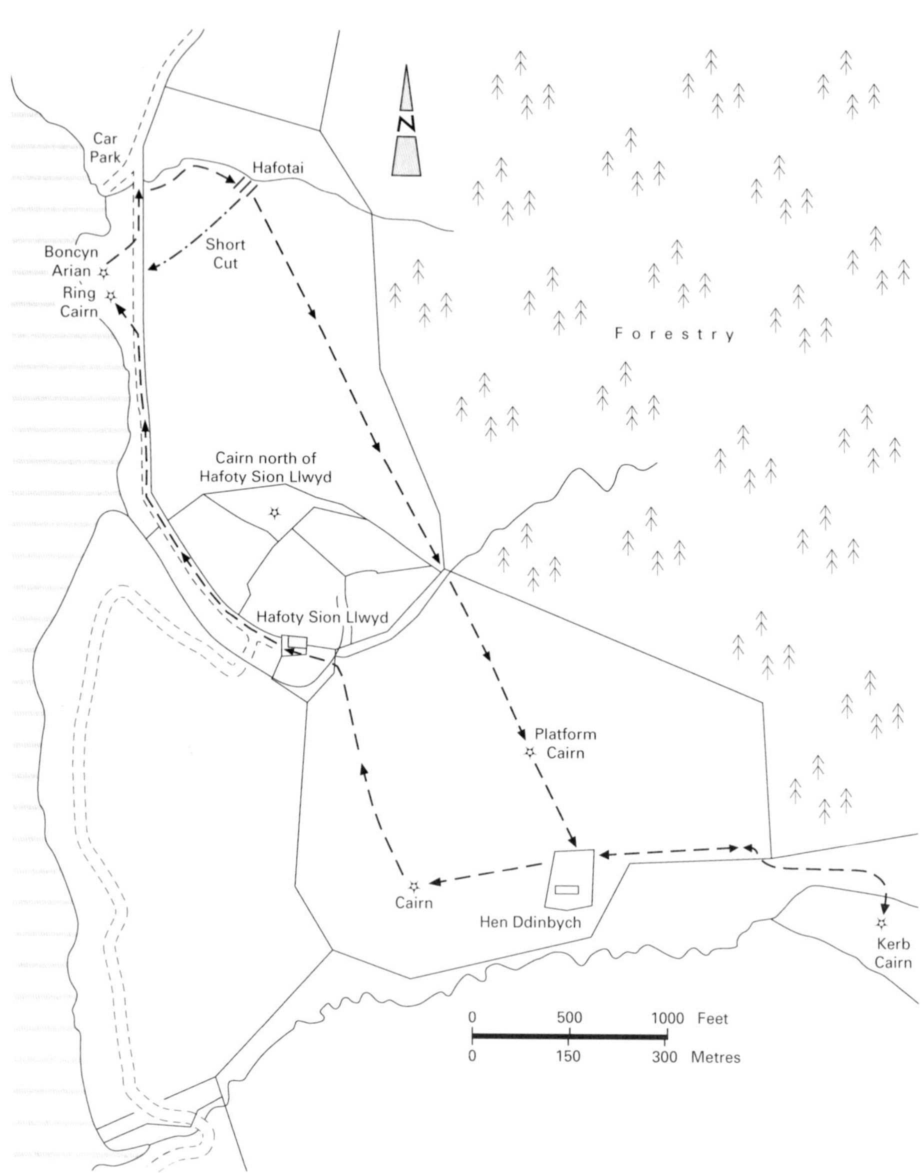

Brenig archaeological trail

being neatly finished with a circle of 26 small standing stones. Beneath this wide ring, on the south, lay the cremated remains of an adult and a child in a pot. There was a child cremation in the central area, while a post, possibly decorated, stood at the centre. The central area was fairly soon filled with stone, finished to a matching flat surface. A small cairn was later added on the north-east, towards the information board, covering a pit in which lay an urn containing charcoal. Despite its complexity, all the activity on this site was radiocarbon dated to the middle phase of the cemetery's development.

In the hollow to the south-east, with an information board overlooking it, lies Hen Ddinbych (no. 132), from which a detour can be made to the kerb cairn (SH 995563), 0.3ml (0.5km) to the east across the stream. Follow the fence to the plantation, cross the stile, and skirt the boggy area; the cairn lies a short way upstream in the valley bottom, with higher ground to north, east and south. It had been badly disturbed before excavation, but clearly consisted of a kerb of large stones, now reconstructed, measuring 5m east–west by 4.6m, with smaller stones filling the centre and overlapping it; traces of a cremation were recovered. To its north lay a hearth, possibly used in rituals; this was radiocarbon dated to around 1100 bc (*c.*1350 BC). It overlay a circular post-built domestic or ritual structure, 5m across with a central hearth; the five posts outside the cairn have been marked. On the hillside to the south is a diamond-shaped natural erratic, Maen Cleddau.

On the spur *c.*200m west of Hen Ddinbych sits another reconstructed cairn (SH 988564), with wide views except to the south-east. All that survived in 1974 was a ring of large stones 12m across, with a few minor gaps. The interior contained at least some smaller stones, possibly the remains of a substantial covering, while a rock-cut grave-pit in the centre produced a cremation.

Return to the lakeside track past Hafoty Sion Llwyd and turn north; after *c.*700m the reconstructed ring cairn and the imposing grass-covered mound of Boncyn Arian (SH 983573) are visible to the left, beyond an information board. The ring cairn remained in use throughout the 500-year life of the cemetery. Its earliest phase consisted of a well-built stone ring, with a turf core, measuring 21.25m across, around which a circle of posts was set at 3–4m intervals, 1.7m from the outer edge; these may have been carved with patterns or even representations of the dead. The interior of the ring had been cleared of turf and levelled. Later, after the posts had gone, clay banks were built against both sides of the stone ring. This monument was probably not used for burial at this stage, but may have been a ritual focus for the cemetery; charcoal was buried in pits, probably during such ceremonies. Later, a central cremation was added, together with three others in a pit near the inner edge on the north-east, although charcoal burials continued. Finally, some of the major deposits were covered by a small cairn, laid against the inner face of the ring on the west.

The ring cairn, Brenig, with Boncyn Arian behind

Boncyn Arian too was first built early in the life of the cemetery, although it was later modified. Three concentric circles of stakeholes underlay the later mound, with traces of wickerwork between them. These were surrounded by a ring of stones, the gaps between which had later been walled across, and the area thus enclosed filled up with turf. Later still, another circle of stakeholes was added outside it, and then a palisade trench beyond this, near the edge of an extended mound. A central grave contained the primary cremation, while six secondary cremations were distributed elsewhere. This impressive grass-covered barrow, 16m across and 1.8m high, has been reconstructed, with a ring of stones indicating where the wall may have pierced the surface. Three more mounds visible across the lake also contained central graves and other complex features. Another barrow to the north-east of the car park, with very wide views, was perhaps a 'marker' for the whole cemetery; it yielded a radiocarbon date of *c.*2150 bc (2650 BC), much earlier than the majority of the features, and contained no burial.

15
Barrows West of Llanarmon yn Iâl

Round barrows

2nd millennium BC

OS 116 start SJ 168558 U4

From Ruthin, take A494 towards Mold. After 4.6ml (7.4km), take B5430 R towards Llanarmon yn Iâl; 2.8ml (4.5km) further on, take B5431 on R. In village (0.4ml, 0.6km), take lane R by Post Office. Keep L at T-junction and after 0.4ml (0.6km), turn R, continue to farm 1.1ml (1.8km) further on. Park on verge just before gate. Offa's Dyke path crosses lane 70m further on; two barrows to L of road here. Follow path past them up hill to stile; turn L across pasture to barrow at top (Moel y Plâs; SJ 170554; 0.6ml, 1km). Fair weather advisable

The two barrows by the lane were described in 1810 as spoil heaps from mining, but there are no other signs of such activity in the vicinity, and the location on the saddle would not be unusual for genuine burial mounds. That nearer the farm is *c.*25m across and 1.3m high, and has been ploughed, while the other, covered with rough moorland vegetation, is *c.*20m across and also 1.3m high.

The Moel y Plâs barrow stands on a summit among the southern foothills of the Clwydian range with outstanding all-round distant views. It is grass-covered, about 15m across and 0.9m high; its top has been disturbed and now carries a modern visitor cairn.

16
Aber Sychnant Barrows, Minera

Round barrows

2nd millennium BC

OS 117 SJ 235496, SJ 238497 U3

From Llangollen, take road up hill off A539 just E of N end of bridge; cross canal, turn R, then L after 0.2ml (0.3km). Continue to T-junction past cattle grid (1ml, 1.6km), turn L. After 2.3ml (3.7km), turn R at Plas Eglwyseg; continue for 3.3ml (5.3km) until Offa's Dyke path leaves to L; park here. Boots advisable

Both these fine barrows are visible from the parking area, although they blend somewhat into the heather background. The first barrow lies not far along the Offa's Dyke path, which cuts its eastern flank. It is about 25m across and 2.5m high, disturbed in the centre – although no excavation is recorded – and may be a stone cairn on which peat has formed. It has good views down the valley to the south-west, and of the other barrow, 330m to its east-north-east.

The second barrow is a very impressive 30m across and 3.4m high. It is difficult to reach across the tall, rough heather, but is readily visible from the road near the boundary stone a short way east of the parking area. These two barrows form part of a group, which may have been positioned to help guide travellers across the watershed, to mark territory, or as prominent memorials to important people. There are several much later mining shafts nearby, including a possible example beside the road.

17
Hafod y bwch Barrow, Rhostyllen

Round barrow

2nd millennium BC

OS 117 SJ 309477 R4

From Wrexham, take B5605 towards Rhosllanerchrugog (also accessible from Croesfoel flyover on bypass). Turn L 0.6ml (1km) W of bypass, and continue for 0.5ml (0.8km); park in lay-by on L of RH bend before railway. Take stile over hedge just W of lay-by. At far side of field, cross stile on to lane; at RH bend ahead, take stile straight on over fence. Site on R here; please keep to footpath

This barrow is a fine example, about 40m in diameter and up to 2.8m high. There are wide views of the surrounding flattish farmland from its gorse-covered top. Its southern side is cut by the track and ploughed in the field beyond, but the remainder is well preserved. The summit appears pointed, suggesting that it has not been excavated. A hollow around the north side may indicate the position of the original ditch.

18
Moel y Gamelin, Llangollen

Round cairn

2nd millennium BC

OS 116 SJ 176466 U4

From Llangollen, take A542 towards Ruthin. After 4.5ml (7.2km), park at summit of Horseshoe Pass. Take path opposite café, keeping L of quarry. Keep straight on over first summit; cairn on second of pair ahead (steep walk; 1.4ml, 2.3km). Moel y Gaer (no. 56) visible on summit beyond. Fair weather advisable

The cairn on the summit of Moel y Gamelin is a particularly large mound, 30m in diameter and 1.8m high, with commanding views across the mountains in all directions. It is built of stony soil, and has suffered considerable wear from trail bikes and visitors' feet in the past. A modern visitor cairn has been built on top of it.

19
Eglwysegs Walk, Llangollen

Bronze Age antiquities

2nd millennium BC

OS 117 start SJ 241429 U4

From Llangollen, take road up hill off A539 just E of N end of bridge; cross canal, turn R, then L after 0.2ml (0.3km). Continue to T-junction past cattle grid (1ml, 1.6km), turn R and follow upper road (L fork) for 1.2ml (1.9km). Park by permissive path running back to L, signposted for Panorama. Boots advisable

The Eglwysegs, particularly their western fringes, are especially rich in traces of Bronze Age activity; the limestone plateau must have been very inviting to farmers moving on to higher ground in this period of improved climate. The monuments, which survive well because of the soil exhaustion which precluded later use, are largely ritual, and include complex types of barrows as at Brenig (no. 14), suggesting a varied range of interrelated activities centred upon the area.

Follow the old quarry track up to the point where two gates form a sheep-pen across it (1ml, 1.6km). Another track doubles back to the right just beyond this, and a circular stone ring known as a kerb circle is visible on its uphill side, roughly in line with the fence running uphill. This circle is about 10m across, with a scatter of drystone, some of which may date from later usage as a sheep-pen, around its circumference. The centre is uneven, making it uncertain whether it was built as a true kerb circle or is merely a robbed cairn.

About 0.3ml (0.5km) further along the main track, a path runs to the left to join that along the top of the crags, which ultimately reaches the summit barrow described overleaf.

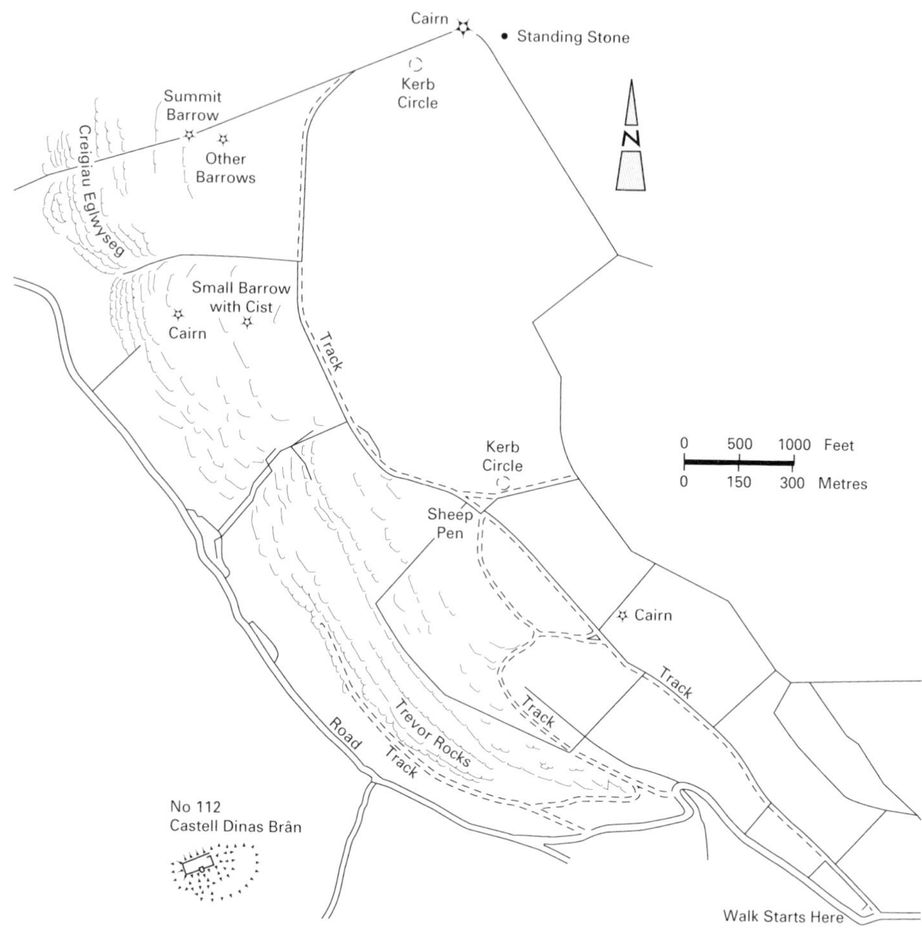

Eglwysegs walk

Continuing along the main track, look out for a small barrow to the left, about 100m from the path and about 150m before the next gate. A flat stone on this mound may be the remains of a cist, although similar stones are scattered nearby.

About 0.7ml (1.1km) beyond the turning, past the gate, and just beyond a sparse plantation on the right, a large summit barrow is visible to the left, along a disused fence line. It occupies a very imposing position near the edge of the crag, with extensive views in most directions, and measures about 20m across and 1.7m high, with a central hollow in which pieces of quartz are visible; excavation in 1879 revealed an urn and a cremation. A related group of features includes smaller mounds 80m to its east and 60m to its south-east, and a circle 75m to its east-south-east. The heather cover and the undulating ground surface make these difficult to distinguish.

About 170m further along the track, a kerb circle is visible 40m away, over the fence; it occupies a patch of higher ground between two marshy areas in the saddle. This circle is about 20m in diameter and is composed of individual stones, quite different from the kerb circle described earlier.

Underlying the next angle in the fence is a large spread stone cairn, about 20m across and 1.3m high. There are traces near the fence of slabs set vertically, which may have formed cists. Beyond this stands a standing stone, possibly contemporary with the cairns, little higher than the fence which it has been bored through to support; nearby lie two large erratic boulders. All these features sit in a saddle with views to the south-east. Two more cairns are visible on the skyline to the north, and the summit barrow described above can be seen to the south-west.

20
Wilderness Barrows, Llangollen

Round barrows

2nd millennium BC

OS 125 SJ 175403 R4

In Llangollen, turn S off A5 at The Grapes, just E of lights. Go immediately R, and fork L after c.50m. After 1.4ml (2.3km) fork L. Keep L at T-junction and 1.1ml (1.8km) further on, park near entrance to Ffynnon Las. Take drive to house, turn L and follow track on to moorland. First barrow (SJ 181405) just visible in last pasture field at top of valley after 1.1ml (1.8km), second (SJ 175403) 0.4ml (0.6km) beyond this on corner with sharp L turn, third (SJ 169400; not readily accessible) off footpath at top of hill 0.4ml (0.6km) beyond this again. Please keep to footpath; take care during shooting season

The first of these three barrows is a low grassy mound, flattened by periodic ploughing, about 100m beyond the fence, barely visible to the untrained eye. The second lies just to the right of the corner in the track, near a small thicket. It is covered, like the surrounding moorland, with heather and some bilberries, and is a low round mound *c.*1.5m high and *c.*10m in diameter. It occupies a commanding position on a natural saddle overlooking both the valley to the east and the top of another running north-west.

The third barrow, on the hilltop to the south-west, with extensive views, has been somewhat damaged. These barrows, which probably contained burials, may have functioned as a group to demarcate territory in some way. Another barrow in the forestry beside the track just above Ffynnon Las is now very difficult to see.

An intriguing circular mound with a hollowed centre lies among dumped material beside the track where it divides on the way up the hill. This may well be the remains of an old shooting butts belonging to the Estate; it may, of course simply be a dump of waste material.

21
Tyfos Cairn Circle, Llandrillo

Cairn circle

Late 3rd millennium BC

OS 125 SJ 028388 R3

From Llangollen, take A5 to Corwen. Beyond village (11.3ml, 18.2km from Llangollen), take B4401 L towards Cynwyd and Llandrillo. After 1.9ml (3km), take first of pair of R turns in centre of Cynwyd. Continue across bridge and turn L at far end; continue up valley, keeping L at junction, for 2.6ml (4.2km). Turn for Tyfos farm on R at LH bend; site in field immediately beyond. Park at farm; please ask permission for visit

The Tyfos cairn circle lies on the edge of the Dee valley floodplain, with rising ground to the north-west. It consists of an earthen mound, about 28m across and 1.25m high, with a circle about 17m across of massive recumbent boulders on its flattened top. This circle now contains 13 stones, and gaps suggest that others are missing; the owners

Tyfos cairn circle

believe that similar stones in the next field came from the circle. There is no sign of a central burial, although this is the most likely purpose of the site. The hilltop where the Moel Ty Uchaf kerb circle (no. 22) sits is visible from here.

22
Moel ty Uchaf Kerb Circle, Llandrillo

Kerb circle

Late 3rd millennium BC

OS 125 SJ 056371 R4

From Llangollen, take A5 to Corwen. Beyond village (11.3ml, 18.2km from Llangollen), take B4401 L towards Cynwyd and Llandrillo. 3.7ml (6km) further on, turn L by phone box opposite campsite. After 0.3ml (0.5km), park at junction; take track through gate ahead on foot. Continue up hill, R at all forks. Pass forestry on R; site visible on hilltop to L at RH bend beyond (1.1ml, 1.8km). Please ask at Ty Uchaf (on R at parking) before visit

Burl 1976; Thom, Thom and Burl 1980

Moel Ty Uchaf kerb circle occupies a commanding hilltop position with outstanding views in all directions, including the Dee and Alwen valleys, although visibility is limited to the immediate north-east. The kerb circle, another of the variants of the ritual and funerary monuments of the Bronze

Moel ty Uchaf kerb circle

Age, consists of a near-circle of stones (the irregularities may be of geometrical interest, or may reflect construction in separate sections), closely set and about 12m in diameter. The stones vary in size, but none is more than 0.9m high; small stones continue the outline across gaps in the main ring (possible entrances?) on the south-east and east.

An outlying stone 12m to the west may have been associated with the site, while the stone at the due north point of the circle is particularly large. Unrecorded old excavations in the centre of the circle have left a stone which may have been part of a cist. There is no trace of any surviving cairn material, though it is probable that any burial would have been covered over with a mound. A fine platform cairn lies a short distance below and to the east of the main circle; there are also a number of undated 'graves' on the way up to the site.

23
Berwyn Summits Walk

Round cairns and standing stone

2nd millennium BC

OS 125 start SJ 098322 U4

From Llangollen, take A5 towards Oswestry. After 5.5ml (8.8km) take B5070 R towards Chirk. 1.5ml (2.4km) further on, take B4500 R for Glyn Ceiriog and Llanarmon Dyffryn Ceiriog (11.6ml; 18.7km). Keep straight on through Llanarmon, 0.6ml (1km) further on, fork L up steep hill; at top (1.8ml; 2.9km from village), keep straight on for Maengwynedd. 1.6ml (2.6km) further on, turn R up hill past Tyn y ffridd farm. Park in quarry beyond first gate, after 1.9ml (3km). Second car can be parked at Pistyll Rheadr, W of Llanrheadr ym Mochnant (SJ 074296; waterfall, toilets, tea shop). Fair weather, appropriate fellwalking equipment and map essential.

From quarry, continue on foot along lane until track crosses stream by disused gateway. Take waymarked footpath over ladder stile to R, over second stile at top of field to third at top of saddle (SJ 081337; 1.6ml, 2.6km). Maen Gwynedd just to L here, over stile, on permissive path; cairn c.*100m beyond it. On circular walk, visit these on return. Continue ahead for Cadair Bronwen*

This mountain walk includes a pass which may have been used in the prehistoric period and encompasses a number of Bronze Age funerary and ritual monuments. The stone at SJ 081337, *c.*2m high, but leaning at an angle of about 60° towards the east, is almost certainly the Maen Gwynedd of the place-name. It is very narrow and slender and its name suggests that it was used as a boundary stone between Powys and Gwynedd, although this would not preclude an earlier origin. The cairn west of Maen Gwynedd (SJ 079336) is 2m high and *c.*20m across, constructed of stones, including fragments of quartz, largely covered with grass and bilberry plants. It has an excavated central hollow 1m deep.

The pass through which the path continues, through the gate to the north, is called Bwlch Maen Gwynedd; the Gwynedd Stone Pass. At the saddle beyond the head of the valley, turn right and follow the fence to Cadair Bronwen (0.8ml, 1.3km). This summit, with impressive wide views, is topped by a modern cairn, but a much larger prehistoric structure, Bwrdd Arthur (Arthur's Table; SJ 077346), is visible beneath it, 23m in diameter at the base, 15m at its top and 1.6m high; its flat top may well be original.

Return across the saddle to the stile at the next summit, beyond which the path from Maen Gwynedd joins from the left (0.7ml, 1.2km). Continue along the ridge, respecting the precipice on your left; the views are magnificent!

The OS pillar on Cadair Berwyn (SJ 072327; 0.6ml, 1km) stands on a mutilated cairn of similar proportions to Bwrdd Arthur and intervisible with it. The convex hill here has good views to north and south, but only more distant views to east and west. Two further cairns lie on the slope of the hill 0.2ml (0.3km)

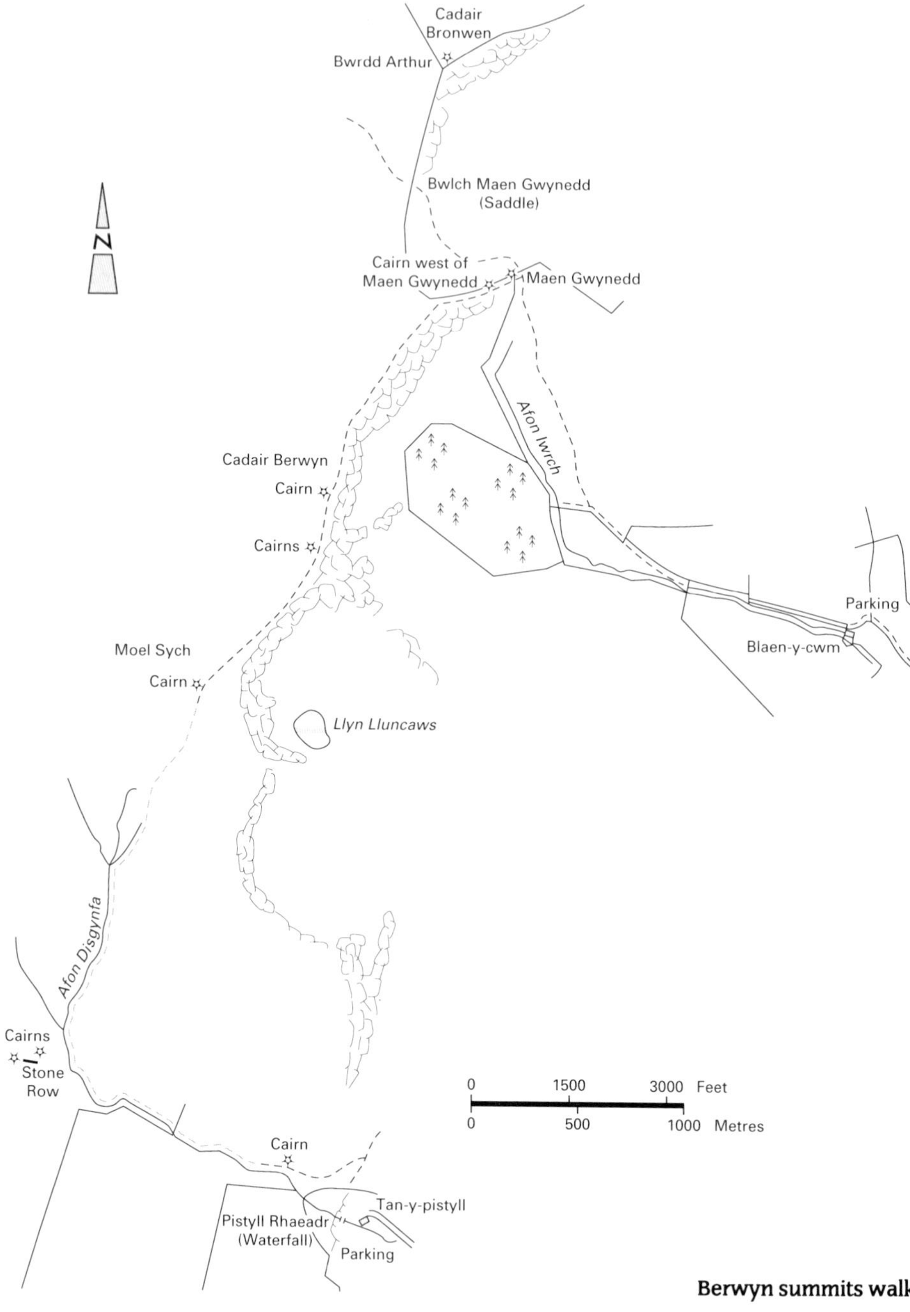

Berwyn summits walk

Cadair Bronwen, Berwyn, seen from the air

to the south (SJ 072324). The main cairn has been rearranged as a shelter; a scatter of stones around it includes traces of possible cists. The smaller cairn to its north-west is a roughly oval spread of stones, *c*.3m long and very low, with no visible cist. These two cairns are on a slight shoulder, with views to east and west; a natural outcrop forms a peak close by on the south.

Continue along the ridge, crossing two more stiles before reaching Moel Sych (SJ 066318; 0.6ml, 0.9km). The ancient summit cairn here is smaller than the other two, only 16m across and about 1m high, surmounted by a modern visitor cairn. There are some larger than average stones towards the south, but no clear trace of the kerb reported by some commentators. Once again there are wide views from this point; the main summit cairns are all intervisible. Permissive paths run to the west from both Cadair Berwyn and this point. To continue to Pistyll Rheadr, follow the path southwards down the ridge (1.9ml, 3km); otherwise return to the end of the precipice and rejoin the original path via Maen Gwynedd.

At Pistyll Rheadr, there is a further cairn (SJ 071297) just north of the track up the valley above the waterfall. This is a pile of tumbled stones, 20–25m in diameter, with a small shelter on top, but no trace of any cist. It is overlooked by a crag on the north, but has good views east, west and south across the valley. About 1ml (1.6km) further west again, off the path (SJ 058302), lies a very fine complex including a cairn, stone circle, stone row and 18th-century boundary stone; this is in a valley-head position similar to sites at Brenig (no. 14), and may have fulfilled a similar ritual function. The path to Moel Sych is not waymarked from this end.

24
Maes Mochnant Standing Stone, Llanrheadr ym Mochnant

Standing stone

2nd millennium BC

OS 125 SJ 137248 R2

From roundabout on W of Welshpool, take A490 to Llanfyllin (12ml, 19.3km). Beyond village, take B4391 towards Llangynog and Bala; after 2ml (3.2km), fork right on B4580 towards Llanrheadr ym Mochnant. After 2ml (3.2km), turn R at T-junction, and after 300m, R again, on B4396. Park in lay-by on R opposite minor road, just beyond junction. Footpath on R heads for far R corner of field; stone in next field on R. Please ask at Maes Mochnant Isaf (farm to E) before visit

This fine standing stone is also known as Post Coch (Red Pillar) and Post y Wiber (Pillar of the Snake). Legend has it that the district was once terrorised by a winged serpent or *gwiber* (English 'wyvern'), which met its death by dashing itself against the stone, which had been wrapped in red cloth studded with spikes. It is an impressive monument, 3.7m high, 0.6m wide and 0.45m thick, standing near a field boundary on relatively level ground in the Tanat valley, between two northern tributaries. The valley is an

Maes Mochnant standing stone

important east-west route, and the stone, although now dwarfed by trees, may have been a landmark on an early trackway or boundary. It belongs to a group of ritual monuments extending from Llanrheadr to Llangedwyn, about three miles further down the valley. Other stones such as that at Cwrt y gollen (no. 43) occupy similar valley-bottom positions.

25
Mynydd Dyfnant Stone Alignment, Llangadfan

Stone row

2nd millennium BC

OS 125 SH 985157 U4

From roundabout on W of Welshpool, take A458 towards Dolgellau; turn R at Foel (17.4ml, 28km). Fork R after 1.3ml (2.1km), gate after 1.9ml (3km). Park on verge before gate or opposite Penycoed Farm 0.2ml (0.3km) further on. Follow track through farmyard, across stream on to mountain. Fork L after 0.3ml (0.5km), head for gate into forest (0.4ml, 0.6km). Through gate, go up ride to forest road, take track opposite. Keep straight on for 0.6ml (1km); stones in clearing on R 0.2ml (0.3km) after quarry on L. Round trip 2.6ml (4.2km); boots essential

This stone alignment, now surrounded by forestry, lies on a gentle south-easterly slope, overlooking the Dyfnant valley. Known also as the Bryn Bras stones, it comprises six original stones, while the seventh, the last-but-one to the north, is remarkably clean and appears to have been only recently (re?)erected. Seven stones were, however, reported in 1910, including one ‘sunk into a bog’.

The first five stones form a straight line, running south-south-west to north-north-east. The southernmost stone is only 0.3m high, but that 4m to its north is 1.7m high,

Mynydd Dyfnant stone alignment

1.2m wide and 0.3m thick, leaning heavily to the south-west and now propped up by a log. Two more stones lie 4m further north, quite close together and 0.4 and 0.6m high respectively, while another, 0.9m high, lies 6m to the north again. The last original stone, 0.5m high, lies 9.5m further north, but is 2.5m to the north-west of the alignment on which the others lie. The new stone has been erected in the 9.5m gap; it may originally have partnered a recumbent stone to its north-west, also about 1m long, to form a cist.

Additional small stones near the northern end, including two more on the original straight line, may have been disturbed by forestry ploughing and are not necessarily in their original positions. Afforestation may have affected the drainage of the area, reducing the stability of some of the stones, especially the largest.

26
Rhosdyrnog Standing Stone, Commins Coch

Standing stone

2nd millennium BC

OS 135 SH 827005 R3

From Machynlleth, take A489 towards Newtown. After 3.7ml (6km), turn R after bridge. Fork L after 3.2ml (5.1km) up lane just after Talywern sign. Follow lane round to L; park at top of hill, beyond drive on R (0.2ml, 0.3km). Stone visible in field opposite drive. To enter, please ask at Rhosdyrnog farm (to R down drive from stone)

This stone, also known as Maen Llwyd, stands in an imposing position on a ridge, with wide views to north and south, more limited views to the east, and dead ground to the west. It is 2.1m high, and roughly hexagonal in shape. Some of the eastern surface has chipped off, but the west side is smooth; animals have worn a hollow at its base. This stone is one of three recorded in the area; unrelated traces of an old chapel have also been found nearby.

Rhosdyrnog standing stone

27
Maen Beuno, Berriew

Standing stone related to cairn circle

Late 3rd millennium BC

OS 126 SJ 203013 U1

From Welshpool, take A490/A483 towards Newtown. After 4.7ml (7.6km), turn L opposite B4390 for Berriew. Park in lay-by on RHS beyond houses after 0.3ml (0.5km); stone on RHS by roadside c.*60m further on*

Lewis and Longueville Jones 1857

Maen Beuno (Beuno's stone), now leaning towards the north-east, is 1.6m tall, 1m wide and 0.6m thick at its base, tapering to a point at the top. The north-west side appears to have flaked away and been stuck back. It may originally have formed part of, or been an outlier of, a stone circle within a now-flattened ditched mound, excavated in 1857 (cf. Tyfos, no. 21), in the next field to the east across the lane. On this mound centred a complex,

The Maen Beuno complex. The stone is outside the picture, to the right

visible on air photographs, including at least three ring-ditches, all in a low-lying, virtually flat area of the Severn valley. Interestingly, it lies only 2.2 miles (3.5km) from another similar complex of Neolithic and Bronze Age ritual monuments south of Welshpool (SJ 218049), including the pit circle at Sarn y Bryn Caled, excavated in 1990–1, a cursus at Brandyshop Bridge, and several more ring-ditches.

St Beuno, to whom the church at Berriew is dedicated, reputedly preached in the area in the 6th–7th centuries AD. The site may still have held pagan associations at this time, and may have been adapted to Christian uses by the saint.

28
Staylittle Barrows

Round barrows

2nd millennium BC

OS 136 start SN 880921 R3

From Llanidloes, take B4518 to Staylittle (7.6ml, 12.2km). On far side of village, turn L. After 0.3ml (0.5km), first 2 of 6 barrows (SN 878923 and SN 877922) visible across field on R. c.*100m further on, 3rd barrow (SN 880920) visible at top of rise on L, to L of forestry track. 0.2ml (0.3km) further on, 4th barrow (SN 877920) visible from entrance to Llwyn y gog Farm on RHS, looking back towards housing. Rough path L near same point leads to 5th barrow in forestry (SN 881915). 0.8ml (1.3km) further on, beyond enclosed field after crossing two cattle grids, 6th barrow (SN 874908) to RHS in open grazing. For scenic return to Llanidloes via Llyn Clywedog, with visit to Bryntail Lead Mine (Cadw, no charge), continue along road, turning L 1.3ml (2.1km) from last barrow (keep R here for Carn Biga, no. 29) and L again for dam 3.4ml (5.5km) further on*

The barrows of the Staylittle or Penfforddlas group occupy relatively low-lying positions on the sides and in the bottom of a pass running north–south between the Clywedog valley and the Llwyd, one of its tributaries. Several of them were probably intervisible, although trees and buildings now block the sight lines. The barrows are all fairly large, and some of them have been dug into in the past.

Of the first two barrows, that on the left (SN 877922) measures 22m by 16m, and is 1.8m high, while the other (SN 878923) is 17m across and *c.*1.2m high; it was damaged by excavation in 1903 which uncovered a Middle Bronze Age urn containing a cremation. Both barrows are grass-covered, and lie on fairly level ground.

The third barrow (SN 880920), beside the forestry track, stands on a north-west facing slope in a false-crest position. Grass-covered, it measures 20m north-east to south-west, but only 16m across; a boundary bank has damaged it on the south-east. The fourth barrow (SN 877920), near the housing, also under grass, is an impressive, apparently undisturbed, mound measuring 29.5m across, and up to 1.9m high, on fairly level ground.

The fifth barrow (SN 881915), in the forestry, is easily reached along a footpath (0.3ml, 0.5km) although it is not visible from the road. It lies on the right, just into the trees, which have encroached upon it, about 100m beyond a bend to the right; an old trench has been dug into it on the north-east. The

Staylittle barrows

surviving remains measure 20m across and 1.6m high. This barrow stands on the crest of a west-facing slope, from which all the others in the group were probably visible.

The sixth barrow (SN 874908) is grass-covered and measures 20m across and 1.6m high; it has been dug into from one side. It lies on the common *c*.50m from the roadside, in a flattish area in the Llwyd valley, some distance south of the others; it was nonetheless probably intervisible with the fifth barrow on the hill to its north-east.

29
Carn Biga, Plynlimon

Round cairns

2nd millennium BC

OS 136 SN 830899 U4

From Llanidloes, take B4518 to Staylittle (7.6ml, 12.2km). On far side of village, turn L. After 3.3ml (5.3km), passing Staylittle barrows, no. 28, and keeping R at junction for Llyn Clywedog, park at Cwmbiga; take stile by forestry gate, signposted for source of Severn. Follow track up mountain to junction (2.3ml, 3.7km); take track slightly R, leaving one to R and two to L. Continue for 0.4ml (0.6km); turn R up gap between trees after RH bend, opposite firebreak. Cross stile by gate and follow green-topped stakes across moorland to site (1ml, 1.6km). Fair weather and appropriate fellwalking equipment essential

Carn Biga, Plynlimon, seen from the air

The summit of Carn Biga, from which there are wide views, supports two impressive cairns, both *c*.15m across and *c*.3m high, built of large stones, with a third smaller one, only *c*.3m across, and *c*.1m high, between them. The tops of the main cairns are painted white, and shelters have been built from the stones on their flanks. A fence with a stile divides the northern cairn from the other two.

Another cairn, Carn Fach Bugeilyn, 12.5m across and 0.6m high, is visible 0.4ml (0.6km) to the north-west, although there is no obvious path to it across the bogs. In 1910 it was described as 5ft (1.5m) high, but it has since been damaged by shelter construction.

30
Rhayader Ridgeway Walk

Standing stones and barrow

2nd millennium BC/7th–9th century AD

OS 147 start SN 931699 U4

From Rhayader, take B4518 towards Elan Valley. After 0.4ml (0.6km), take mountain road R for Aberystwyth. 2.9ml (4.7km) further on, park on L; take bridleway signposted on R. Esgairperfedd (no. 70) can be visited from same point. Total length of walk described 3.1ml (5km); boots essential

Nash-Williams 1950, no. 407

Follow the bridleway diagonally uphill until it joins another path; from here Maen Serth (Steep Stone; SN 943698) is clearly visible on the skyline to the south-east. It stands at the western side of an undulating flattish hilltop, with natural outcrops and traces of quarrying, dominating the approach from the north-west. The stone may have been intended to guide travellers along the old road, avoiding the crags to the south; it is not so readily seen from the other direction, where the route follows the farther shoulder of the hill. It is a thin slab of local shale, 2.06m tall, but only *c*.0.5m wide at the base. On the south side, partly broken away, is a roughly carved cross of possible 7th–9th century AD date. It has been reset in modern cement.

From Main Serth, return along the middle track, following the ridge. On the next spur, a barrow, Clap yr Arian (Silver Lump; SN 937699), can be distinguished by its vegetation, lying perhaps 20m left of the track. It enjoys wide views across the valley from south-west to south-east, and is intervisible with Maen Serth. It is about 16.5m in diameter, with a central crater 10m across; the bumps to its south may be the spoil heap from an antiquarian investigation which yielded a Bronze Age axe-hammer. Five of the eight kerb stones surviving on its west are readily visible.

Continuing along the track to the north-west, Maen Gwyngweddw (White-widow Stone; SN 926706) is visible on the right not far before the modern road is reached. This is a striking white quartz boulder about 0.76m high and 0.84m across, roughly polygonal in cross-section. The limited views from this stone are mainly south and west towards the valley, although the barrow is still just visible along the track to the south-east.

31
Beguildy Barrows, Knighton

Round barrows

2nd millennium BC

OS 148 SO 210783, SO 222770 R3

From Knighton, take B4355 towards Newtown. After 6.9ml (11.1km), park on R opposite Vedwllwyd entrance. Meagram's Corner barrow in field beside road, footpath runs past. Retrace route for 1.4ml (2.3km). Just beyond Pennant Pound farm, park in gateway on L opposite gate halfway along straight stretch. Barrow visible in field on L, over gate. No public access

The Meagram's Corner barrow is a large, turf-covered mound 21m across and 2m high, occupying an unusually low-lying position

Beguildy barrows: the Meagram's Corner barrow

near the river Teme. Some stones revealed on the south (away from the gate) during scrub clearance some years ago were interpreted as part of a kerb around the foot of the barrow, but this is not clear today. A slight hollow in the top of the mound may also be the result of scrub clearance, or may be the remains of an unrecorded antiquarian investigation.

The Pennant Pound barrow is very similar, measuring 21m across and 2m high. It too occupies an unusually low-lying position in the bottom of the Teme valley, very close to the present, if not necessarily the past, course of the river. Another single, similarly located mound lies just over the border, on private land at Skyborry Green (SO 269741), 1.5ml (2.5km) north-west of Knighton.

32
Beacon Hill Barrows, Knighton

Round barrows

2nd millennium BC

OS 148 SO 176768 U4

From Knighton, take A488 towards Llandrindod Wells. After 4.7ml (7.6km), take B4356 R for Llangunllo; 2.4ml (3.9km) further on, turn R in village for station. Turn L at crossroads after 0.5ml (0.8km), R after 0.3ml (0.5km). Continue past station to L turn beyond (2ml, 3.2km from village), park and continue up lane on foot (waymarked). Go straight on beyond Upper Ferley cottage, and turn R at staggered crossroads; take Glyndŵr's Way at junction in forestry. Lanlluest short ditch (no. 97) visible here. Continue across shoulder into hollow beyond; barrows visible on hilltop to R. Follow track round head of valley; fork L at top of rise. Head for OS pillar once visible. Total distance to site 4.1ml (6.6km). Fair conditions essential, boots advisable if ground wet

Beacon Hill barrows occupy the summit of an imposing, rather convex, heather-covered hill, the highest for some way around, with good views in all directions. Further barrows, on Rhos crug, are visible on the skyline to the south.

From the barrow with the OS pillar, the other three in the group are readily seen, one 100m to the north-west, and the other two to the south-east, the farther of them occupying a local summit 150m away. The barrows average 22m across, with the most northerly being the largest; they vary in height between 1.4 and 1.7m, with that beneath the OS pillar being the highest. The most south-easterly barrow has relatively recently been heavily burnt, probably by use as a beacon; the name suggests a long tradition of such use.

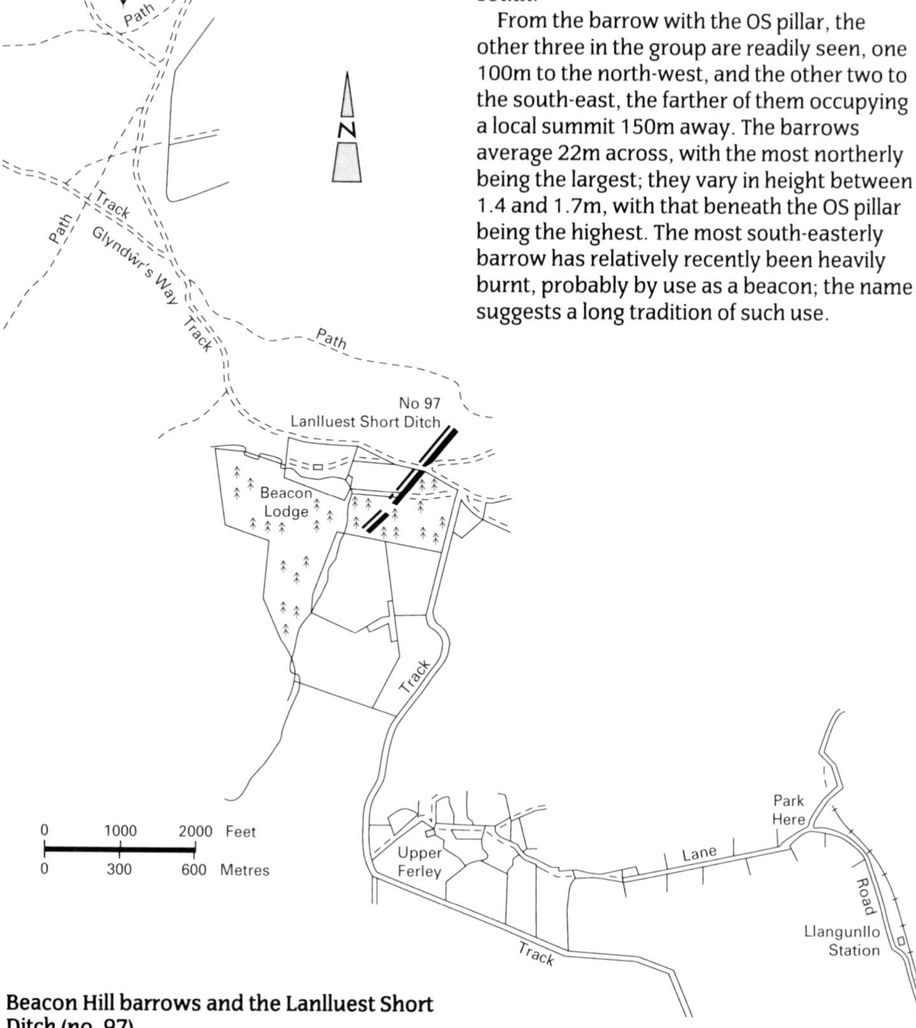

Beacon Hill barrows and the Lanlluest Short Ditch (no. 97)

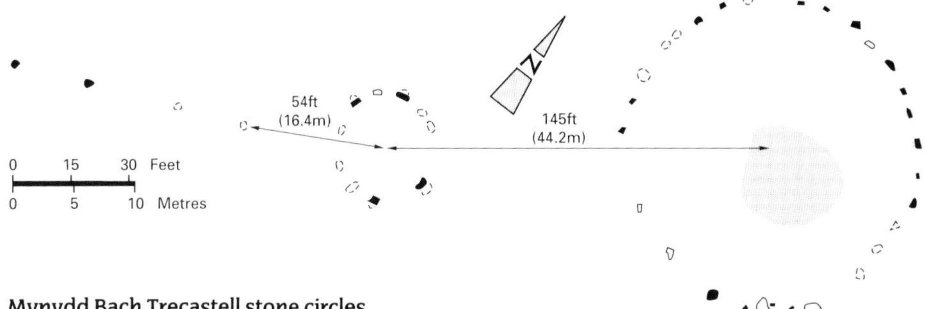

Mynydd Bach Trecastell stone circles

33
Mynydd Bach Trecastell Stone Circles and Barrow

Stone circles, alignment and round barrow

2nd millennium BC

OS 160 SN 833311 U4

From Brecon, take A40 towards Llandovery; turn L at far end of Trecastle (11.8ml, 19km). After 0.5ml (0.8km), take lane R along ridge; park at gate after 1.9ml (3km). Follow track to first rise with marker (0.8ml, 1.3km); fork R and R again, and head across saddle towards top corner of improved pasture to R of hill ahead (Y Pigwn, no. 72). Stone circles about halfway across saddle, 0.3ml (0.5km) from marker. Barrow to SW (SN 831309), c.*80m to R of track at large rock, 0.5ml (0.8km) from marker*

Grimes 1963; Burl 1976; Thom, Thom and Burl 1980

A complex of ritual sites lies grouped together on this now exposed and desolate hillside. The smaller of the two stone circles lies astride the path, while the larger is a short distance to the north-east. An alignment composed of two low stones and two sockets runs for a total of 27m west-south-westwards from the smaller circle. This latter is only about 8m across, with four good surviving stones, and another very low in the grass; holes indicate the positions of at least four more. The larger circle is 23m across, with at least 21 surviving stones, and pits suggesting at least three more. On the south-east, stones on the ground may have formed a ritual entrance; a slight mound inside the circle possibly covers a burial.

The circles and alignment lie towards the top of a rise, with wide views south, south-east and south-west, but more limited views along the ridge. About 100m south-east of the larger circle is an isolated stone, lying flat, nearly 3m long and 1.5 to 2m wide, broken into two pieces. This, it has been suggested, may have aligned with the rising midwinter sun when viewed through the circle's entrance.

The barrow, a large grassy mound, about 15m across and 1–1.5m high, with a slight central hollow, occupies a false-crest position with good views except to the north-west; it is prominent from the west but not visible from the circles. A bank to its south, of uncertain date and purpose, curves round towards the north a little way further east.

34
Gwar y felin Cairn, Sennybridge

Round cairn

2nd millennium BC

OS 160 SN 925349 U4

From Brecon, take A40 towards Llandovery. In Sennybridge (8.3ml, 13.4km), turn R after overbridge for Pentre'r Felin and Llandeilo'r

Fan. After 1ml (1.6km), turn R across bridge at T-junction; follow road L for Pentrebach. After 0.5ml (0.8km), fork R for Llanfihangel Nant Bran. Park at moorland junction just before second cattle grid, 1.8ml (2.9km) further on; continue on foot along track ahead. Cairn on summit of second hill, after 1.2ml (1.9km), track branches L to it. Boots advisable in wet weather

Gwar y felin cairn is turf-covered, 17.3m across and 0.8m high; an unrecorded antiquarian excavation has clearly taken place in the centre. Traces of concrete and metal lie close by, the remains of a military marker, revealing the fact that this area was until recently part of the Sennybridge artillery range.

The best views from the cairn are to the north, although there are more distant views in other directions, apart from the south, where the ridge continues. Immediately to the south-east is a boundary bank, probably representing an abandoned part of the field system still in use beyond the track.

35
Nant Tarw Stone Circles, Usk Reservoir

Stone circles and cairn

2nd millennium BC

OS 160 SN 819258 U4

From Brecon, take A40 towards Llandovery. After 11.4ml (18.3km), turn L in Trecastle in front of Castle Coaching Inn. Beyond bridge, follow Usk Reservoir road, continuing straight on at last turning through forestry to bridge beyond (5.5ml, 8.8km); park. Follow track L along river until streams fork at ford; cross and take grassed track on to ridge above stream to L (0.8ml, 1.3km). Boots essential; streams to ford

Grimes 1963

The ritual complex on the south-western side of Nant Tarw consists of a cairn, now very ruined and nondescript, on a ledge above the steep ravine, two stone circles, intervisible with each other and with the cairn, on flattish sites within rather marshy areas further from the stream, and an apparently natural glacial erratic on a pile of moraine debris to their west. There are some local views from the site, but it is relatively low-lying. The western circle appears on the near skyline from both the cairn and the eastern circle, and the erratic is in a similar position as seen from the western circle.

The eastern circle is 21m across, and contains about 15 stones (more are visible in very dry weather), mostly very low, although some reach 0.8m high, particularly on the west. The western circle, 112m to its north-west, is 19.5m across. It also contains about 15 stones, ranging up to 0.7m high on the south. Immediately east-south-east of this

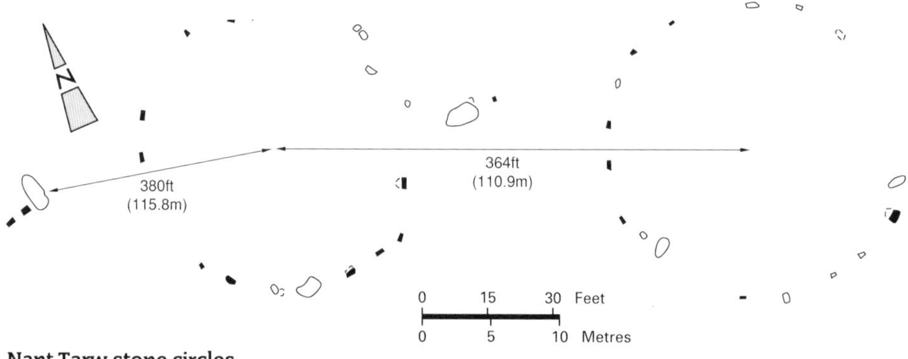

Nant Tarw stone circles

circle lies a monolith, similar to the large western stone, with two small stones beyond it forming a line 'pointing' to the eastern circle.

The large, slender western stone, 2.7m long and 1.8m wide, also has two stones on its farther side, forming a line pointing west-south-west. These stones lie at right angles to the southern end of the main stone, suggesting that it may have fallen from a position aligned with them. These stones are not in line with the circles, although they may be with the cairn; this is not in sight, however. 'Pointers' like these are also seen at Cerrig Duon (no. 36).

Cerrig Duon, looking from behind Maen Mawr

36
Cerrig Duon, Craig y nos

Stone circle, standing stone and avenue

2nd millennium BC

OS 160 SN 851206 U4

From Brecon, take A40 towards Llandovery. After 11.4ml (18.3km), turn L in Trecastle in front of Castle Coaching Inn. Follow main road for 1.5ml (2.4km); turn L. Continue over watershed for 4.8ml (7.7km); park on R after small bridge. Site visible to R coming down hill but not from parking. Cross stream on foot (easier upstream from bridge); site at top of rise beyond. Boots essential, preferably Wellingtons

Grimes 1963

The site known as Cerrig Duon (Black Stones) stands on a roughly level knoll west of the Tawe not far from its source. The most prominent feature is Maen Mawr (Big Stone), a large standing stone visible for some distance both up and down the valley. A stone circle lies just to its south, and an 'avenue' of small stones approaches at a tangent to the circle from the north-east. Another standing stone 0.5ml (0.8km) to the north has its narrow edge aligned on Maen Mawr, although the latter only becomes visible a little to the south of it.

Maen Mawr stands 1.9m high, and averages 1.3m wide and 0.9m thick. It is aligned north-south, towards the centre of the circle, and has two much smaller stones to its north, on the same alignment. About 10m from it lies the circle, slightly egg-shaped, measuring 18.5m north–south by 17.5m east–west, with 20–22 stones (more are visible in very dry conditions), standing up to 0.6m high. Another stone on the north-west, about the same distance from the site as Maen Mawr, may also be part of the complex.

A particularly interesting feature of this fine site is the avenue of very small stones, which can be difficult to see in extremely wet conditions. The stones, cut from the local flat-bedded rock, have been placed with their flat faces along the line, in two not quite parallel rows; the western survives for 42m, the eastern for 25m. They start together, 5m apart, at the south end, and diverge slightly before the western row continues alone to the north. The avenue follows one of the easier approaches from the valley bottom, and may have been used for ceremonial processions; it runs, however, at a tangent some way east of the circle, so may not be related to it. Small cairns lie on the slopes further down the valley.

Saith Maen, Craig y nos, from the south-west

37
Saith Maen, Craig y nos

Stone row

2nd millennium BC

OS 160 SN 833154 R4

From Brecon, take A40 towards Llandovery. In Sennybridge (8.3ml, 13.4km), take A4067 L towards Swansea. After 11ml (17.7km), park in car park on L for Craig y nos country park (small charge, other activities). Take track opposite through farmyard (path may be moved to south) on to mountain, go L past stile to follow small valley; keep well to R above stream. Stones eventually visible to R on shoulder of hill (0.6ml, 1km). Please ask at bungalow to L of track before visit

Saith Maen is, as the name suggests, an impressive row of seven stones; they are aligned north-north-east to south-south-west, high on the shoulder of the mountain, with particularly wide views to the north and north-east. The Tawe valley can be seen forking left, and the Tywyni, with the main road, forking right.

The stones are all flattish, with their flat sides running along the row. The most northerly, the tallest of those still standing, is 1.6m high; the second (2.3m) and fourth (2.9m) have fallen, to west and east respectively; some of their present length would originally have been beneath the ground. The third stone stands about 1m, the fifth and sixth about 0.8m and the seventh about 0.7m high. All are 0.7 to 0.8m wide, and stand about 1m apart, except for the fifth and sixth, and the sixth and seventh, which are wider and closer respectively.

There is a possible outlier 7.9m to the south-west, and three low stones, which may or may not be part of the monument, on the same line 13m, 26m and 53m north of the most northerly stone. The crater immediately to the north is probably a natural kettle hole in the limestone, although there are traces of quarrying in the area.

38
Maen Llia, Ystradfellte

Standing stone

2nd millennium BC

OS 160 SN 924192 U3

From Brecon, take A40 towards Llandovery. In Sennybridge (8.3ml, 13.4km), take A4067 L towards Swansea; after 1ml (1.6km) take A4215 L towards Merthyr Tydfil. 1ml (1.6km) further on, turn R towards Ystradfellte. After

2.2ml (3.5km), turn L at T-junction; 0.3ml (0.5km) further on, turn R. Site clearly visible on L c.*70m from road after 3.2ml (5.1km). Parking, access over stile; can be very wet*

Maen Llia is an impressive flat slab of conglomerate 3.7m high, 2.8m wide, but only 0.6m thick, set on edge. Its greatest width is partway up, making it look rather like a square set on one corner. It stands on the desolate moorland watershed between the Llia valley to the south and the Senni to the north, although, interestingly, it is not at the highest point, but occupies a false-crest position so that it is visible some considerable distance away down the Llia valley. It was probably intended to guide travellers across the watershed, its thin side pointing along the route.

Faint Latin and Ogam inscriptions of 5th-6th century AD type, interpreted in the 1940s as reading ROVEVI/S.... SOVI and VASSO(*G*?) respectively, are not readily visible today. The inscription was probably a personal memorial, possibly indicating activity along the Roman road from Brecon to Neath which passes about 300m to the east. Other more recent graffiti on the stone include some dating back to the 19th century.

Maen Llia

39
Mynydd Llangorse Cairn, Llangorse

Round cairn

2nd millennium BC

OS 161 SO 166261 U4

From Crickhowell, take A40 towards Brecon. After 1.8ml (2.9km), fork R on A479. 5.3ml (8.5km) further on, turn L at Waunfach Forge. Fork L again after 0.8ml (1.3km), continue for 0.5ml (0.8km) past Blenau Draw farm to junction with track. Very limited parking; note boundary stone inscribed 'Mrs Macnamara 1821', similar to that beside road at no. 7. Follow track a short way, then head L for mountain, leaving boundary on L. Good path from R joins near foot of slope; follow this up mountain; cairn on summit. Site can be included in walk between nos 7 and 40

This cairn on the summit of Mynydd Llangorse, probably a burial mound or territorial marker, has spectacular views, especially to the north and south. A modern visitor cairn now caps the rather battered original, 23m across and 1.8m high, from which some stone appears to have been removed. The path continues along the ridge past several other cairns including no. 40, and may itself be of some antiquity.

40
Bwlch Cairn

Round cairn

2nd millennium BC

OS 161 SO 154229 U4

From Crickhowell, take A40 towards Brecon. After 6ml (9.7km), find parking near top of hill in Bwlch. On foot, take turn R by Post Office, continue to T-junction, go R, then after c. *100m L up drive to large white house. Path continues on to mountain beyond house, following boundary; cairn at top. Can be combined with nos 7 and 39 to make a longer walk*

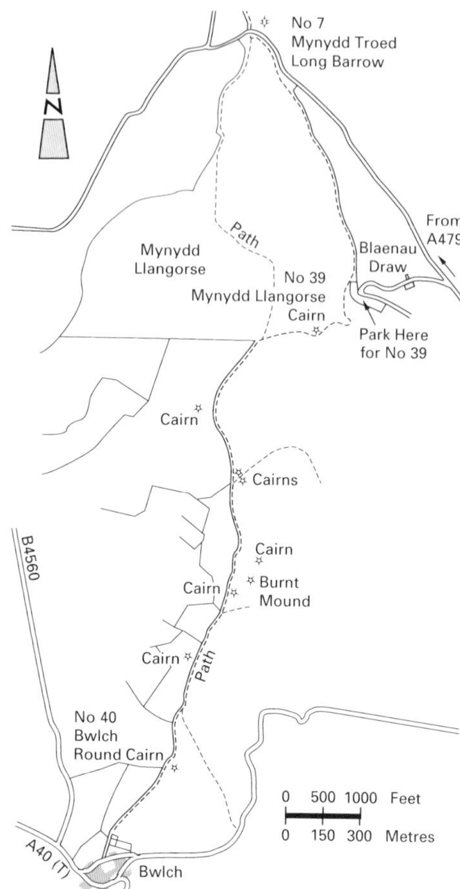

Mynydd Llangorse and Bwlch cairns

This cairn occupies a convex hilltop with good distant views on all sides apart from the north and, to a lesser extent, the south-west; they include a vista across Llangorse lake. The cairn itself is 19m across and 1.2m high, turf-covered, and has been dug into, probably by antiquarians, leaving a central hollow. A modern visitor cairn sits on its north-west side. The path continues along the ridge past several other cairns including no. 39, and may itself be of some antiquity.

41
Twyn y Beddau, Hay on Wye

Round barrow

2nd millennium BC

OS 161 SO 241386 U1

From B4350 in Hay, take minor road SE towards Craswall and follow signs for Capel y ffin and Abergavenny. Site on L after 3.2ml (5.2km), about 150m beyond start of moorland. Limited parking close by. No. 42 further along same road

Thomas 1872

Twyn y Beddau appears today as a barrow 22.7m across and 2m high, occupying a false-crest position with rising ground to the south and the most open view towards the north. It has been excavated several times (some trench outlines are still visible), but the best reported work was in 1871, when five 'cists', irregularly distributed within the mound and containing cremated human bone, were discovered. The core of the cairn contained an organic layer, over which lay, successively, a rough stone surface, a layer of charcoal, a band of soil and a second rough stone surface.

These remains, recovered from a roughly T-shaped trench, may represent some sort of mortuary structure, allowed to decay before the mound was built. Other, upright, stones reported around the edge of and close to the site, and two stone cists to the west or north-west, are not visible today.

42
Blaenau Stone Circle, Hay on Wye

Stone circle

Late 3rd millennium BC

OS 161 SO 239373 U2

From B4350 in Hay, take minor road SE towards Craswall and follow signs for Capel y

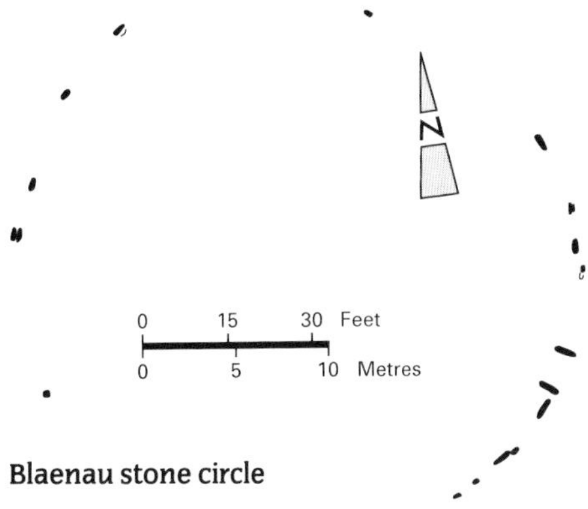

Blaenau stone circle

ffin and Abergavenny. Pass no. 41; site on R after 4.1ml (6.6km), beside car park

Blaenau stone circle has only fairly recently been recognised as an entire circle and, it must be said, is difficult to follow on the ground; the stones immediately beside the car park, now protected by recently laid boulders, provide a useful starting point. The largest original stone, possibly marking an entrance on the east of the circle, is a slightly sloping flattish slab 1.5m high and 1.1m wide, with an OS benchmark (broad arrow and horizontal bar). Others to either side form the arc of a circle 29.8m across, a little larger than others in the area (cf. nos 33, 35 and 36); three very low stones, and a hummock possibly concealing a fourth, are visible on the far side, with another small stone further south. There are no obvious features in the undulating grassy interior. The site occupies a level plateau below and to the north-west of Hay Bluff, with good views north and west, especially from its outer edge.

43
Cwrt y gollen Standing Stone, Crickhowell

Standing stone

2nd millennium BC

OS 161 SO 232168 U3

From Crickhowell, take A40 towards Abergavenny. 1.4ml (2.3km) from town centre, park in lay-by on RHS opposite main entrance to barracks. Stone clearly visible on grass L of drive

This magnificent standing stone, over 4m high, but relatively narrow, is made of red sandstone, giving it a dark appearance. It is one of several standing stones in this part of the Usk valley; others (on private land) are at Penmyarth (SO 183198), Llangynidr (SO 156204) and Gilestone (SO 116237). All lie north of the river, at or near junctions with other valleys; in this case, the Grwyne joins from the north not far to the east. More stones lie further north, in the Rhiangoll valley at Bwlch (SO 150219) and near Tretower (SO 180219), and in the Grwyne valley near Llangenny (SO 240178 and SO 236188). While not all of these are definitely ancient, they can plausibly be seen as route or territorial markers of some sort.

Cwrt y gollen standing stone

3
The Iron Age

The arrival of iron working in the 7th century BC seems to have had little impact in Clwyd and Powys, at least to begin with. Early iron objects were cast, like bronze, suggesting limited mastery of the material; iron tools are not plentiful until about 300 BC, when forging techniques had been perfected and local sources of iron presumably exploited. Bronze continued to be used throughout the period for objects such as personal ornaments and horse trappings.

A continuing fall in average temperatures, except between 300 and 100 BC, reduced the potential of the uplands still further, and many valley bottoms probably became too wet for cultivation. Woodland was cleared from valley sides, especially in the Marches, and stock-rearing became more important, perhaps with some transhumance. The balance of farming would have varied in different areas. Cereals continued to be grown, including emmer wheat and, increasingly, the hardier spelt, together with oats and rye. Manuring and liming were probably practised to help maintain the fertility of the land and reduce its acidity; lime is also needed for iron smelting, and may have been traded. Containers for salt, from the West Midlands, used in the preservation of meat and vegetables, are found on excavated sites throughout Clwyd and northern Powys.

The main surviving Iron Age monuments are defended settlements; with few exceptions, disposal of the dead left no trace. The larger settlement enclosures are generally known as 'hillforts', while those below 1.2ha (3 acres) are often differentiated as 'small enclosures'; both types come in many different shapes and sizes, some with multiple lines of defence, and may have fulfilled a range of different functions. Some occupy strongly defended positions, on hilltops or natural promontories, while others are overlooked by higher ground which would make practical defence difficult; others again have widely spaced ramparts or annexes which may have served as areas for marshalling or penning stock. The defences were built of soil, wood or stone in a variety of combinations, sometimes with external ditches, sometimes without. Even sites in poor defensive positions sometimes had substantial ramparts. Many defences were partial, focused usually upon the entrance, and probably intended chiefly to impress. Some sites undoubtedly saw action, however; widespread traces of burning have been found in excavations along the Marches.

Relatively few sites have been extensively excavated, and the wet and acid soil

Reconstruction drawing of an Iron Age hillfort interior

conditions prevailing over much of Clwyd and Powys mean that few materials survive well. Even buildings, like the tenuous final-phase structures at Moel y Gaer, Rhosesmor (no. 48), may be elusive. Dating is also difficult. Radiocarbon dates for this period often produce multiple possible calendar dates when calibrated (see Summary of Dates), while few sites used pottery before about 300 BC; what little is found after this date, mainly produced in the Malvern area, remained much the same in appearance right through to the Roman conquest.

Some larger sites in Clwyd and the Marches, such as Moel y Gaer, The Breiddin (no. 58) and Ffridd Faldwyn (no. 59), have excavation evidence to suggest unusually early foundation dates, some as far back as 800 BC. At a later stage, inturned gate passages with guard-chambers become a particularly distinctive feature of hillforts along the Marches. The tribes in this region were probably the Deceangli in north-east Wales and the Cornovii on the central Marches; the inturned entrance design is also found in Brecknock, usually taken to belong to the Silures.

The main distribution of hillforts and small enclosures lies in the drier areas in the rain shadow of the Cambrian range. Such settlements are relatively widespread in Clwyd, with a concentration of particularly fine sites along the Clwydian Hills (e.g. nos 49, 50, 51), but further south they cluster in particular areas. The larger sites tend to occupy better defended positions at higher elevations, while the smaller enclosures lie on slopes and valley floors, in weaker positions but on generally better land. In Montgomery there is a great concentration of sites around the Severn valley, continuing eastwards into Shropshire. In Radnor, sites cluster around the Ithon valley, north and east of Builth, and west of the Radnor Forest massif; another group lies across the border to the east, probably within the same Iron Age tribal territory. In Brecknock, the main concentration lies along the Usk and Llynfi valleys.

These enclosures, particularly the larger ones, are often within easy reach of both upland and more sheltered valley slopes, and probably exploited both these environments. Excavated sites such as Moel y Gaer, The Breiddin and Ffridd Faldwyn have yielded traces of timber round-houses, presumably used as dwellings, and also of 'four-posters', generally regarded as storage buildings, probably granaries to hold corn for both consumption and future planting. In one of the phases at Moel y Gaer, the four-posters occur in planned rows, separate from round-houses of the same date, and there are hints of similar functional zoning elsewhere. These stores were presumably controlled by a chieftain or by the community, and redistributed to both farmers and craft specialists according to need.

Reconstruction drawing of a small Iron Age enclosure

While the larger sites seem to have had at least some permanent residents, most of the population probably lived either in smaller enclosures, or in undefended sites which are usually discovered only by chance. Many smaller enclosures, especially on more heavily cultivated land, are known only from cropmarks on air photographs, although excavations at Collfryn, about 10ml (16km) north of Welshpool, showed that considerable remains can survive the plough. Three widely spaced concentric banks and ditches were built here in about 300 BC, and the site continued in use, with modifications, into the Roman period; the central enclosure contained round-houses and four-posters, with three or four houses and four or five four-posters in use at any one time during its first two centuries of occupation. Traces were found of bronze and iron working and containers for salt. This site has been interpreted as the homestead of a fairly wealthy extended family practising mixed farming, and is probably fairly typical of many of the smaller enclosure sites.

Defended sites were constructed, modified and abandoned throughout the period, and it is not altogether clear how many remained in use by the Roman conquest. The local balance of power probably shifted frequently as a result of the successes and failures of individual petty leaders. Tribes in southern Britain had made treaties with Caesar on his visit in 54 BC, and probably controlled the export to the Roman world, now just across the Channel, of the corn, cattle, gold, silver, iron, hides, slaves and hunting dogs mentioned by the historian Strabo; several of these probably came from Wales. The Romans themselves invaded Britain in AD 43 and subdued Wales piecemeal in the course of the following 30 years.

44
Bryn Euryn, Colwyn Bay

Iron Age/early medieval hillfort

Late 1st millennium BC/5th–6th century AD

OS 116 SH 832798 U4

At Colwyn Bay, take B5115 exit from A55 westbound. Turn R at lights and R again at next lights on to A547; take B5115 on R at roundabout. Cross A55, go straight on at lights and at next roundabout. Turn L at next lights into Rhos Road. Continue to next crossroads, park down lane opposite. Walk to sharp RH bend, take rather slippery path to L; keep climbing to top. Llys Euryn (no. 131) close to parking

Although probably originally Iron Age, Bryn Euryn was almost certainly refortified in the post-Roman period, as were Deganwy and Dinorben nearby. They were used by the elite as refuges in the 5th and 6th centuries AD, when central rule had broken down and the Irish were raiding along the coast. Despite the absence of archaeological confirmation of early medieval occupation, tradition links the place-name with Maelgwn Gwynedd, who fortified Deganwy in the 6th century. The strongly defended inner and outer enclosure and the traces of rectilinear buildings are both reminiscent of sites with dated early medieval material.

This prominent site overlooks lower-lying ground in all directions, including the sea coast to the north; it occupies the two grassy

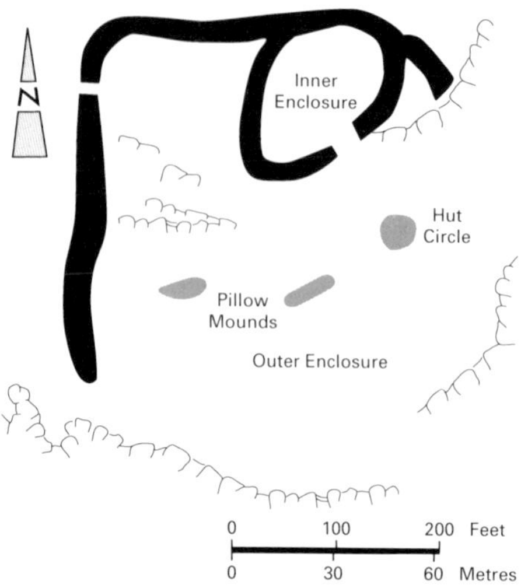

Bryn Euryn hillfort

summits and the intervening scrub-covered hollow of an imposing naturally defended hilltop. The northern summit, the higher of the two, now surmounted by an OS pillar, forms the site's main stronghold. There are slight traces of a surrounding wall, especially on the east; the entrance was probably on the south-west beneath the modern path.

Some remains of buildings survive within this enclosure, including a scrub-filled oval outline on the west, and a possible room to its east running north–south and divided by an east–west partition. The rock outcrop at its north-east corner, beneath the OS pillar, suggests that the floor would have been at a rather higher level. A viewpoint panel stands on the room's south-west corner. To the north-east of the pillar is a hollow, surrounded by traces of footings suggesting a square structure.

The outer enclosure bank is clearly visible on the north-west, running west from its junction with the inner circuit; scrub makes the eastern connection more difficult to see. Within the outer enclosure lie two medieval pillow mounds (artificial rabbit warrens) and a hut circle. All these, except for part of the western pillow mound, which is crossed by the path between the two summits, are hidden beneath the scrub, as is a further pillow mound outside the bank on the west.

The blackthorn scrub also makes the western bank of the outer enclosure difficult to trace, although it is visible where the path crosses it; the suggested entrance on the north-west is overgrown too. There are no Iron Age or early medieval buildings in the outer enclosure, except perhaps the hut circle; this may however have been a shelter for the medieval warrener, supervising the rabbit farm. Excavation might help to answer some of the many questions about the site.

45
Mynydd y Gaer, Llannefydd

Iron Age hillfort

Late 1st millennium BC

OS 116 SH 973718 U4

From Abergele, take A548 towards Llanfair Talhaiarn. After 3.3ml (5.3km), take second turning of pair on L. After 1.4ml (2.3km), turn L

Aerial view of Mynydd y Gaer, Llannefydd, from the south-east

and immediately R. Keep straight on, then turn L after dam (1.9ml, 3km) and park in triangle. Walk up lane to L; at junction, turn up hill; take footpath L at Bron Hwylfa. Site to L at top of hill. Boots advisable

This 4ha hillfort occupies the summit of a rounded hill with fine views in all directions. The eastern half, higher and rockier than the western, is crowned by a modern summit cairn. The Iron Age defences, a single line for the most part, have been confused in places by later activity, including the construction of a small farmstead and its improved fields, a number of other boundaries, and quarrying in the north-eastern quarter. The features on the south-east, including a possible outwork, have been particularly affected.

Around much of their circuit the defences consist of a ditch, over 2m deep on the north-west, with a counterscarp bank outside it, presumably built from the dumped fill. Only on the east, adjoining the improved field, is an inner bank visible; ploughing close alongside it has destroyed any ditch. Unfortunately this stretch is isolated from the remainder by quarrying on the north-east, and by the earthworks of the probable entrance on the south-east.

The other likely entrance is on the north; here the two ends of the ditch are offset from one another, forcing anyone entering to turn right; the ditch is larger to the west of the entrance than immediately to its east, although it increases in size again a little way further eastward.

On the south-east there is an additional inner bank protecting the entrance, which also deflects entering traffic to the right. The outwork may be part of this entrance, although older maps show both entrances reused for access to the farmstead. The inner bank at the south-east entrance has been damaged by field clearance, and is crossed by a boundary bank as well as by the present path; the original track is disused. The wet area beside the entrance may have provided a seasonal water supply. No obvious hut positions survive in the interior.

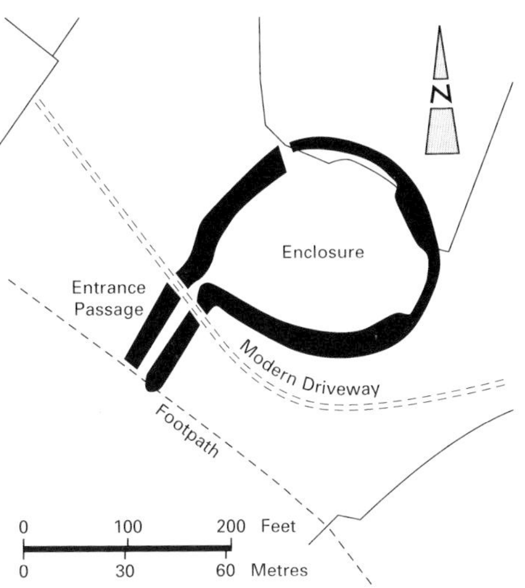

Old Foxhall enclosure

46
Old Foxhall Enclosure, Henllan

Iron Age enclosure

Late 1st millennium BC

OS 116 SJ 035674 U4

From Denbigh, take B5382 to Henllan (2.5ml, 4km). Park near track climbing sharply back on L. Follow track on foot past houses, over stile, over stone stile at end of field and hurdle at end of rough patch. Go through gate on R at end of wood. Turn L, keeping buildings to L, cross track and go into next field. Site lies c.75m beyond corner of wall (0.8ml, 1.3km)

The Old Foxhall enclosure is clearly visible as a low bank in the pasture; it is roughly circular, about 60m in diameter and 0.8m high, with two parallel banks about 8m apart and 35m long flanking its approach from the south-west. The metalled track from the nearby buildings crosses these banks just where they meet the enclosure. A stone field boundary, now disused, has been built on part of the bank on the north; a gap near the west of the affected stretch may have been an entrance. The modern boundary east of the point where the wall leaves the enclosure bank preserves the only trace of the ditch.

The site lies on a slight rise within a relatively flat area. The views on all sides were adequate for defence, although those to the south and west are now blocked by trees and buildings.

A short distance to the south are two further very substantial banks running west-north-west to east-south-east, parallel with one another and about 40m apart; there is another similar bank a short way to the east. These may be the remains of a field system, although this may not relate to the enclosure. The site, which is similar to small Iron Age enclosures elsewhere, was probably occupied as a farmstead, although there is no visible trace of any internal buildings.

47
Bron Fadog, Caerwys

Iron Age enclosure

Late 1st millennium BC

OS 116 SJ 141721 U2

From Denbigh, take A543/A541 towards Mold. After 7.3ml (11.7km), turn L at Afonwen for Babell (second turning of pair). After 1ml (1.6km), pass bridleway on R; very limited parking on R opposite field entrance c.*100m further on. Take footpath on R through scrub after* c.*30m; site to R a short distance across field*

Bron Fadog is a small near-circular earthwork enclosure, similar to that at Old Foxhall (no. 46). It measures 40m north-north-east to west-south-west, by 25m at the north end and 35m at the south, on almost level ground with a slight slope to the south. It has been ploughed over, but the bank, 0.4–0.5m high, is still visible around most of the circumference, and is clearest on the south. There is a possible entrance gap on the south-

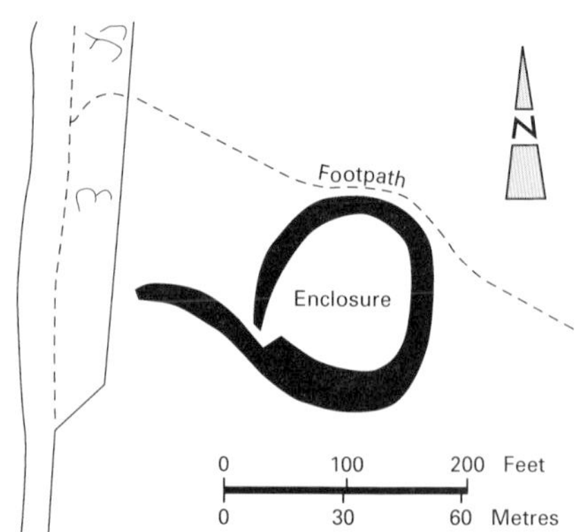

Bron Fadog enclosure

east, and an additional length of bank, possibly relating to a lost field system, runs westward towards the road. The site may have enclosed a small farmstead, or may have been a stock enclosure.

48
Moel y Gaer, Rhosesmor

Iron Age hillfort

1st millennium BC

OS 117 SJ 211690 U3

From Mold, take A451 towards Denbigh. After 2.2ml (3.5km), take B5123 on R. Site 2.1ml (3.4km) further on, beyond village on L. Parking in service road at foot of hill. Continue on foot along track round L of hill to old quarry fenced with stone posts; turn R through original entrance into fort. View from road to NE

Guilbert 1975; 1976

Moel y Gaer occupies an isolated grassy hill, with a commanding outlook. Despite the relatively gentle slopes there is only a single bank and ditch around most of the circuit with an inturned entrance on the east. On the north-east, a second ditch has been added, in two separate sections; the spoil from the more northerly has been added to the counterscarp bank outside the main ditch, producing a double defence, while that from the more southerly forms a separate bank. These extra defences may have been part of an unfinished circuit or may have been intended to impress anyone approaching the entrance. A low bank, which excavation showed to have supported a palisade, is visible 10m outside the main ditch on the south and west. Gaps across the defences on the north and south are probably relatively modern, while parts of the west side have been disturbed by mining trials. There is a mound, probably a damaged Bronze Age barrow, at the highest point of the site.

Extensive excavations, covering a fifth of the interior and two sections of the defences, were carried out in 1972–4 before the large covered reservoir was built. Three main phases were identified in the interior, although there were also traces of one possible rectangular Neolithic building. The first main phase consisted of round-houses, 6.5–11.5m in diameter, each supported by a ring of posts some way inside its wall line; the latter was largely untraceable and usually deduced from the position of the post-holes for the porch. These buildings seemed to have spread from the middle of the site towards the outside, since those nearer the centre had lasted long enough to be renewed in the same style. Most faced south-east, but did not follow any planned layout. Three small 'four-posters', probably storehouses or granaries, may have been associated with this phase.

The early round-houses were replaced by a new design, with an outer wall 5.6–8m in diameter supported on a ring of small stakes, and no internal posts. These buildings, which also faced south-east, were interspersed in an apparently organised plan with groups of neatly spaced four-posters, up to 4m square.

This phase was followed by a period of disuse, after which the site was radically remodelled. Rectangular concentrations of stone, assumed to be the floors of buildings founded on timbers lying on the ground, were linked together by features which looked like boundaries forming yards. Although pottery was found from all the phases on the site, it was very difficult to date precisely.

The different phases of the defences seemed to relate to those in the interior. The earliest settlement was defended by a simple palisade, not now traceable on the surface. A much more substantial defence enclosed the second settlement with the stake-walled houses; its inner bank overlay the remains of one of the earlier post-ring buildings, which, like a number of the others, yielded a radiocarbon date very early in the Iron Age. The complex structure of the second-phase rampart was fully understood only because a considerable length of it was excavated. It consisted of a 6m-wide bank with timber uprights at close intervals along its front face, the intervening spaces filled with drystone walling; massive slabs stood on edge at its base. Further timbers tied those at the front into the core of the bank; some of these were pinned into the ground at the back by further posts. The core of the bank was constructed in 'cells', so that should part of the rampart collapse the adjoining cells, retained by walls across the width of the bank, would remain intact.

Despite these precautions, this defence eventually fell into disrepair, and a further rampart was built over its remains. This had a

Aerial view of Moel y Gaer, Rhosesmor, from the north

sloping front, and probably a breastwork for defence on its crest. The outer embanked palisade, visible on the south and west, may well have belonged with this phase, which might logically be seen as defending the rectangular stone-floored buildings of the latest settlement. None of the buildings is now visible.

49
Pen y cloddiau, Nannerch
Iron Age hillfort
Late 1st millennium BC
OS 116 SJ 128676 U4

From Denbigh, take A525 towards Ruthin. At southern bypass roundabout, take minor road towards Llangwyfan and Llandyrnog. After 2.7ml (4.3km), go straight on at roundabout; 0.5ml (0.8km) further on, turn L at crossroads. After 2.4ml (3.9km), park on L at end of forestry. Follow Offa's Dyke path (on R through forestry gate) to top of hill (0.6ml, 1km). Moel Arthur (no. 50) accessible from same spot

The 21ha hillfort of Pen y cloddiau occupies an imposing heather- and bilberry-covered hilltop in the Clwydian range with wide views in most directions. Its defences consist for the most part of a single substantial grass-covered rampart with an internal quarry ditch, an outer ditch and a counterscarp bank beyond, although extra defences were provided on the north and north-east where dead ground was unavoidable.

The visitor arrives at the south, where a simple original entrance is flanked by inturned banks in a design common in Marcher hillforts; the passage would have rendered attackers approaching a gate at the inner end vulnerable to defenders on either side. The path continues along the hillfort's south-western side, where a field bank caps the rampart, while the counterscarp bank had until recently been lost in forestry. It is now clearly visible beyond the ditch, and becomes more substantial further north.

The quarry ditch is not generally wide enough for huts, which occupy this position on many sites. There are, however, some level platforms, possibly more recent, behind the rampart midway along this side, clearly visible on a rising slope as one approaches. A gap in the bank to their south-east may relate to them. The vegetation masks features in the interior, although numerous hut positions were recorded close to the bank on the north-east in 1962 after heather-burning.

Aerial view of Pen y cloddiau from the north-east

At the northern end, a third and fourth bank help to cover dead ground; interestingly, there is no entrance. The path follows the upper bank to the top of the hill, then drops away over the defences to the north. Moel Arthur hillfort (no. 50) can be clearly seen looking back from here. The ramparts on this side are largely of stone; it is worth going a short way down the path to appreciate their full impact. A path continues around the remainder of the circuit, passing a modern shelter built into the rampart.

The single bank and ditch are more pronounced on the north-east, where there are two possible entrances, fairly close together. The northernmost is relatively slight, and does not look original; it has been considerably worn by farm vehicles. The other, to the south of a stretch of triple bank, is more complex, exploiting a steep-sided natural valley which runs into the fort here. A bank joining the ends of the three banks provides a slight inturn, while only a single low bank continues across the valley bottom. No track is now visible here.

At intervals on the south-east, and towards the southern end, the quarry ditch is rock-cut. The ditch and counterscarp fade out, but the main bank persists. At the south end, the much reduced bank sits above a row of crags, with a second row further down the hill providing an intermittent outer defence.

50
Moel Arthur, Nannerch

Iron Age hillfort

Late 1st millennium BC

OS 116 SJ 145660 U4

From Denbigh, follow directions for Pen y cloddiau (no. 49) to car park. Take Offa's Dyke path on opposite side of road to saddle at top of hill; turn R at field gate on to broad green track up hill. If approaching from S, follow path to same point; direct approaches on both sides seriously eroded

Aerial view of Moel Arthur from the north-east

Moel Arthur is a steep-sided, conical hill on heather moorland, with spectacular views from the summit cairn, including Pen y cloddiau (no. 49) to the north. It is crowned by a roughly circular hillfort, 5ha in extent, defended by two strong banks and ditches on the weaker north side, at the eastern end of which is the entrance, through which the green track enters. Elsewhere, the slopes are steeper and the defences are just scarps. The outer scarp on the south-west is surmounted by a field wall, with improved land beyond. A hollow in the centre of the site may mark the site of an excavation in 1849, which revealed slight traces of stone structures. Hut circles are visible in the interior after heather-burning, but are not otherwise apparent. A Bronze Age hoard of early Irish flat axes is also known to come from the vicinity.

51
Moel Fenlli, Llanbedr Dyffryn Clwyd

Iron Age hillfort

Late 1st millennium BC

OS 116 SJ 163601 U4

From Ruthin, take A494 towards Mold. After 2ml (3.2km), turn L just after RH hairpin bend. 1.2ml (1.9km) further on, park in car park either on L before cattle grid or on R beyond.

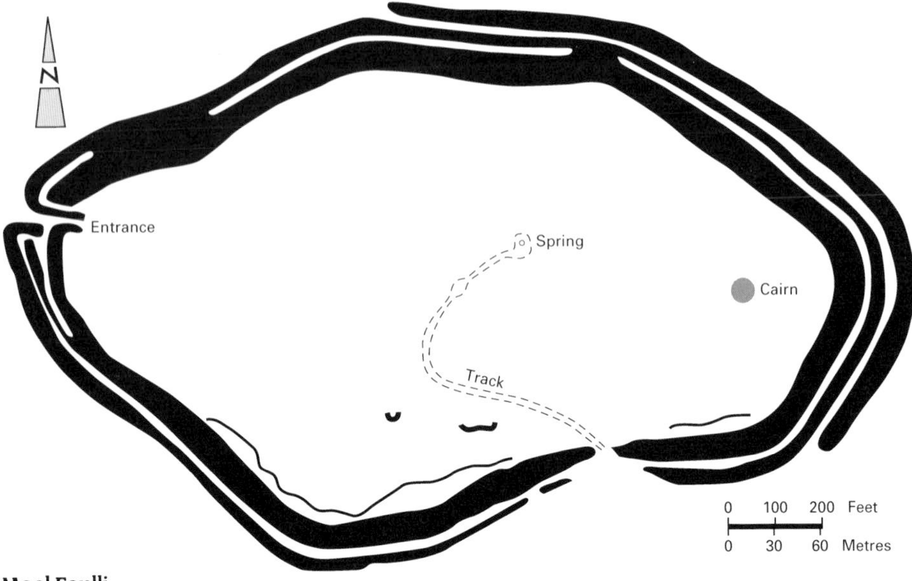

Moel Fenlli

Follow Offa's Dyke path up hill on R, from gate to R of cattle grid. Site surrounds summit. Please keep to path to avoid erosion

Moel Fenlli lies at the western end of a ridge running west-south-west to east-north-east, overlooking passes through the Clwydian Hills to both north and south. The hillfort defences enclose 10ha, including a domed summit and a quite steeply sloping area to its west. Much of this would have been suitable for building, and numerous hut platforms have been reported; these are clearly visible only when the heather has been burnt off, but undulations can be seen even beneath it.

The main entrance is on the west, and the terrace followed by the path up the hill from the north might be an original approach. The banks are inturned a short way, although they have been disturbed by 19th-century excavation and by more recent visitor erosion. The strongest defences are on the north, and especially on the north-east and east, where the approach along the ridge is easiest. The northern defences are double, with a quarry scoop behind each of the banks; the inner scoop may well have contained huts. Along the eastern half of the northern side the outer bank also has an outer ditch with a slight counterscarp bank, while the inner bank gradually increases in size. On the east the outer bank divides into two, a smaller bank rising out of its inner face.

The summit of the hill is marked by a modern cairn fairly close to the eastern defences. The peak to the north is Moel Famau, with the remains of a monument built for George III's golden jubilee in 1810; to its left, on the second skyline, is the domed outline of Moel y Gaer, Llanbedr, another strongly defended hillfort, on a westward-facing spur overlooking the Vale of Clwyd.

As the defences of Moel Fenlli continue from the east round to the south the outer counterscarp bank gradually peters out, followed by the outer bank. This corner has been badly eroded by the path. Further west, the terrace of a probable later trackway runs up the hill towards a break in the defences just before they drop steeply to the west, and crosses them to continue into the interior. This is unlikely to be an original entrance. The defences beyond this are much weaker, with only one bank along most of the south side, although a second reappears briefly about halfway along, resuming beyond the south-west corner and continuing to the western entrance.

The hillfort would have been well supplied with water, having a spring in the interior and others immediately outside on the south-east.

52
Pont Petryal Enclosures, Clawddnewydd

Iron Age enclosures

Late 1st millennium BC

OS 116 SJ 044522 U4

From Ruthin, take B5105 towards Clawddnewydd and Cerrigydrudion. After 6.8ml (11km), park at RHS by forestry track marked R101, opposite Glan y Gors Farm. Walk along track into forest (0.3ml, 0.5km) and take first L. Both sites in clearings a little way down hill on R

Two clearings in the forest, separated by a shelter belt, each contain a roughly circular enclosure with very low but visible banks, 0.3m high and 3m wide. The banks are covered with tussocky rank grass typical of ungrazed areas within plantations, and a scattering of bracken. The sites lie on a gentle south-westerly slope.

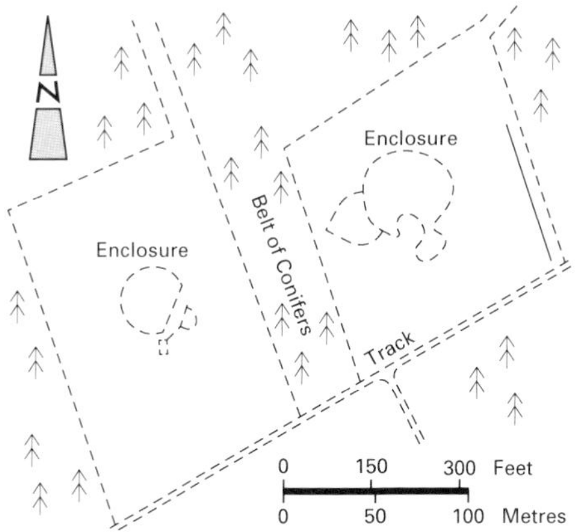

Pont Petryal enclosures

The eastern enclosure averages 48m across, with annexes to the south and west formed by narrower walls. A rowan tree stands on its south-west side. You can walk through the shelter belt to the western enclosure, which is very similar.

These enclosures are fairly typical of the smaller type of Iron Age site, which might have been used either as a small farmstead, containing one or more huts, or a defended stock enclosure; possibly even a combination of the two.

53
Bryn Alyn Promontory Fort, Gwersyllt

Iron Age promontory fort

Late 1st millennium BC

OS 117 SJ 332537 R4

From Wrexham (or Wrexham bypass), take A541 towards Mold. 1.4ml (2.3km) beyond bypass, turn R towards Bradley. At roundabout after 200m, go straight ahead. Continue for 0.6ml (1km) to junction with B5425, turn L. Turn R at top of hill beyond cutting after 0.6ml (1km); turn immediately R again, and fork R again shortly. Park at Bryn Alyn Community complex, about 0.3ml (0.5km) from main road. Skirt round left of buildings and cross playing field to RH end of fence; note barrow in field to L of track near first corner. NB: Please contact Bryn Alyn Community (01978 855811) before visiting, and report to reception on arrival

Bryn Alyn promontory fort is very strongly defended, enclosing only about 1.25ha. It occupies the western side of a narrow tongue of land enclosed within a bend in the river Alyn, the steep-sided valley of which provides

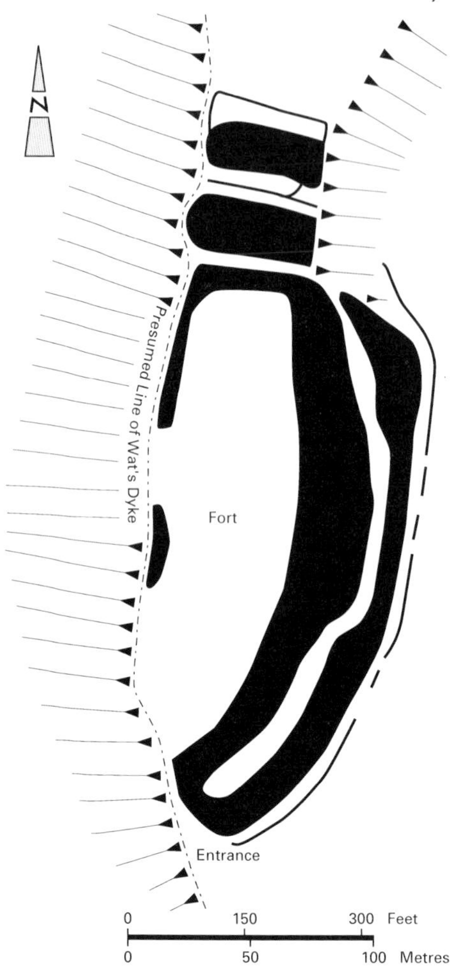

Bryn Alyn promontory fort

the site with excellent natural defences. The steepest slope leads directly down to the river on the west of the enclosure; faint traces of a bank along its top may be part of the early medieval Wat's Dyke. At the south end, the ridge, including the line of the Dyke, runs down to the river somewhat more gently, and there are remains of a probable entrance. The relatively steep slope on the eastern side of the promontory has a pair of defensive banks and ditches as additional protection.

The most impressive defences are, however, the three banks and ditches across its narrow northern neck. The innermost bank is fairly slight, possibly damaged by ploughing, but the remaining features are all substantial. The middle bank has a level berm along its outer edge, between its base and its ditch. There is no evidence for an entrance at this end, although the area has never been excavated; the present track appears quite recent. The site would have been extremely strong if the southern entrance was the only one, but it would have been difficult for a farming population to exploit the level area to the north. This might suggest that the site was used only as a refuge, at least in its present form; it fits a pattern of strongly defended small promontory forts which may have been refurbished, or even first built, in the early medieval period. No traces of occupation are visible in the wooded interior, which has been ploughed in the past.

54
Caer Drewyn, Corwen

Iron Age hillfort

Late 1st millennium BC

OS 125 SJ 088444 U4

From Llangollen, take A5 to Corwen (10.6ml, 17km); turn R in centre of village. At T-junction after 0.6ml (1km), take B5437 L. Continue for 0.8ml (1.3km) to junction with A5104; turn R. After 1ml (1.6km), park in lay-by near R turn; follow waymarked path S along lane on foot to L turn; take L track through gate up hill round south of site to entrance on E (1ml, 1.6km). Please do not move stones

Bowen and Gresham 1967

Caer Drewyn occupies an imposing hilltop position, overlooking an important natural route focus: the Dee valley runs south-west and east from here, the Alwen, west and the Morwynion, north-east; northwards, a pass gives access to the Vale of Clwyd. The first enclosure on the site appears to have been relatively small, with a single U-shaped bank against the natural scarp to the north; only the portion outside the later fort, the bank of which seems to have more or less bisected it, is now clearly visible. The junction between the two can be seen from the access track; the later rampart is stony, while the earlier is grass-covered.

The entrance into this early enclosure, beside the track, is unusual, with the banks turned outwards past the ends of the ditches. This layout may however date from the site's last phase, possibly in the Roman period or even later, when a small enclosure containing two well preserved hut circles and traces of other features was made, reusing parts of the earlier work, by joining the first and second phase ramparts with a further bank on the north.

The main entrance to the large second-phase fort lies to the north of this final-phase blocking-bank. This entrance has been described as inturned with probable guard-chambers at the inner end, but the detail of this is difficult to trace among the rubble. The main enclosure continues down the slope across a pronounced scarp, below which it is more slightly built, with a higher soil content, suggesting an addition, although no rampart is apparent along the scarp itself. This drystone rampart can be seen in several places to retain part of its original facework, an unusual survival on such early sites.

At the lower end is another, simpler entrance, with a slight inturn; in it are the remains of a rectangular building, probably of medieval date, while another similar and better preserved building lies just beyond. Looking back up the inside of the northern rampart from this western gate, there are traces of terraces, which may have supported buildings belonging to the fort. The only certain hut site in the main fort, a flattened round platform, lies on the east opposite a very large stone in the base of the rampart.

Aerial view of Caer Drewyn from the south-east

55
Craig yr Ychain Enclosure, Llandrillo

Iron Age enclosure

Late 1st millennium BC

OS 125 SJ 024366 U4

From Llangollen, take A5 to Corwen. Beyond village (11.3ml, 18.2km from Llangollen), take B4401 L towards Cynwyd and Llandrillo. In Llandrillo (5ml, 8km) turn L beyond church; fork R after 150m; turn R at Rhos uchaf 0.3ml (0.5km) further on. Parking by trackway on L at beginning of moorland or on R beyond Ysgubor newydd, after 0.6ml (1km); also at far end. Take track L up hill opposite house, keep straight on at top of rise, settlement lies on L after track bears R into bracken a little further on (0.3ml, 0.5km). Permissive right of way only, no dogs please. Best when bracken down

The Craig yr Ychain enclosure, measuring 63m east–west by 45m, exploits a steep natural slope on the south and east, and has a single bank and ditch on the north and west. It occupies a spur with good views to the north and east, although it is overlooked by higher ground on the south and especially on the west, where the defences are strongest. The entrance was probably on the east. There are

Craig yr Ychain enclosure from the air

Aerial view of Moel y Gaer, Llangollen

traces of drystone walling at intervals around the site, especially where the ditch is rock-cut. Even with the bracken on, possible hut positions are visible in the interior, although it is difficult to see detail. This site would probably have been used as a small farmstead, in all likelihood by a single extended family.

56
Moel y Gaer, Llangollen

Iron Age hillfort

Late 1st millennium BC

OS 116 SJ 167464 U4

From Llangollen, follow directions for Moel y Gamelin (no. 18). Moel y Gaer lies on the next summit, some way lower (2.1ml, 3.4km). Fair weather advisable

Moel y Gaer is a 0.8ha hillfort on a low rocky summit on Llantysilio mountain. It has reasonable views in most directions, but is rather overlooked by Moel y Gamelin to the east; this would however have been well beyond the range of contemporary weapons.

The single bank is up to 3.1m high externally and 0.6m internally, with an inturned entrance 20m long on the east. It is fronted by a ditch around the north of the fort, while on the west it has been worn away by motorcycles and walkers using the path along the ridge. There are numerous possible positions for hut platforms in the interior, although the ground cover of bilberries and heather makes it difficult to distinguish detail.

57
Gaer Fawr, Guilsfield

Iron Age hillfort

Late 1st millennium BC

OS 126 SJ 224130 U4 WT

From roundabout on W of Welshpool, take A490 towards Llanfyllin. After 1.8ml (2.9km), take B4392 R to Guilsfield. At far end of village, 1.4ml, 2.3km from last turnoff, turn L towards Geuffordd. Park in small WT car park on R after 0.5ml (0.8km)

Gaer Fawr occupies the summit of a long hill, running south-west to north-east; the slope is somewhat steeper on the south-east side than on the north-west. An information board in the car park provides a good introduction to the site, which is of interest for its woodland as well as its archaeology. The walk begins from the stile on the right, although there is an easier path to the fort's north-eastern entrance through the gate.

The path leads up the hill and through a kissing gate, a short distance beyond which lie the earthworks of the south-west entrance. These are staggered, requiring an attacking force to expose their unshielded right sides to the defenders above, while confined to a passage between two ramparts. A long inturned entrance passage at the inner end may have contained two or more wooden gates, producing a 'kill zone' comparable with that in some medieval castles. The path enters the upper fort through this passage, although it passes over the outer works rather than following the full original route. Much of the interior is open grazing but there are no obvious hut platforms.

The south-eastern defence is mainly a double scarp, with a 'ditch' platform interrupting the slope, although at one point towards the north-east there is only one scarp. A disused field boundary exaggerates the height of the 'bank' above the scarped slope. Along the north-west side there are apparently two sets of defences, an inner scarp, largely a natural feature of impressive size, running virtually down the middle of the total enclosed area, and an outer scarp with a rock-cut ditch and a stony counterscarp bank. These probably represent two different phases, with an increase from *c.*1.25ha to *c.*2.7ha at some stage. A slight bank across a natural constriction of the hill, towards the north of the inner enclosure, may represent a still earlier phase. The ground level of the western area is considerably below that of the presumably earlier part of the fort, into which both the entrances lead.

The simpler north-eastern entrance, through which the main path leaves, consists of a trackway straight down the hill, passing through gaps in two main banks, probably protected by gates, but channelled past the ends of two more short outworks further down. The path to the left just inside this entrance returns along the outer defences on the north-west; from it both these and the inner scarp can be well appreciated.

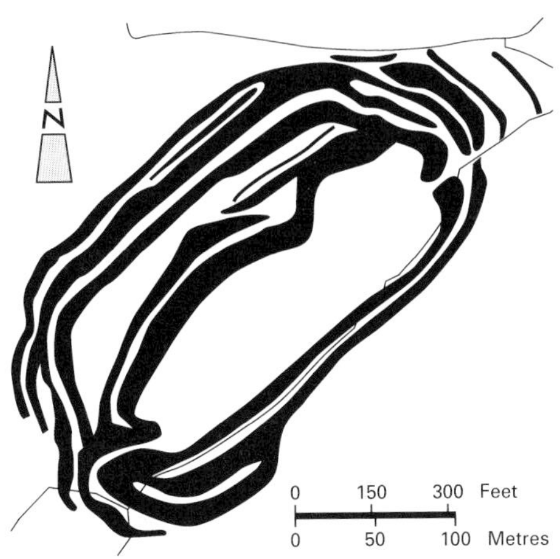

Gaer Fawr, Guilsfield

58
The Breiddin, Welshpool

Bronze Age and Iron Age hillfort/ Roman period occupation

1000 BC–AD 400

OS 126 SJ 295144 U4

From Welshpool, take A458/A483 towards Oswestry. 0.7ml (1.1km) beyond northern bypass roundabout, take A458 R towards Shrewsbury. 3.2ml (5.1km) further on, turn L by phone box at Trewern. At T-junction after 1.8ml (2.9km), turn R. Continue through quarry; after 1.3ml (2.1km), take forestry track on R signposted Rodney's Column. Limited parking on L before gate. Continue on foot. After 0.6ml (1km), path branches R, climb steepens; after 0.1ml (0.2km), fork R again. Continue to top (0.3ml; 0.5km), White Well (spring) to L, outer defence visible on R beyond gate. Continue along saddle, then take track R through hillfort entrance to quarry gate, turn R along ridge to monument. Return straight down hill across ramparts. Boots advisable in wet weather

St John O'Neil 1937; Musson, Britnell and Smith 1991

Breidden Hill is the north-westernmost of an isolated group of hills of volcanic origin, overlooking the confluence of the Severn and the Vyrnwy. The 28ha hillfort, one of the largest in the Marches, known to archaeologists since excavations in the 1930s as 'The Breiddin', is not the only defended site on these hills; the univallate enclosure on Middletown Hill is clearly visible to the south-east, while to the east, the much lower Bausley Hill sports a smaller but strongly defended site. It is unknown whether all three were in use at the same time. Another enclosure, excavated in the 1930s, lies on sloping ground in the forestry on New Pieces, between Breidden Hill and Middletown Hill. This was occupied during the Roman period, chiefly in the 2nd and 3rd centuries AD, although its origin may lie much earlier; a post-Roman glass fragment found there also hints at later use. Two banks from its associated field system can be seen running down firebreaks in the forestry towards the saddle below the main hillfort.

The Breiddin itself occupies a ridge running south-west to north-east, with precipitous slopes on the north-west. The hilltop is rocky and narrow at the north-east, but widens towards the lower centre and south-west, where settlement may have concentrated. Much of this end has, however, been forested or quarried away, though parts were excavated beforehand between 1969 and 1975; the readily visible portion, from the entrance north-eastwards, is only about half of the original site; perhaps a fifth of the

Aerial view of The Breiddin, with New Pieces enclosure (lower right)

enclosed area would have been suitable for building.

The visible defences consist of a strong stone inner bank, originally 5–6m wide with revetment walls to front and back, sited well up the slope from the base of the saddle, with a rather weaker outer bank up to 60m outside it. At the entrance, excavated in the 1930s, the two banks join together on either side of a passage trending diagonally to the left, overlooked and defended by natural outcrops and by the innermost bank to the right. The outer bank, which had two gaps on the south-west, may have enclosed an area for stock. A further strong outer rampart, perhaps added later, runs north-east from the entrance at the foot of the slope above the saddle. It has a clear outer ditch and traces of a counterscarp bank, and is visible to the right of the footpath up, capped by a recent field wall; all three banks can be seen on the way down from Rodney's Column. The modern track follows a probably original terrace across the saddle and through the hillfort entrance.

The 1970s excavations, all in areas now quarried away, looked at three areas: a length of the inner rampart and occupation deposits at the southern end of the hill; part of the summit ridge nearby; and a waterlogged area, until recently a pond, further to the north-east. The hilltop had apparently been used sporadically in the later Neolithic and Early Bronze Age, and a hard-standing was laid around the pond in about 1200 bc, well before the first phase of hillfort occupation.

Beneath the inner rampart, a Late Bronze Age defensive line from the 10th or 9th century BC consisted of two parallel lines of post-holes, about 0.8m apart, forming a timber framework for a carefully placed dump of stones and soil, which continued about 2m behind it to a low stone kerb. This rampart apparently received patchy repairs, but eventually collapsed, in places as the result of fire. The Bronze Age fort may, surprisingly, have enclosed the same enormous area as the subsequent Iron Age work.

A sharp drop in oak pollen from the pond deposits coincided with the construction of the Bronze Age rampart. Internal features from this period included a circular post-built structure, not necessarily roofed, a series of furnaces used by bronze-smiths for recycling scrap, and three small 'four-posters' of rather lighter construction than the later Iron Age examples.

At much the same time as the Iron Age defences were built, around 300 BC, a cistern 8m by 6m and over 2m deep was dug into the pond area; this had silted up completely within about a century, but contained valuable Iron Age finds, especially of wood. The numerous buildings within the Iron Age fort consisted of round-houses, mainly 5-7m in diameter, best preserved behind the rampart, but not present near the pond, and rectangular four-posters of variable size, found in all three excavated areas. Round-houses were probably domestic, and four-posters used for storage. No street system was noted in the excavations, although an apparent increase in the proportion of four-posters through time may reflect a change in the 'zoning' of activities within the fort.

Iron Age finds indicated various activities: spinning and weaving (presumably wool); leather working; wood working (good examples were excavated from the cistern); and metal working. Remains of salt containers suggest meat preservation, while threshed grain may indicate processing or storage on site, perhaps for a wider population. It was unclear whether the Iron Age occupation continued beyond about 100 BC.

In the later Roman period, a hard-standing was laid behind the disused rampart; two hearths, one associated with a possible rectangular structure, were found above this, with 3rd- and 4th-century pottery. These remains may reflect agricultural activity, perhaps related to the settlement and fields on New Pieces.

The monument commemorates George Brydges Rodney, Admiral of the White, 1781. Rodney played an important part under George III in restoring British sea power after the American War of Independence.

59
Ffridd Faldwyn, Montgomery

Iron Age hillfort

1st millennium BC

OS 137 SO 217969 U4

Continue up lane from Montgomery Castle car park (no. 118) for 0.5ml (0.8km) to stile on R beside gate (very limited parking between gates opposite). Cross stile and head up hill towards further stile leading to main part of site. Better when bracken down

St John O'Neil 1942; Hogg 1975; Guilbert 1981

Ffridd Faldwyn occupies a prominent hilltop commanding the Severn valley near its confluence with the Camlad and its crucial crossing at Rhydwhyman. It is the precursor of a series of Roman and medieval sites in the area (see nos 117 and 118).

The excavations, in 1937–9, were among the earliest on a hillfort to examine an open area, so that the excavators had little previous evidence to compare with the features they found. Fortunately the work, despite being abandoned in 1939, was conducted and written up to a sufficiently high standard to allow reinterpretation in the light of more recent discoveries, although some problems remain, largely because there were disappointingly few datable finds.

Some Neolithic material was recovered, and the remains of a Bronze Age barrow on the summit were trenched with no result. The earliest Iron Age settlement appears to have been a fairly small enclosure, measuring 170m by 80m (1.2ha), exploiting the natural summit of the hill. It had a double timber palisade, built in two parallel rows *c.*2m apart, the post-holes for which lay beneath the earthwork defences now visible. This enclosure had an entrance on the south, and probably also on the north. In the next phase, the palisade was apparently replaced on the same line by a timber-framed rampart, with an outer ditch; at either this or a later stage a

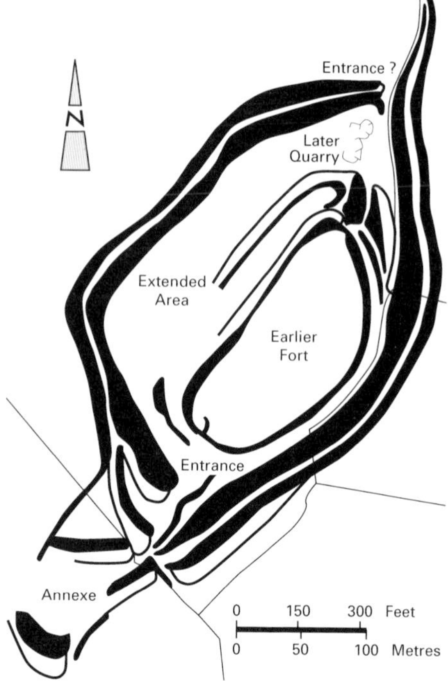

Ffridd Faldwyn

second ditch was added around much of the west side. The distance between the two ditches was increased at the north entrance, and their ends joined by ditches along the entrance way, providing a 'barbican' in front of the gate. Outworks, some of which have become confused with the outer enclosure, were provided at the vulnerable south-west end. The inner rampart is today reduced to a scarp for most of its circuit, although some stretches towards the south-west appear more clearly as a bank.

At a later date, a timber-laced rampart, with a second rampart outside it, was constructed at a lower level, completely surrounding the earlier work, and obscuring any earlier outer ditch on the east. It enclosed a greatly increased defended area, 300m by 200m (4.4ha). The main entrance of this larger enclosure faced south-west, and an annexe was built at this vulnerable end, visible in the field next to the road, before the entrance proper is reached over the second stile. A 'barbican' like that on the north of the earlier fort was provided at the entrance, which was probably modified a number of times. A simpler entrance was provided on the north.

After the timber-laced rampart of this phase had become ruinous it was replaced around the main fort by a simple earthen rampart; this work was originally interpreted as a hasty refortification in the face of the Roman approach, since the new rampart contained human remains, but this may reflect ritual practice. Both banks survive as substantial scarps, the inner 5–8m high, the outer 3–6m, separated by a terrace 3–4m wide.

The inner enclosure contained numbers of large post-holes, almost certainly for 'four-posters', which might have served as granaries. The excavators believed that these were built after the outer enclosure, and protected by a limited refortification of the inner defences, but this now seems unlikely. The date of the structures is uncertain; they may belong to the smaller fort or represent a specific zone within the larger. A number of round hut sites containing hearths and occupation debris were uncovered between the inner and outer enclosure, to the west of the south-western entrance; much of the rest of the plateau between the two lines of defence would also be suitable for building, but bracken makes it difficult to see any detail. Parts of the site are wooded and scrub-covered, but the summit is open and much of the detail can be appreciated from it.

60
Castle Ring, Presteigne

Iron Age enclosure

Late 1st millennium BC

OS 148 SO 267636 U4

In Presteigne, take B4355 towards Kington. Turn R almost immediately into Warden Road, and take first R past castle (no. 123). Site in plantation on L after 3.2ml (5.1km); car park through entrance or lay-by beyond. Take track from car park, at right angles to road; track bends R round site, then enters. Boots advisable in wet weather

Castle Ring is a roughly oval earthwork, measuring 136m north-west–south-east by 106m, on the south-western edge of a plateau. It is strongly defended by a fine single bank, rising over 3m above the base of the ditch, with a counterscarp bank in places. There are entrances at either end of the oval, the north-west (from which the track enters) and the south-east. Part of the bank on the north-east has been damaged by quarrying. The interior is fairly flat, but there is no trace of structures.

The forestry makes it difficult to appreciate the wider setting of the site, although the interior is not now planted and the banks support mature deciduous trees. The enclosure lies just to the west of Offa's Dyke (no. 94), although the two are probably not related.

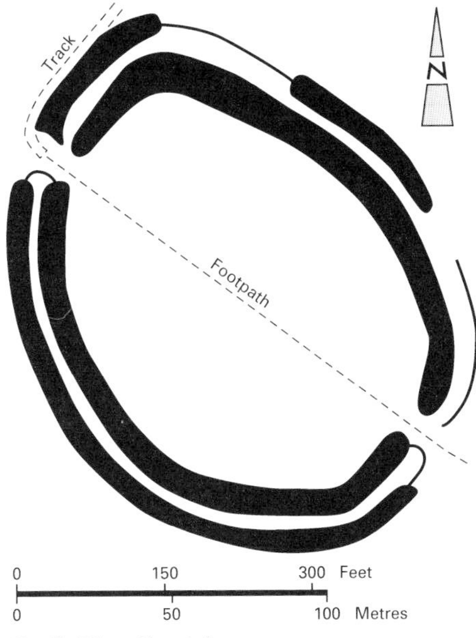

Castle Ring, Presteigne

61
Pen y crug, Brecon
Iron Age hillfort
Late 1st millennium BC
OS 160 SO 029303 U4 BBNP

In Brecon, turn off B4601 immediately N of bridge. In Cradoc, after 2.2ml (3.5km), turn R. 0.8ml (1.3km) further on, park in lay-by on L; path signposted opposite. Best access to site from farther (S) side; follow path to next marker beyond crest to reach this. Boots essential in wet weather; bottom of path can be slippery. Better when bracken down

RCAHMW Brecknock ii, HF 33

Aerial view of Pen y crug, Brecon, from the north-west

The imposing hillfort of Pen y crug occupies the summit of a prominent, steep-sided hill, which overlooks the valleys of the Usk and the Honddu, including modern Brecon, to the south and east respectively, and looks towards the more distant Yscir further west. A walk round the top of the inner rampart shows off the site and its commanding setting to advantage.

Despite its good natural position, it is strongly defended. The defences were built by throwing material down the hill, a common technique where slopes are steep, so that there is a quarry ditch inside the innermost bank and a counterscarp bank outside the outermost ditch. The number of banks, not including the counterscarp, varies between three on the steeper west side, and at the north-east, and four elsewhere; the fourth bank and ditch merge with the third where not required. The innermost bank is individually the most impressive, with an outer scarp between 4.0m and 5.2m high, although it is the overall effect of the defences which renders the site so outstanding. A simple, slightly inturned, entrance lies on the south-east; its passage narrows towards the innermost rampart, which probably supported a gate. The defended area measures 182m north to south by 134m; bracken makes it difficult to identify any hut positions although the interior, which has been ploughed in the past, does undulate suggestively.

There are traces of an annexe with a single bank and ditch adjoining the site on the south, although later quarrying has obscured its relationship with the main defences. This earthwork might have provided extra protection on the side with the easiest approach, or have contained animals or equipment. Earlier commentators suggested that, together with a section of scarp and ditch in the south-west of the main fort's interior, it represented the remains of an earlier enclosure, but detailed survey now makes this seem unlikely.

Small-scale quarrying has damaged the ramparts at a number of other points, although only limited areas are affected; visitors scrambling on the banks are causing erosion, so please try to avoid this. Traces of field banks nearby are probably more recent than the hillfort.

62
Slwch Tump, Brecon
Iron Age hillfort
Late 1st millennium BC
OS 160 SO 057284 R4

In Brecon, take A4062 Free Street/ Cerrigcochion Road NE from B4601. Path, signposted Ty'n y caeau and YH, begins 0.3ml (0.5km) up, through gap on R above hospital, opposite lane on L. Parking on verge, or in car park c.*300m down hill. Total round walk 1.3ml (2.1km); please keep to path. Boots advisable in wet weather*

RCAHMW Brecknock ii, HF 30

Slwch Tump, though in an imposing position above Brecon, is largely concealed from below by trees and field boundaries. At the junction *c.*250m along the path, take the footpath straight on. Keep the hedge on the right to the gap, go through, then follow the terrace to a further stretch of hedge. The western bank of the site can be seen from about here, running down the hill from the left to meet the path at its southern corner; beyond the fence the path follows the south scarp of the fort, with wide views across Brecon and the Usk valley to the south.

The fort itself is roughly oval, except for the sharp angle at the south-western corner, already mentioned; it measures 242m east–west by 187m. The summit of the small dome-shaped hill which it encloses lies towards the north-west corner. The defences today consist of a single scarp, between 3.0m and 4.6m high, with traces of a ditch on the north and especially on the east, where there are also hints of a counterscarp bank. Most of the area has been ploughed, destroying any evidence for structures in the interior; 18th-century sources suggest that the counterscarp bank may previously have been more extensive, although it was probably deemed unnecessary on the steeper south and west. Field boundaries run just inside the rampart on all sides but the west, where the two coincide. The original entrance was probably a simple inturned gap at the north-west, since damaged by quarrying and by use as a field access. Quarrying has also taken place in the south-east of the interior and outside the defences to the north-east.

The path continues along the crest of the scarp around the eastern end of the site. As it reaches the north side, it gradually runs away from the defences, which remain visible for some distance (ignore an earlier sharp right turn), and returns to the bridleway, completing the round walk. The hill was formerly known as Penginger or Pen cefn y gaer, 'the hilltop ridge with the hillfort'.

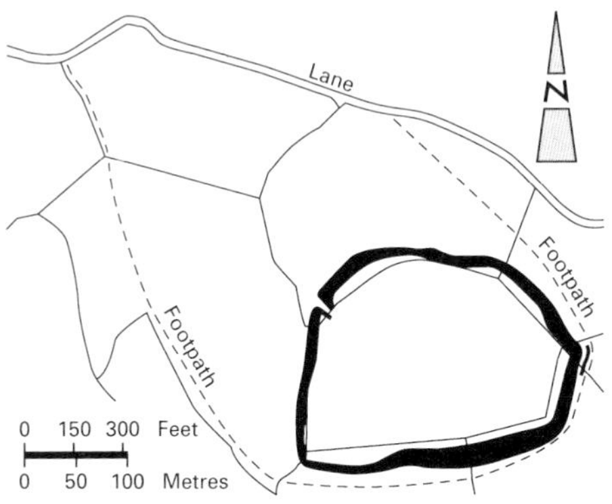

Slwch Tump, Brecon

63
Allt yr Esgair, Llangorse

Iron Age hillfort

Late 1st millennium BC

OS 161 SO 126245 U4

From Crickhowell, take A40 towards Brecon. After 6.6ml (10.6km), take R turn for Pennorth; 0.2ml (0.3km) further on, park near entrance to Middlewood Farm (very limited). On foot, take bridleway through gate to L of drive, follow to top of hill (forestry on RHS) (1.3ml, 2.1km). Earthworks begin just after stone cross-wall near top of hill. Boots advisable in wet weather

RCAHMW Brecknock ii, HF 47

The hillfort on Allt yr Esgair occupies the top of a steep-sided ridge running north-north-west to south-south-east; it consists of a main enclosure measuring 566m by 114m, and an annexe on the southern end a further 130m

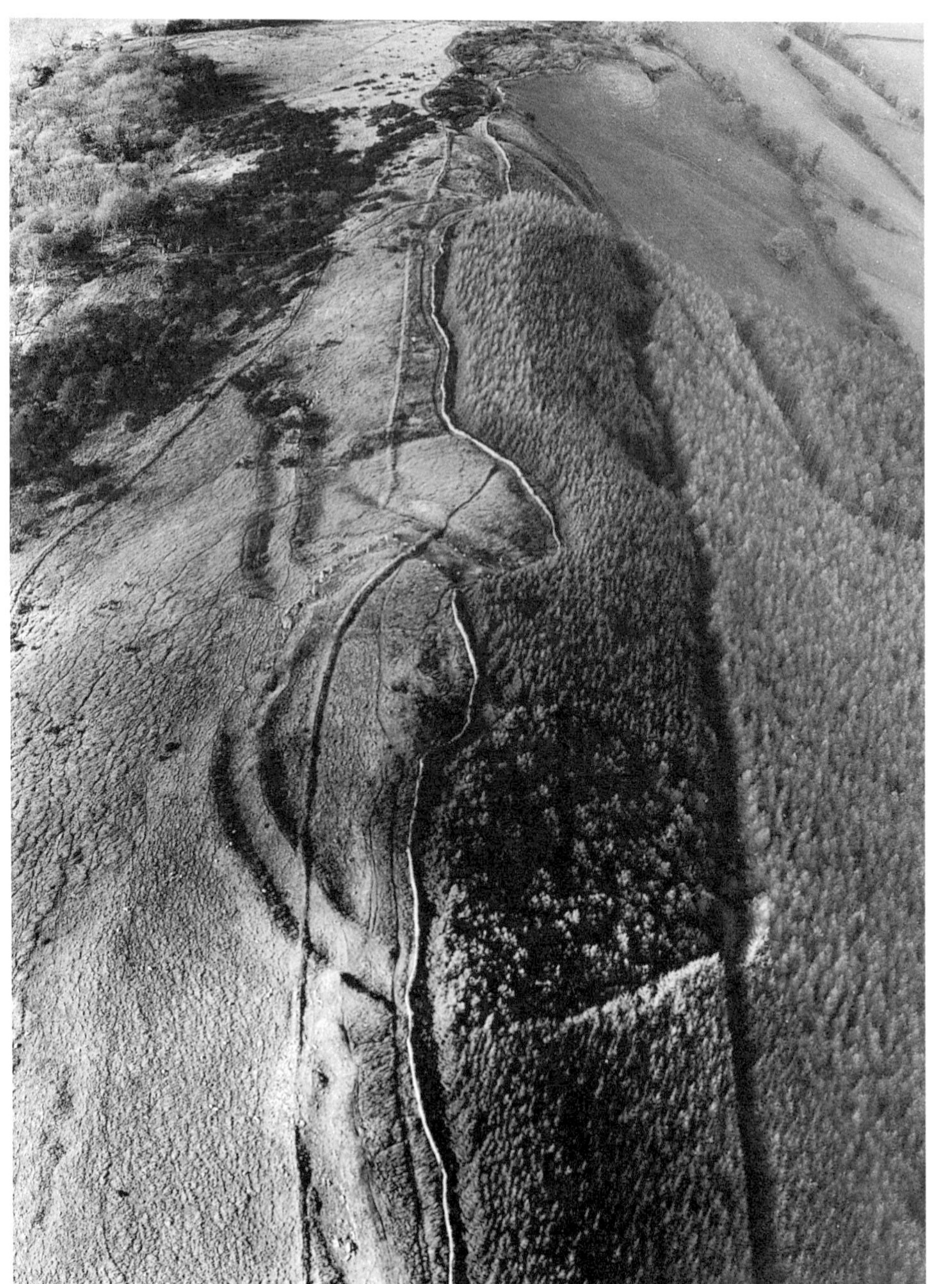

Aerial view of Allt yr Esgair from the south

long. The detail of the site is somewhat confused by past quarrying on and around parts of the remains, and by a disused boundary bank running along the ridge beside the path. There may have been a smaller, earlier fort enclosing only the high point at the south end of the main fort, and the annexe may originally have been part of an earlier arrangement; the junctions between the annexe and the main site are not altogether clear.

The site commands magnificent views to both sides of the ridge, covering the Usk valley on the west, and the Llynfi valley and Llangorse lake on the east and north-east. The recently felled forestry plantation also makes it difficult to appreciate the archaeological features on this side of the fort, which lie for the most part along a track which has caused some damage to them. Fortunately the most impressive features are clearly visible in the pasture on the western side of the hill.

The site is defended by a scarp between 2m and 8m high, except on the western side of the annexe where a natural cliff serves instead. In places this scarp was crowned by a bank, built by quarrying material from behind it, where quarry ditches and irregular pits can be seen. Some parts of the circuit, particularly the north-west, south and south-west of the main fort and the south of the annexe, were further reinforced with a shelf or ditch at the base of the scarp; where the ditch is best represented the upcast from it has been used to form a substantial counterscarp which gives the appearance of a second bank.

The later quarrying makes it difficult to reconstruct the positions of the entrances, although there can be no doubt about the main access at the northern end, through which the bridleway passes as a very distinct hollow way. Other entrances have been postulated halfway along the west side, where the double defences to the south meet the simpler scarp further north, and at the south-east end of the annexe, although the evidence for the latter is debatable. There are no obviously prehistoric features visible in the interior.

Aerial view of Crug Hywel from the north

64
Crug Hywel, Crickhowell

Iron Age hillfort

Late 1st millennium BC

OS 161 SO 226207 U4

In Crickhowell, turn N off A40 opposite castle (no. 130). Take Standard Street R at T-junction; go L at next junction. After 2.6ml (4.2km), park in lay-by on L, just before cottage; take path L signposted 'Table Mountain'. A short distance beyond top of plantation, take track on L and follow along side of ridge (1.2ml, 1.9km in all). Site on summit at far end. Route joins shorter path up (steeper, less parking) at its foot. Boots advisable

RCAHMW Brecknock ii, HF 64

Crug Hywel, from which the town takes its name, is a very distinctive hilltop overlooking the confluence of the Grwyne Fechan and Usk. The hill commands spectacular wide views, and offers an ideal site for a defensive hillfort, with very steep natural slopes on all sides apart from the north, where there is higher ground beyond a saddle.

The relatively level triangular hilltop has been enclosed, more or less following a contour, with a rampart constructed at least in part from the underlying stone. This is accompanied by an external ditch, which varies from a true ditch with a counterscarp bank (probably resulting from the dumping of spoil on its outer side) on the north-west, north and east, to little more than a shelf elsewhere, reflecting the steepness of the slopes and natural erosion. The defended area measures 162m north-west to south-east by 59m. At the pointed north-western corner there is a particularly impressive rock outcrop, and the height between the ditch and the top of the bank here reaches nearly 8m; elsewhere it is about 7m.

There is one entrance, on the eastern side, where the bank is slightly inturned. It was approached from the north, although quarrying to the north and north-east has obscured the course of the trackway except in the immediate area of the entrance.

A number of hut platforms are visible in the interior. These are especially impressive and well preserved on the north, between the entrance and the north-western corner, where there are at least four examples. Others survive towards the south end of the west side. Unfortunately, a number of shelters and cairns have been constructed in more recent times, which confuse the picture somewhat. In particular, a possible hut platform immediately to the south of the entrance is now difficult to appreciate. On the slopes south-west of the site a small stone enclosure and lengths of bank may relate to an associated field system.

65
Coed Cefn Enclosure, Crickhowell

Iron Age enclosure

Late 1st millennium BC

OS 161 SO 228186 U4 WT

In Crickhowell, turn N off A40 opposite castle (no. 130). Take Standard Street R at T-junction; go straight on at next junction. Limited parking on LHS at end of woodland, 1ml (1.6km) from original turning. Take path into wood; fork L, then R up hill. Site on hilltop, straddling path

RCAHMW Brecknock ii, HF 63

Coed Cefn enclosure is a small sub-rectangular site, measuring 68m north–south by 51m, with a single defensive bank and intermittent ditch. It now lies in woodland, which makes it difficult to appreciate as a whole, or to see more than a glimpse of the views it commanded; nonetheless, most of the defensive circuit , 0.2–0.8m high internally and up to 1.75m high externally, can be followed. There are traces of an outer counterscarp bank on the north and north-east. The entrance probably lay on the east, beneath the present path.

Quarrying has damaged parts of the site, particularly at the north-west corner, internally at the south-west, and outside the bank on the south, where the ground falls away steeply.

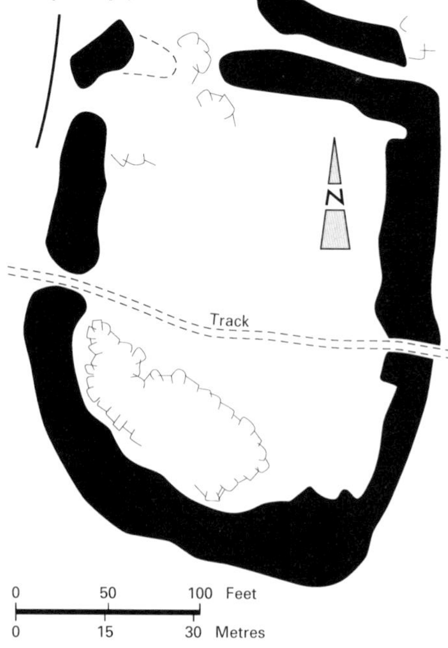

Coed Cefn enclosure

4
The Roman Period

It is quite possible that the Romans did not originally intend to conquer Wales at all, judging that the inhabitants would be unlikely to respond to Romanisation and were not ready to settle down in comfortable (and easily controlled) towns. While this assessment proved correct, with civilian *civitates* ultimately being established only in south-east and south-west Wales, and over the border to the east, conquest nonetheless became necessary because the 'free' areas harboured dissidents; Welsh mineral resources must also have proved an attraction. In the early years after the invasion of Britain by Claudius in AD 43, Welsh resistance centred upon Caratacus, the fugitive heir to the powerful eastern Thames kingdom of the Catuvellauni.

Although Caratacus had taken refuge with the Silures of south-east Wales, the Romans started their campaign against him by crushing the Deceangli of eastern Clwyd, in the hope of severing contact between the hostile elements in Wales and their sympathisers in the client kingdom of Brigantia, to the north. While military steps to cordon off Siluria were underway, Caratacus moved on to the Ordovices, who were centred in mid-Wales. After making a last stand (the identity of the site is a subject of lively debate), he escaped to Brigantia, but the pro-Roman Queen Cartimandua handed him over in AD 51.

Despite the removal of Caratacus, the Silures won a notable victory over Roman forces in AD 52. Other factors meant that it was AD 57 before the Roman campaign could be seriously resumed, but this time it proceeded smoothly and culminated in the capture of Anglesey in AD 60. These conquests could not be not consolidated, however, since Boudica's rebellion, already underway in south-east England, demanded the withdrawal of most of the troops from Wales.

Archaeological evidence for the military sites belonging to this initial conquest is very thin, and almost entirely concentrated in the Marches and along the Glamorgan and Gwent coast. Caersws I (see no. 68), Clyro (north-east of Hay), Colwyn Castle (at Hundred House, east of Builth) and a possible site at Nantmel, east of Rhayader, may date from this period, as may some of the temporary camps in the Leintwardine, Kerry (south of Newtown) and Walton areas. The lack of consolidation at this stage may well have meant that the forts remained relatively slight in their construction.

Under the Flavian emperors, the breakup of Brigantia made the reconquest of a

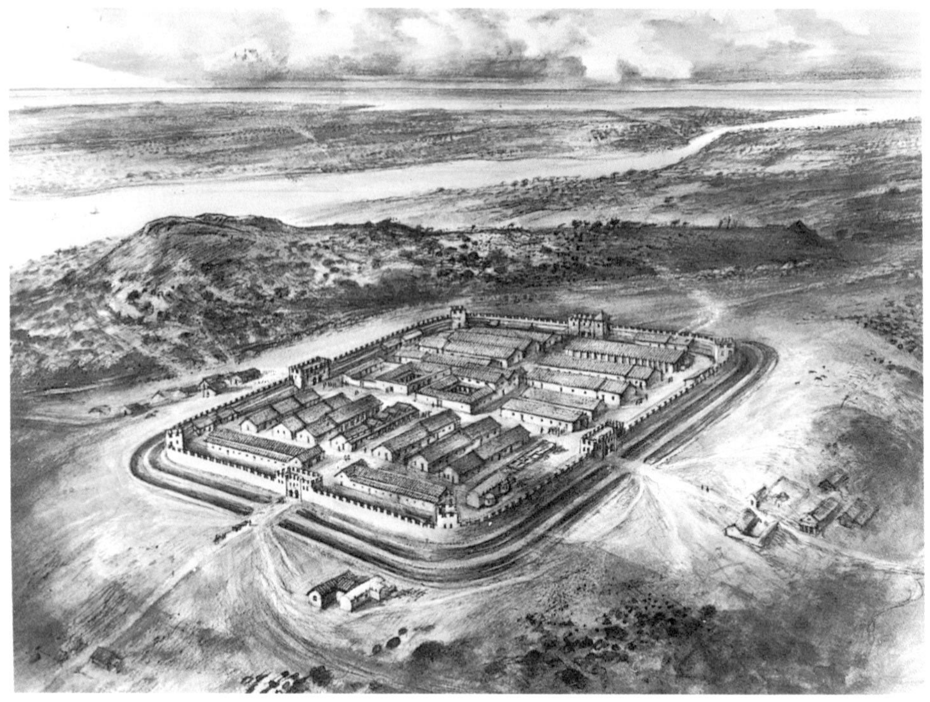

Reconstruction drawing of a Roman fort

newly restive Wales once more a pressing issue. The campaign, starting in about AD 74, probably proceeded from the south, with forces working inland from Neath, Cardiff, Caerleon and possibly also Carmarthen; from the east, the upper Severn, the Teme, the Walton gap and the Wye were probably also used as lines of penetration. Temporary camps from this period survive along these routes in a number of areas (e.g. Y Pigwn, no. 72); in Powys, there are particular concentrations around Kerry (if not from the earlier campaign), in the mountains north-west of Castell Collen (no. 71) (e.g. Esgairperfedd, no. 70), at Walton and near Beulah. In the north, the progress of the campaign is less clear, although scattered temporary camps lie along the Corwen–Bala–Dolgellau axis; the only one of these in Clwyd is at Penrhos, west of Corwen.

The campaign was complete by AD 77; numerous forts were built to consolidate the position, although most of them had been abandoned by the AD 120s. Several of these are known from Powys, but although Roman material has come from Corwen, Ruthin, St Asaph and Prestatyn, excavations have failed to produce conclusive evidence of forts from Clwyd. Clwyd was however within the military orbit of the site at Rhyn Park, across the river from Chirk, and later of the legionary fortress at Chester; another fort lay on its north-western boundary at Caerhun, and another not far to the south-west, at Llanfor, near Bala.

While there is a shortage of forts, Clwyd is well endowed with sites which almost certainly came under military patronage, including the important legionary works depot at Holt, which produced tiles and pottery, the settlement at Ffrith, north-west of Wrexham, the lead-processing sites in the Pentre area, near Flint, and the manufacturing centre and possible port at Prestatyn (no. 66). These last would have related to the lead and copper deposits of Halkyn Mountain, exploited in the period from AD 60 onwards, perhaps initially by C. Nipius Ascanius, a contractor also recorded in the Mendips, and later, after about AD 74, under direct Imperial control. Copper was also mined at Llanymynech Hill, on the Severn north of Welshpool, and lead may have been won in western Montgomeryshire, around Pen y crocbren (no. 67).

The majority of Clwyd and Powys probably remained under military rule throughout the Roman period; while the fort at Brecon Gaer (no. 73) lay in what had been Silurian territory, its remarkable longevity suggests that the Civitas Silurum with its centre at Caerwent was confined to the south of the mountains, leaving Brecon to control an administrative area to the north. A 3rd-century villa at Maesderwen, Llanfrynach, about 5 miles (8km) south-east of Brecon, may however suggest that the habits of the *civitas* were spreading. The forts at Castell Collen, Caersws and Forden Gaer, near Montgomery, were also retained for long periods, albeit with some breaks, together with Leintwardine over the border; these sites must have formed the core of the security system in central Wales.

It is difficult to be certain where the bulk of the population lived during the Roman period, although many of the small enclosures of the Iron Age very probably remained in occupation. Traces of an agricultural settlement were found at Rhuddlan, while excavated material from rural sites at Arddleen and Collfryn, north of Welshpool, suggests that these enclosures were occupied into the 4th century. A number of forts, attracting their own associated trading settlements (*vici*), were placed in areas which evidence from cropmarks on aerial photographs suggests were already densely populated. During the first three centuries AD, the climate improved somewhat, and the more widely available iron tools may have allowed new areas to be taken into cultivation, but in the fourth it started to deteriorate again. Some hillforts such as The Breiddin (no. 58), Cefn Carnedd (see no. 68) and a number of Clwyd sites appear to be reoccupied at this time, probably reflecting growing insecurity.

In the limestone areas of Wales, including north-eastern Clwyd and western Brecknock, caves have been found reused for burials during the Roman period. Little is known of the local religious practices, although what appear to be temple precincts on the normal Romano-Celtic pattern have been found near Ruthin and

Forden Gaer. Towards the end of the period, traditionally taken as AD 410, and in the years which followed, Wales gradually became the repository of much of the Romanised, and now Christian, tradition of Britain, as pagan Germanic peoples began to move into the more easterly parts of the island.

66
Prestatyn Roman Site

Roman bath house and settlement

c. 100 BC/2nd–4th century AD

OS 116 SJ 062818 U2

Leaving Prestatyn by A547 towards Rhuddlan, turn R along Melyd Avenue (2nd turn after bridge over old railway). Bath house at far end of cul-de-sac; parking provided

Blockley 1989

Roman baths worked much like a Turkish bath; there was a hot room (*caldarium*) where steam would induce sweating, followed by a tepid room (*tepidarium*), and a cold room (*frigidarium*). The usual Roman practice was to cover the body with olive oil, and to scrape it off, together with the dirt, with a special tool known as a *strigil*. Bathing was probably a leisurely affair, with the *tepidarium* providing an opportunity for relaxation in warmth and comfort, and the *frigidarium* acting as a meeting place where gossip could be exchanged and board or ball games enjoyed.

The Roman baths at Prestatyn

The baths at Prestatyn are very small; larger suites sometimes have a sports ground or swimming pool adjoining the *frigidarium*.

The floor in the heated rooms was raised on columns (*pilae*) made up of square tiles, an arrangement known as a hypocaust. A metal boiler probably sat over the stokehole area (*praefurnium*), providing steam for the hot *caldarium* immediately next to it, while heated air passed beneath the floor. The hot air then continued under the floor to heat the cooler *tepidarium*, before being drawn out up flues in the thickness of the wall. Excavation here suggested that these two rooms were the first to be constructed, around AD 120, and that the cold room and plunge bath with drain, which now form the end nearest the road, were added some 30 years later; the whole building seems to have gone out of use around AD 160. Some modern *pilae* tiles have been added in the original positions.

A portion of the settlement around the baths has also been excavated. The earliest remains discovered were those of a native farmstead dating to *c.*100 BC. Between the AD 70s and the 160s, a succession of bronze workers' workshops occupied the site, together with, from *c.*AD 150, an aqueduct carried on wooden posts with two structures which probably served as water towers. This apparently industrial settlement seems itself to have been abandoned, and the only feature later than *c.*AD 160 was a late 3rd- or early 4th-century timber building, perhaps for agricultural use.

Tiles from the baths with the stamp of the XX legion, made at Holt (SJ 404546) suggest that the site at least received military assistance, but it does not itself appear to be a fort. The excavators suggest that it may have been connected with early Roman lead mining nearby, perhaps as a port, since water transport of the heavy ingots would have been much more economical than movement by land.

Some commentators have argued for the presence of a fort a little way to the north of the site, but trial excavations in the school playing field have proved inconclusive.

67
Pen y crocbren, Dylife

Roman fortlet

2nd century AD

OS 136 SN 856935 U4

From Llanidloes, take B4518 towards Staylittle and Llanbrynmair. After 8.6ml (13.8km), N of Staylittle, turn L for Dylife. After 2.4ml (3.9km), park on L by Rhyd y porthmyn and follow waymarked footpath (Glyndŵr's Way) past house and up next hill. Site on RHS after 1ml (1.6km)

Putnam 1962

This small rectangular fortlet, perched high on a moorland ridge, measures 27m north–south by 23m, and is defended by an earthen bank, 0.6m high, with typically Roman rounded corners but, unusually, no ditch. A single entrance, centrally on the north, faces the well-worn road along the ridge, which may date back to Roman times.

Excavation showed that the bank had been built of turf and clay, cut from the immediate vicinity, while the gateway had two pairs of posts, front and back, flanking an entrance 3.2m wide. The gate passage and the interior had been surfaced with mudstone chippings at an early stage; early 2nd-century pottery beneath this surface probably dates the site's construction. By this time, the conquest of Wales was complete, but troops remained at strategic points; this site lay midway between Caersws (no. 68) and Pennal (SH 704001).

Later, the entrance passage was resurfaced with a crude layer of broken stone roofing tiles. This may indicate a domestic or agricultural reuse of the abandoned fortlet, probably still within the Roman period or soon afterwards, and perhaps associated with the lead workings just to the south, which are very probably of Roman origin. No trace was found in the interior of any buildings of either phase.

On the hilltop about 100m west-south-west of the fortlet, visible from it on the near

Aerial view of Pen y crocbren from the west

skyline, lies an interesting circular feature which probably held the gibbet from which the hilltop takes its name (Gibbet Hill). The remains consist of a circular rock-cut ditch, most pronounced on the south, 1m wide and up to 0.3m deep, 17m in overall diameter, with a dump of spoil on its inner edge 2m wide. A set of gibbeting irons, dating to about 1700, and a skull were apparently found in the central mound in 1938.

68
Caersws

Roman fort and associated features

1st–4th century AD

OS 136 SO 030920 R3

From Newtown, take A489 W towards Machynlleth. After 6.1ml (9.8km), follow A470 R at level crossing. After 0.5ml (0.8km), park on

L by toilets in Caersws village. (Remains visible from car but traffic busy.) Continue over crossroads with B4569 to road junction on L. SE bank of fort (cut by main road; corner lost) visible on far side; NE bank runs gently away from main road on R beyond. Follow main road past farm track on R; N corner of fort visible beyond with NW bank turning back towards and across road; clear profile on L. Bank turns again on far side of field and runs back to SE. Fort annexe adjoins it on NW, and vicus *on S and E; not readily seen. View from road only*

Jarrett and Nash-Williams 1969; Britnell 1989; Jones 1993

Caersws lies at a natural crossroads of enormous strategic importance, where the Severn valley, flowing north, is joined by tributaries from the west and north-west, before running eastwards towards Newtown; five Roman roads meet here. One of the largest Iron-Age hillforts in the area, Cefn Carnedd, occupies the prominent hilltop just to the south-west which is also intermittently visible from the A470 between Caersws and Llandinam. In its time, it too would have dominated the route centre here, and its presence may have been a factor in the siting of the Roman fort. Occupation on a reduced area of this hillfort may be late Roman or immediately post-Roman.

The first Roman stronghold in the area (Caersws I) was at Llwyn y brain, on a spur overlooking the river 0.7ml (1.1km) to the east of the later fort; this 3.8ha site was probably abandoned before AD 70. The main fort (Caersws II), built in a more central but low-lying position in the valley bottom, was long-

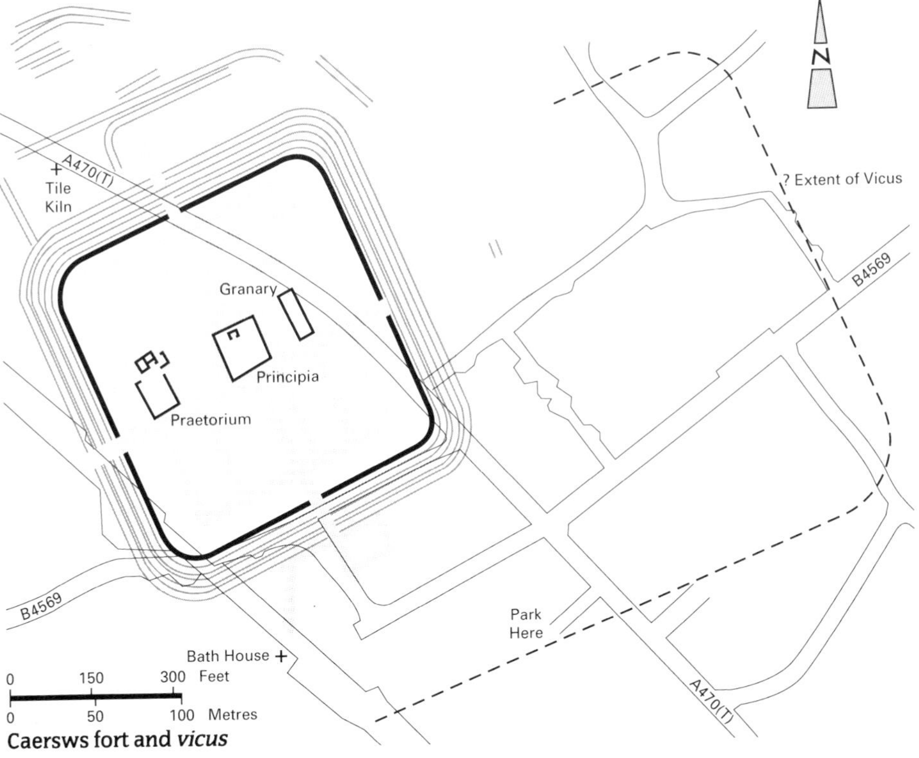

Caersws fort and *vicus*

lived by comparison with many others in Wales, and at 3.1ha was one of the largest of those maintained after the initial conquest. The water table is high today, and there were very probably flooding problems during the Roman period. Various excavations on and around the site have identified three main periods of activity.

The fort visible today was probably constructed in the early AD 70s, although finds suggest some earlier activity. It had a clay rampart on a timber corduroy foundation, with a turf front revetment; three ditches outside this provided additional defence. The relatively crowded buildings inside the fort were all of timber.

South and east of the fort, now largely under the present village, lay the *vicus*, a community of craft specialists and camp followers providing the luxuries and amusements appropriate to a well-paid garrison. Soldiers were allowed, within reason, to have items of personalised equipment made, which may have provided a living for the leather worker and the coppersmith, who was also apparently producing enamelled jewellery. A building outside the south gate of the fort, dated to the later AD 70s, which contained gaming pieces and was interpreted as a tavern, suggests that the *vicus* was probably developing, on this side at least, fairly soon after the construction of the fort. The quality of the finds suggests that this period was the most prosperous on the site, probably reflecting the garrison at its maximum size.

The fortunes of fort and *vicus* were inevitably closely linked; they may have been abandoned briefly in about AD 100, when a number of buildings in both were burnt down, perhaps reflecting deliberate clearance. Not long afterwards, however, the fort was remodelled, with a higher turf rampart and a new, less crowded layout, presumably to accommodate a smaller garrison. At the same time, the *vicus* was more formally laid out, with a corridor building south of the fort providing space for shops and workshops, probably including a bakery.

Activity on the site apparently decreased considerably after about AD 120, by which time many troops had left Wales, chiefly for duties in northern Britain. Caersws, however, as a critical communication centre, would have been the obvious place to keep a reduced garrison ready for emergencies. The fort defences were remodelled again at about this period, and a sandstone revetment wall on rammed pebble foundations replaced the turf rampart revetment of the second period. A few years later, clay was spread across the interior of the fort and parts of the *vicus*, possibly to raise the level in response to flooding. The fort's main administrative buildings were rebuilt in stone, although the new barracks were still of wood. The *principia*, or headquarters building, largely underlies the modern Pentre Farm, while a stone granary (*horreum*) lies just south-west of the A470 in an old orchard. Between the farm and the railway lie the remains of the commandant's house (*praetorium*). Later still, a set of rooms with underfloor heating, probably a bathing suite, was added to the latter; this apparently continued in use after the demolition of the main building. Another baths building, which also survived relatively late, lay south of the fort alongside the railway.

To the north of the fort lay a defended annexe, possibly laid out in the second phase. The fort ditches were gradually filled in on this side, and much of the area was metalled. Excavations within the annexe in 1990, immediately south of the A470, revealed an early to mid 2nd-century tile kiln, producing among other things hexagonal floor tiles like those used in the baths south of the fort mentioned above. Further craft activities are also likely to have been undertaken, providing equipment and materials for the garrison.

Flooding may have forced the *vicus* to move eastwards. While the area south of the fort was in use only until about AD 130, occupation further east, between Main Street and Manthrig Lane, dates mainly to the 2nd and 3rd centuries. The main buildings of the fort were, however, demolished and metalled over by the later 3rd century; some of the *vicani* must have left with the forces, but the remainder presumably survived somehow once the garrison had gone. They may have gone elsewhere (back to Cefn Carnedd?), or have become invisible to archaeology by ceasing to use pottery and turning to the organic materials and simpler construction techniques which seem to have been their mainstay in the early medieval period.

69
Cae Gaer, Llangurig

Roman fort

1st century AD

OS 136 SN 824819 U3

From Llanidloes, take A470 to Llangurig (5.4ml, 8.7km). At roundabout, take A44 for Aberystwyth; after 5ml (8km), park in small car park on L at beginning of forestry track, just before farm on R. Continue on foot along track to T-junction, go R. Follow track to fork (1.3ml, 2.1km); site lies on rise between tracks. A fair amount visible from both tracks; access on to site very rough and boggy; tough boots essential. Good view from bend on A44 1ml (1.6km) W of car park, especially eastbound; no parking though

Pryce 1914

Cae Gaer lies on a small rise within a boggy hollow in the mountains. It overlooks the Tarenig valley, an important pass and a tributary of the Wye, the upper reaches of which it joins about one mile (1.6km) to the east. This fort would have lain between Caersws (no. 68) and Trawscoed (SN 671728) on the Flavian front line of the early AD 70s; troops from Esgairperfedd (no. 70) could have reached it up the Diluw valley from the south. It was probably abandoned by AD 80.

The fort is a slightly irregular rhomboid in plan, measuring 170m along the north and south sides by 230m, with rounded corners. A small valley (visible from the track on the east) and a marshy rill lie within it. Its defences consist of a single bank, 5m wide and 1.5m high, fronted by a shallow ditch 2m wide with a counterscarp 2–3m wide beyond it.

Excavation in 1913 showed the bank to be built of turf and clay in typically Roman fashion, although there were no datable finds. It had been surmounted by a palisade of timbers spaced 0.6m apart, and post-holes

Aerial view of Cae Gaer from the north-west

indicated the positions of wooden corner- and gate-towers; there were entrances to north and south, although that on the south has since been lost to the bog. These defences enclosed an area of 1.1ha, although the undulating ground probably rendered some of this unusable. The only find in the interior was the remains of an oval stone floor with a hearth, again undated. A later miners' track, now disused, passed through the north entrance and breached the south bank near the south-west corner.

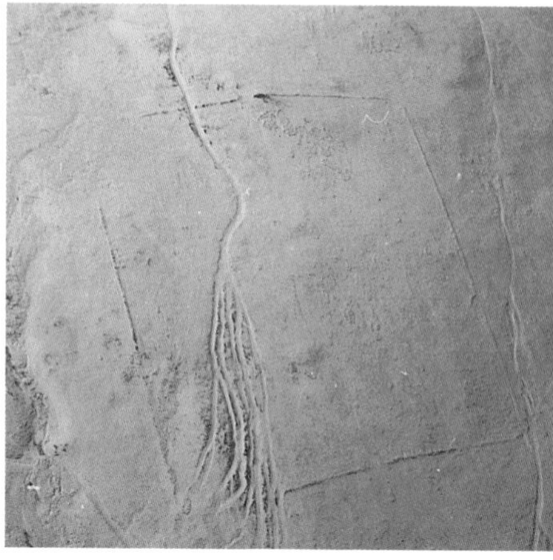

Aerial view of Esgairperfedd from the south-east

70
Esgairperfedd, Rhayader

Roman temporary camp

1st century AD

OS 147 SN 927699 U4

From Rhayader, take B4518 towards Elan Valley. After 0.4ml (0.6km), take mountain road R for Aberystwyth. 2.9ml (4.7km) further on, park on L and take 2nd signposted bridleway on L, past sheep-pens. Site lies 0.7ml (1.1km) from road; boots essential. Ridgeway walk (no. 30) from same parking place

Hogg and Jones 1968

The size of this temporary camp, 6.2ha, does not readily correspond with any standard Roman army unit, though the dimensions may have been adapted to allow for ground lost in steep, rocky or boggy areas; it might have accommodated a detachment about 4,000 strong. This force would probably have been moving north-westward during the conquest of the area in the AD 70s; the site commands the Gwynllyn valley, which forms part of an east–west route, followed by the modern mountain road, while a tributary of the Ystwyth, the Diluw, runs north to a point near Cae Gaer (no. 69).

The low bank of the camp, 0.3m to 0.5m high, is most easily seen running up from the path to a crest a short distance to its right, towards the top of the hill. The main entrance, protected by a *clavicula*, a curving bank on the inner side of the gateway which, unlike the other three examples, forces the person entering to turn right, can be seen just as the bank reaches the crest. From here, the layout of the site on the undulating slopes below, overlooking the Gwynllyn valley on the north and east and protected by a tributary on the south-east, can be appreciated. The position, sheltered from the west, meant that views this way were poor, although signals from watchmen some distance away could have been seen from this purposely elevated portion of the rampart.

Away from the path, the bank continues to the north-west corner, a clearly marked curve of typical Roman design. The bank along the north side beyond is rather faint at times, but a very clear *clavicula* lies about two-thirds of the way along; this entrance probably marked the main cross-street of the camp, suggesting that the layout was similar to more permanent establishments. The north-east corner is also well marked, just above another branch of the track, while the eastern side has another good *clavicula*, centrally placed. The south-eastern corner lies about 50m beyond the main track, but is not very clear because of boggy rills, which may have provided a water supply for the garrison. The southern side of the site is visible again a little way further on, running roughly parallel with the track, until it disappears into a boggy area at the south-west corner. Another well preserved *clavicula*, corresponding to that on the north, sits just before the top of the rise.

71
Castell Collen, Llandrindod Wells

Roman fort

1st–4th century AD

OS 147 SO 056629 U2

In Llandrindod, take A4081 towards Rhayader. After 1.4ml (2.3km), turn R down lane beyond bridge. Continue past farm and right-angle R bend, to far end (0.7ml, 1.1km). Very limited parking by outhouses before gate. Site lies through gate ahead, almost immediately R through second gate and pedestrian wicket. Boots advisable in wet weather

Evelyn-White 1914; Alcock 1964; Newman 1981

The fort at Castell Collen is strategically situated on a spur to the west of the river Ithon, commanding the flat land of the river valley. Although the easiest access is from the west, the only known Roman road in the area approaches from the south; a large bath house found outside the fort on this side may suggest that the *vicus* or civil settlement, providing goods and services for the garrison, lay here, but it has never been investigated. The road south is very clear across Llandrindod common, beyond the modern town, where there are numerous 'practice camps', training earthworks consisting of little more than corners and entrances (on private land).

Castell Collen is fascinating in that it shows not only Roman archaeology, but the trenches used by the excavators in 1911–13, allowing us to reconstruct their strategy. They started by putting narrow cuttings diagonally across the site, hoping to hit buildings sooner or later; when they did, they followed the walls, revealing the plan, but in the process losing any relationship with the floors, where dating evidence would be more likely to survive. The trenches have been left open, but unfortunately much of the masonry exposed has weathered away. Most of the work at this date concentrated on the internal buildings of the fort, although the defences were examined, with inconclusive results.

Fresh work in 1954–7 showed that there were four main defensive phases, apparently with periods of decay between each, although these cannot be precisely dated. The first fort was probably built between AD 75 and 78, during the initial conquest of Wales. It was defended by a turf and clay bank, fronted by a double ditch, and with a foundation raft of pebbles beneath its front face; the palisade on top of it, the gateways and all the internal buildings would have been of wood. Some traces of these structures were noted during the early excavations. The early fort was larger than some of its successors; the remains of the abandoned line, a flattened bank and ditch outside the fort on the west, are still visible. This first fort probably held a garrison of 800 to 1,000 infantry.

The fort was probably rebuilt, still using the larger plan, in the Antonine period, *c.*AD 140 or later, as at Brecon Gaer (no. 73). The alterations were broadly similar at both sites; the old bank was fronted by a drystone wall, founded on pitched stone dug into a trench in the collapsed front of the earlier bank. The rear of the bank was built up, and a revetment of wooden stakes provided. The north, east and south gateways were rebuilt in stone with a double passage and a guard-chamber to each side (no longer clearly visible); these chambers had rounded outer faces and stood forward of the wall, in accordance with a new plan just being introduced; their presence here and not at Brecon Gaer, where the gateways are simpler, suggests that the refurbishment here was slightly later. The

Aerial view of Castell Collen from the north-west

west gate was more basic, with only one simple chamber and one passage.

The major buildings, aligned along the west of the main north-south road, fit better into the larger, rather than the later smaller fort. They include, from the north, a granary, with characteristic buttresses, the headquarters building and the commandant's house. The last two apparently had at least two phases of stone construction, besides their timber precursors, but these phases are difficult to relate to those of the defences. The stone headquarters building may date from the early 2nd century, while the first-phase defences were presumably still in use.

In the third phase, a wider stone wall bonded with white mortar was built into the ruins of the earlier defences, except on the west, where a new bank was built for it some way inside the earlier line, which was flattened and the stone reused. The three surviving gates were extensively refurbished, again using white mortar, while the new west side was given an unusual gateway with two simple guard-chambers flanking a single passage. This reduced fort probably held an infantry regiment 400 to 500 strong, half the size of the previous garrison. The granary may belong to this phase, although its position would also fit the earlier plan; the unusual building in the north-western corner is probably part of the new layout, although it appears to predate the new west defence. Two phases of timber barrack blocks were identified in the 1950s, but it is uncertain whether either of them relates to this later plan, which probably belongs to the Severan period, in the early 3rd century.

Later still, the walls and gates of the third phase were refurbished and the ditch replaced by one with a broad, flat profile typical of late 3rd- or early 4th-century defences. This may have been part of a general reorganisation at this period, which concentrated mainly on frontier sites since raiding from all sides of Roman Britain was increasing. No internal structures of this phase were identified, and it is not clear how long it continued in use.

The site today lies under pasture, and the high water table may mean that organic remains are preserved, which could yield interesting results for the archaeologist using modern analysis (the 1911–13 excavators threw away the contents of a wooden drain!). The condition of the buildings already discovered is, however, still deteriorating, and it is to be hoped that they can be preserved for the future.

72
Y Pigwn, Trecastle

Roman temporary camps

1st century AD

OS 160 SN 828312 U4

From Brecon, take A40 towards Llandovery; turn L at far end of Trecastle (11.8ml, 19km). After 0.5ml (0.8km), take lane R along ridge; park at gate after 1.9ml (3km). Follow track to first rise with marker (0.8ml, 1.3km); site on rise ahead, 0.6ml (1km) further on. Stone circles (no. 33) can be visited on way, barrow on return

RCAHMW Brecknock ii, RMC1 and 2; Frere and St Joseph 1983

The trackway along the ridge between Trecastle and Llandovery perpetuates the Roman and medieval road from Brecon to Llandovery. This follows the Usk valley between Brecon and Trecastle, then strikes out westwards over the ridge for Llandovery and the Tywi valley. Three and a half miles (5.5km) to the south-west lies another temporary camp of similar date, at Arosfa Garreg (see *Dyfed* volume in this series, no. 83), presumably also covering this crucial watershed between east and west. Y Pigwn commands very wide views in all directions except westwards, where the approaches are covered by a small fortlet on a rise above the road about half a mile (0.8km) to the west, visible from the south-western side of the main site (for access, see *Dyfed* no. 83). A mound in one corner of this fortlet may be a Norman motte, but could equally be a signal platform. Another possible Roman fort lies near the foot of the escarpment on this side.

In view of the site's strategic importance, it is hardly surprising that temporary camps were built at Y Pigwn on two separate occasions during the Roman campaigns in Wales. The earlier of the two is the larger, at 15.2ha, but is not as well preserved as the later (10.3ha), built inside and at an angle to it; this survives very well apart from on the south-east, where both camps have been damaged by later quarrying. The extent of

Aerial view of Y Pigwn from the west

these camps gives some impression of the size of a Roman army on campaign, even if one makes allowance for space lost to bog and steep slopes; the camp needed to be sufficiently large to defend soldiers sleeping in leather tents; animals for the baggage train and for scouts, possibly even for cavalry, would also have needed accommodation.

The entrances to both camps feature the *clavicula*, a short length of curving bank inside a gateway, usually used to force an armed man entering the camp to turn his unshielded right side towards the defenders. An excellent example can be seen in the middle of the north-western side of the later camp. This type of entrance was current between *c.*AD 70 and 138, so that both camps must belong to the Flavian campaigns of AD 74–7.

73
Brecon Gaer

Roman fort

1st–4th century AD

OS 160 SO 003297 U2

In Brecon, turn off B4601 immediately N of bridge. In Cradoc, after 2.2ml (3.5km), turn L; 0.7ml (1.1km) further on, fork L down track, opposite turn on R. After 0.4ml (0.6km), park near house (very limited), continue on foot along lane into farmyard; take gate to L before far shed. Site on R beyond gates. Please keep to edge of field; no access to S or W gates during May, June or July until harvest

Wheeler 1926; RCAHMW Brecknock ii, RF 2

The Roman fort at Brecon Gaer lies on a spur overlooking the confluence of the rivers Usk and Yscir. The ground falls fairly steeply towards the valleys on the west and south, while on the east it is marshy. The easiest approach is that used today, from the north; indeed, the bend in the lane by the house perpetuates a Roman crossroads outside the fort, with one road coming from an angle just north of the present lane, another from the north-east along the green lane, and another along the hedgerow on the west, from a ford on the Yscir. A *vicus* offering various goods and services to the garrison probably lay in this area; a bath house and a possible official guest-house (*mansio*) have been excavated.

The visitor enters the Roman fort by a modern break in the north side, slightly to the east of the original north gate. The fort itself is rectangular, with the longer axis running east–west; there is a gateway in each side, but whereas those on the east and west are central to their sides, those to north and south are offset towards the west, giving the unequal division typical of the classic fort plan. The fort was also provided with internal towers on each of the rounded corners.

The stretch of wall to the left of the entry point is the best preserved in the fort, showing the construction of the stone defences well. Wheeler's excavations in 1926 demonstrated, however, that these were not the earliest; the original earthwork rampart had a sloping clay facing at the front, while the rear was made up of soil, beneath a 0.3m-thick capping of clay. This bank, founded on a raft of pebbles, would have supported a palisade and was fronted by two ditches. The gateways were also constructed of timber; traces were found at the west and south entrances.

This fort was probably built in about AD 75 during the conquest of Wales. An inscription gives one of the early garrisons, probably the first, as the *ala Hispanorum Vettonum civium Romanorum*, a 500-strong cavalry unit originally recruited from Spain.

The rebuilding in stone is dated by pottery, the chronology of which is still disputed. It is currently believed to have been *c.*AD 140, relatively late for a site in Wales, where many of the units appear to have been withdrawn during the AD 120s, probably for duty on the northern frontier. Castell Collen (no. 71) was however redefended at about the same time. The rebuilding involved infilling the outer of the two ditches, and cutting back the front of the clay rampart to insert a stone wall. This was strengthened by the addition of further soil to make a higher bank behind it, into which it was pinned by large stones projecting from its rear face. All the four gates were rebuilt in stone as part of the same plan, with double entrance passages flanked by a tower to each side; the guard towers on the west projected forward of the line of the wall, unlike at the other three entrances. The plan suggests that this would be the main gate, leading to the headquarters building. Traces of sockets for the gate hinges may be seen at the west and south gateways.

The headquarters building (*principia*) lay in the middle of the fort, just beyond the main north-south road. To its south lay the commandant's house, unusually laid out at right-angles to its normal position, and to the north was a granary. The north-western sector of the fort contained a bath house, in an area normally devoted to barracks, but this may have been a late adaptation. The long barrack blocks which occupied the eastern end of the fort were built in wood; a charred timber indicated their north–south alignment.

After the construction of the stone defences, there were a number of other additions and adaptations, but these are not easily dated. Immediately to the east of the south gate, the wall subsided and was rebuilt on two separate occasions. The first was probably soon after its initial construction, using the same stone and similar neat masonry. It collapsed again, however, and was not repaired for some time, and then very roughly.

At both the south and west gateways, the roads were raised substantially at some stage, new thresholds forming a step up into the fort. The hinge-sockets of the gates were covered over and the gates themselves apparently not replaced; this work also obliterated a drain leading from the commandant's house through the south gateway. This late work is puzzling, since there are few finds much later than the AD 140s. The fort may have been maintained by a skeleton garrison, or reoccupied for only a very short period.

The south gate at Brecon Gaer

One later feature which is clearly not Roman is the walling running around most of the site except the west, blocking both the towers and the gateways. This consists of a new revetment wall some distance behind the Roman wall, with a rough infilling inserted between the two. It was clearly built when the Roman remains were already ruinous, although the exact context is not clear. Wheeler suggested that it might represent a temporary Norman strongpoint thrown up during their conquest of the area. Whatever the case, the masonry is not good enough to belong much later in the medieval period.

Not all the fort is accessible, but the stretch near the entrance, which shows both the original and the late wall, the north-east and south-east towers, the south gate, the west gate and the northern tower of the east gate are displayed to visitors today. The interior of the site is farmed, so that access is limited during the growing season.

5
The Early Medieval Period

The period of upheaval between the 5th century AD when effective Roman rule in Britain broke down, and the Norman Conquest in the 11th century, has with some justification been called 'the Dark Ages'. It was in these shadowy centuries, however, that Wales assumed its political and linguistic identity and established its major regional kingdoms. The Anglo-Saxons posed a constant threat to the east, initially as an expanding military force, and later as a pre-eminent political power; Irish incursions on the south-west occurred early in the period; and the Vikings raided around Welsh shores in the 9th to 11th centuries and may have settled to a limited extent in Anglesey, on the north-east coast of Clwyd, and in parts of the south.

Although there are some historical documents, none is easy to use: there are annals (annotated calendars with brief notes of important events); a few other works, notably the 6th-century attack by the cleric Gildas on the moral laxity of the royalty and clergy of his time; and the *Historia Brittonum*, a rather uncritical 10th-century collection of 'historical' information. There are also collections of poetry, legends (such as the *Mabinogion*) and a number of 'Lives' of the Welsh Saints, who were active in the 5th and 6th centuries; much of this material appears to have been passed on as oral tradition, written down only from the 10th century onwards, so that the genuine historical detail has been heavily intermixed with later anachronisms and myth.

Archaeological evidence is gradually adding to our picture of Wales at this time. Unfortunately for us, most of the native people apparently adopted a way of life which has left little archaeological trace; the majority of buildings were probably rather makeshift, and little pottery or metalwork is found. Some of the hillforts seem to have been reoccupied, possibly as the centres of local kings, who, with their warbands, were the main foci of secular political power during the period. In the coastal areas of both north and south Wales, these forts, such as Dinorben near Abergele, are marked by the presence of high quality imported pottery from Gaul and north Africa, although similar sites may well have existed inland without access to this trade. There are a number of very small but strongly defended promontory forts, and a few other defended sites which may date to this period. The great 8th-century Anglo-Saxon earthworks along the eastern borders of Wales (principally Offa's Dyke and Wat's Dyke) are discussed in the following chapter.

Reconstruction drawing of the graves at Tandderwen

Burials and memorials are the chief remains from the early medieval period. Between the 5th and 7th centuries a number of inscribed stones have been found commemorating individuals (e.g. nos 76, 81 and 82); this practice is reminiscent of contemporary Gaulish Christianity, and shows that links with the Continent continued. Some of these stones, particularly in West Wales and Brecknock, have the Latin inscription repeated along the angle in the Irish Ogam alphabet, suggesting strong influence from that country. In Clwyd, long-cist graves from the early part of the period have been found at Pentrefoelas, while cemeteries from Tandderwen, where the graves were enclosed by rectangular ditches, and from Trelystan in Powys may belong a little later. From the 7th century, the inscribed stones are largely replaced by crosses, simple to begin with, but increasing in complexity towards the end of the period, culminating in the remarkable 10th- to 11th-century monuments of Maen Achwyfan (no. 74), which shows some Viking influence, and the Cross of St Meilig (no. 80).

Information on pre-Norman churches is scanty, but there are a number of probable Celtic foundations in Clwyd and Powys. An ecclesiastical community is attested at Bangor-is-y-coed in the 7th century, while pre-conquest churches are either certain or highly likely at (from north to south) Abergele, St Asaph,

Llangollen, Meifod, Llanmerewig, Llandinam, Llangurig and Presteigne, together with a number of sites in southern Radnor and Brecknock.

As the stability of Roman rule in Britain ended in the early 5th century, the northern and western parts of the island became a refuge and a stronghold of Christianity for those unwilling or unable to remain in the lowlands, where the pagan Germanic Angles and Saxons were settling in increasing numbers. Irish raiders and settlers were pushing into south-west Scotland and consolidating their hold on western Dyfed, where they probably followed an Irish contingent established under the Romans. According to the *Historia Brittonum*, Cunedda and his warband came to Gwynedd from the North British kingdom of the Gododdin (Votadini), near Edinburgh, and drove out the Irish; many of the later royal dynasties of north and west Wales claimed descent from him, as well as from Macsen Wledig (Magnus Maximus), a later 4th-century British contender for the Roman imperial purple. Cunedda's migration may have occurred while the area was still under Roman rule, possibly even as part of Maximus' arrangements to cover his rear, or at some date in the 5th century.

The kingdoms of Gwynedd, Powys and Deheubarth (part of Dyfed) appear to have taken shape relatively early, while Morgannwg in the south-east developed somewhat differently, perhaps as a result of its stronger Roman heritage. Maelgwn of Gwynedd was probably the greatest of the 6th-century kings castigated by Gildas, and Gwynedd continued to hold a leading position for much of the period and beyond. There was intermarriage between the royal families, which enabled Gwynedd to take over Powys after the death of Cyngen in 855, followed by Ceredigion in 872; this enabled Rhodri Mawr, who was also successful against the Vikings, to become king of much of Wales, an achievement consolidated by his grandson Hywel, known as Hywel Dda (the Good) for his work in codifying the Welsh Laws. Hywel married the heiress of Dyfed, and held both kingdoms from 942, but the Welsh custom of partible inheritance (sharing property among members of a fairly wide family group, including those we would regard as illegitimate) meant that different claimants succeeded and the two kingdoms remained separate, with kings of either coming from either branch of the family. Nonetheless, Gruffudd ap Llywelyn was able, from 1055 to 1063, to rule virtually the whole of Wales including the south-east as a result of his conquests; once again, however, his death, during an unsuccessful campaign against earl Harold of England, saw a return to fragmentation.

The church was also an important influence on society. While contact with Gaul apparently continued for a period after the end of Roman rule, allowing early ideas on communal life to reach Wales and take hold, it had clearly been lost by the time St Augustine's mission arrived from Rome in AD 597 to convert the Anglo-Saxon settlers. Although the main disagreement between the two parties was about the calculation of the date of Easter, the Welsh church was in many ways very different from its continental cousin. Marriage was permitted among the clergy, and indeed some families held ecclesiastical offices over several generations. Ecclesiastical settlements contained a self-sufficient community of men, women and children, including both clerics and lay people, their main distinguishing feature being a commitment to the Christian way of life; some were notable centres of learning. Those in search of a more ascetic way of life formed their own separate communities of hermits or anchorites. The church was a powerful political force providing some protection against the depredations of the nobility and their warbands, who had not yet developed a paternalistic model of kingship, but many probably also found it a very real spiritual comfort in a period of considerable insecurity.

Key to Transcriptions

This chapter uses the following conventions in the transcriptions of early Christian gravestone inscriptions:

> The inscriptions are written in capital letters. Editorial insertions within the inscriptions (also in capitals), and the translations of the inscriptions themselves, appear in italics.
>
> Square brackets indicate letters which are assumed, but indecipherable in the inscription.
>
> Round brackets indicate letters or words which are inserted for comprehension or translation, but which are not present in the original inscription.
>
> An oblique line indicates the beginning of a new line in the inscription (quite frequently in the middle of a word).

74
Maen Achwyfan, Whitford

Early Christian cross
Late 10th–11th century AD
OS 116 SJ 129788 U2 Cadw

From Holywell, take A5026 towards St Asaph. After 3ml (4.8km), take A5151 R towards Prestatyn. 0.8ml (1.3km) further on, turn R at roundabout; keep L at next junction and continue for 0.8ml (1.3km) to T-junction; turn R. Stone in field on L after 0.4ml (0.6km), by sharp LH bend; parking at R turn just beyond; kissing gate opposite

Nash-Williams 1950, no. 190

Maen Achwyfan is a particularly fine early Christian slab-cross, fashioned from one large stone. It stands some 3.4m high, and has a small disk-head and a tapering shaft. Probably still in its original position, it is mounted in a sunken quadrangular base-block, and is now fenced for protection from

Maen Achwyfan

animals and machinery. It is ornamented all over with patterns carved in low to medium relief, mainly interlace designs; these are generally well preserved, although weathered in parts. The cross-head has a large central boss and splayed arms, surrounded by a pronounced ring. At the base of the eastern face, a small figure holding a staff or spear is framed by the loops of the design, while figures and stylised animals are included in the patterning on the sides.

The cross may commemorate an individual or an event. It has similarities to others found in Cumbria, Cheshire and elsewhere in north Wales, which belong to a Northumbrian tradition heavily influenced by Viking design. The cross is one of the few hints remaining to us of the presence of the Vikings in this area.

75
Llangernyw Churchyard Stones

Early Christian pillar-stones

9th–10th century AD

OS 116 SH 875674 U2

From Abergele, take A548 towards Llanrwst. At Llangernyw (9.9ml, 16km), church entrance on L just beyond Stag Hotel at crossroads. Parking in Stag car park, on R 50m before crossroads. Stones on far side of church from entrance, to W of transept

Nash-Williams 1950, nos 178 and 179

There are two stones, one close to the transept wall on the south side of St Digain's church, the other *c.*3m to its west, near a buttress. Both are of similar size, 1.4m high, 0.4m wide and 0.3m thick; they may have been used as headstones. The stone nearest the transept has a fairly deeply incised cross potent, with two dots symmetrically placed in the upper interspaces. The cross on the stone near the buttress is more lightly incised, and more difficult to make out, partly because of the greater lichen growth. The arms of this cross are open, and each of the inner corners is decorated with a hollow. The forms are late, probably 9th to 10th century AD.

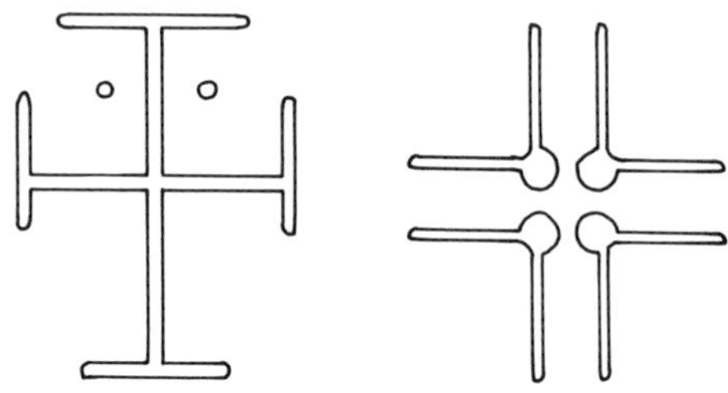

Llangernyw churchyard stones

76
Gwytherin Churchyard Stones

Stone row and early Christian inscription

5th–early 6th century AD

OS 116 SH 877615 U2

From Abergele, take A548 towards Llanrwst. After 5ml (8km), take A544 L at Llanfair Talhaiarn. After 4ml (6.4km), take B5384 R at Llansannan. At Gwytherin (5ml, 8km), turn S into village; park on L by church gate and toilets. Stones on farther side of church from door

Nash-Williams 1950, no. 177

Gwytherin churchyard stones

A row of four small standing stones, running east-west, lies alongside the north side of the church, not far from the edge of a steep drop. The stones are fairly even in size, about a metre high, although the easternmost stone is marginally shorter and thinner than the rest. Each stone lies *c.*3m from its neighbour, although the westernmost pair are a little closer than the others.

The westernmost stone has a Latin inscription in incised capitals running vertically in two lines on its eastern face, which reads VINNEMAGLI FILI / SENEMAGLI , or: (*The stone*) *of Vinnemaglus, son of Senemaglus*. In each line, 'ma' has been written as a single character. The right-hand edge has been partly broken away. This style of inscription can be dated to the 5th or early 6th century AD, and is usually interpreted as a personal memorial. The other stones are plain and the date of the row itself is uncertain. St Winifred (see no. 140) is said to have lived as a nun here.

77
Eliseg's Pillar

Early Christian cross

9th century AD

OS 117 SJ 203445 U3 Cadw

From Llangollen, take A542 towards Ruthin. After 1.9ml (3km), park on R just beyond turn for Abbey Caravan Park (and abbey: no. 146). Site on R about 100m further down main road

Cadw Guidebook (Valle Crucis Abbey); Nash-Williams 1950, no. 182

Eliseg's Pillar is the remaining portion of a tall round-shafted cross of Mercian type, which gave its name to the valley and the neighbouring abbey (no. 146; Valle Crucis means 'valley of the cross'). All that survives today is part of the rounded lower shaft, on one side of which it is just possible to see weathered traces of early lettering. The roll mouldings at the top of the surviving section mark the point at which the squared and

The back face of Eliseg's Pillar

tapering upper portion of the cross would have originated; this may have continued to a height similar to that of the rounded shaft before being surmounted by a cross-head.

The cross was pulled down in the 17th century, during the Civil War, and the rest had been removed before this column was re-erected in 1779 by T Lloyd of Trevor Hall, an event commemorated in the late inscription on the rear. The mound was excavated at this time, and a skeleton found in a long cist, but it is not clear from the description whether this burial was prehistoric or early medieval.

Fortunately, a detailed record of the original inscription was made in 1696 by the antiquarian Edward Lhuyd, before the lettering deteriorated to its present extent. Where his reading can still be checked, it appears reliable. Much of the wording was illegible, even in Lhuyd's time, but sufficient survived to allow an interpretation of the purpose and date of the monument.

There seem to have been at least ten main phrases in the inscription, each usually beginning with a small carved cross. The first phrase names successive generations of the ruling house of Powys in the 8th and 9th centuries AD, running from Gwylog through Eliseg, Brochwel and Cadell to Cyngen, and the second states that Cyngen erected the stone in memory of Eliseg. Cadell is known to have died in AD 808 and Cyngen in AD 854, while on a pilgrimage to Rome. The third phrase celebrates Eliseg's success in reuniting the inheritance of Powys by fire and sword after a struggle with the English, while the fourth asks the reader to pray for his soul.

The fifth and sixth phrases are very incomplete, but may celebrate the achievements of Cyngen himself. The seventh and eighth appear to contain a more distant genealogy of the kings of Powys, linking them to the late-Roman figures of Gwrtheyrn (Vortigern) and Macsen Wledig (Magnus Maximus), and claiming a blessing from St Germanus too. This need not be taken literally, but was a device commonly used by early medieval ruling houses to claim greater legitimacy. The ninth phrase indicates that the lettering was painted by Cynfarch at Cyngen's command, while the tenth asks for a blessing on Cyngen and his household and on the land of Powys in perpetuity.

The monument was probably erected in the early 9th century, celebrating the exploits of a king up to a century earlier. Eliseg's campaigns may have provoked the construction of Offa's Dyke by the English, as a defence against the Welsh, in the mid 8th century.

78
The Carno Stone

Early Christian cross-inscribed stone

7th–8th century AD

OS 136 SN 963964 U2

From Newtown, take A489 towards Machynlleth. After 6.1ml (9.8km), follow A470

R at level crossing. Continue past Caersws (no. 68). After 6.1ml (9.8km), park in lay-by by church on RHS. Stone inside church, against wall L of door

Spurgeon 1961

This stone was discovered in 1960 acting as a gatepost near the junction 0.8ml (1.3km) north of the church; this was probably not its original position. As then recorded, it stood 1.5m high, and tapered slightly from the base to the head. A further 0.5m of the stone, originally below ground level, is now also visible. The holes used for the gate hinges can still be seen.

The design is an incised ring-cross with a central ring and three-pronged arm ends. It appears to have been punched rather than chiselled, and it can be dated on stylistic grounds to the 7th to 8th centuries AD.

The Carno stone

Bryngwyn stone

79
Bryngwyn Stone

Early Christian pillar-stone with cross

7th–9th century AD

OS 148 SO 186495 U2

From Hay on Wye, take B4351 towards Clyro. After 1.3ml (2.1km), cross A438 into Clyro. Turn R in front of church, and L for Rhosgoch after 0.4ml (0.6km). 3.1ml (5km) further on, take B4594 R at T-junction in Rhosgoch. 0.5ml (0.8km) further on, turn L for Bryngwyn Church; church is 0.9ml (1.4km) up lane; limited parking, more nearby

Nash-Williams 1950, no. 405

The stone stands on the south side of the chancel inside the church; it was moved here from the churchyard in 1958. It is 1.7m high, and is inscribed with a plain deeply incised Latin cross with a ring-and-dot design at its centre and at the end of each of its arms. Much smaller incised Latin crosslets occupy the spaces between each of the four arms. The top left-hand corner has been broken away at some stage, and there are signs of later graffiti. There are said to be traces of an Ogam inscription on the angles, not deciphered. The form of the cross is characteristic of the 7th to 9th centuries AD. The interpretation on the label provided should be treated with caution; local tradition is likely to have been the main influence on the design of the cross.

Front face of the cross of St Meilig

80
Cross of St Meilig, Llowes

Early Christian cross

11th century AD

OS 161 SO 193417 U2

From Hay on Wye, take B4351 towards Clyro. After 1.3ml (2.1km), take A438 L at T-junction. 2ml (3.2km) further on, turn R by phone box and immediately R across bridge. Parking by church ahead

Nash-Williams 1950, no. 408

The great cross of St Meilig is now displayed inside the church, towards the west end opposite the font. Until 1965, it stood in the churchyard, but tradition states that it was brought here in the 12th century from a position on the mountain known as Croesfeilig (Meilig's cross; SO 180446).

It is one of the finest slab-crosses in Wales, standing 2m high, with a Latin cross carved in high relief on each side. That on the front face also has a wheel linking the arms, which have rounded armpits. On this face, the surface of the cross itself has been divided into seven roughly square fields, one on each arm, one in the centre and two on the shaft below. Each of these fields contains a lozenge. The cross on the reverse is similar, but plainer and with no wheel. It has been suggested that the decoration may show Northumbrian or Irish influence.

St Meilig is said to have come to the area from his native Clydeside around AD 650 and founded a religious community nearby. He is mentioned in the Book of Llandaff and also in the *Mabinogion*.

81
Defynnog Pillar-stone

Early Christian pillar-stone

5th–6th/10th–11th century AD

OS 160 SN 925279 U2

From Brecon, take A40 towards Llandovery. In Sennybridge (8.3ml, 13.4km), take A4067 L towards Swansea. In Defynnog, church on R behind houses after 1ml (1.6km); parking by phone box just beyond

Nash-Williams 1950, no. 44

The stone, previously in the masonry of the tower, now stands in the south porch of the church. It is particularly interesting because

Defynnog pillar-stone

the carving on it appears to be of two different dates.

It was probably first carved in the 5th or early 6th century, as a personal memorial in Latin and Ogam. The Latin inscription, which was originally set the other way up, is in Roman capitals, and reads vertically: RUGNIATIO / [*FI*]LI VENDONI , or: (*The stone*) *of Rugniatio, son of Vendonus*. The name Vendonus is also found on a similar stone at Clydai in Pembrokeshire, again as the dedicatee's father (see *Dyfed*, no. 85).

The stone was reset the other way up, probably in the 10th or 11th century, and decorated with a carved design incorporating a cross within a ring adjoining three triangular panels and part of a fourth, arranged to form an expanded-arm cross. A horizontal line cut across the earlier inscription may mark the depth to which the redesigned stone was set in the ground.

82
Maen Madoc, Ystradfellte

Early Christian pillar-stone

5th–6th century AD

OS 160 SN 918157 U4

From Brecon, take A40 towards Llandovery. In Sennybridge (8.3ml, 13.4km), take A4067 L towards Swansea; after 1ml (1.6km), take A4215 L towards Merthyr Tydfil. 1ml (1.6km) further on, turn R towards Ystradfellte. After 2.2ml (3.5km), turn L at T-junction; 0.3ml (0.5km) further on, take next R. Limited parking at entrance to forestry track on R after 5ml (8km); walk up track for 0.7ml (1.1km); stone on LHS on moorland

Nash-Williams 1950, no. 73

Maen Madoc is a tall thin column of old red sandstone, 2.8m high. Its narrowest edge, on the south-west, has an inscription carved vertically in Latin letters, probably a personal memorial dating to the 5th or early 6th century AD. It reads downwards: DERVAC–

Maen Madoc

FILIUS / IUST– (*H*)IC IACIT , or: (*The stone*) *of Dervacus, son of Justus. He lies here*. The lettering is very roughly carved and a number of the characters are either back to front or upside down, suggesting that the carver was not very familiar with written Latin. The stone occupies a prominent false-crest position when seen from the Neath valley on the south-west, which, together with the placing of the lettering, suggests that Dervacus may have come from a settlement on this side of the hill.

Excavation in 1940 revealed that the monument originally stood just over 5m to the south of its present position, alongside the Roman road from Neath to Brecon (no. 73) via Coelbren (appendix), which runs on the farther side of the stone, roughly parallel with the modern track. The platform of stones on which the monument stands today appears to date from a 19th-century restoration; the actual grave of Dervacus was not located.

The slight remains of a 1st-century AD Roman temporary camp (predating the road) can just be made out in the plantation as one goes up to the stone. The lines of the defences have been left unplanted; one side can be seen running away to the right just beyond the right turn near the bottom entrance of the plantation, with another, at an angle to it, on the left. Some way further up, the track crosses the far side, which runs from behind on the left to in front on the right. The forestry unfortunately makes it very difficult to appreciate the siting of this camp in relation to its surroundings.

83
Llanspyddid Pillar-stone

Early Christian pillar-stone

7th–9th century AD

OS 160 SO 012282 U2

From W roundabout on Brecon bypass, take A40 towards Llandovery. Church lies on L after 1.4ml (2.3km). Parking in lay-by alongside

Nash-Williams 1950, no. 63

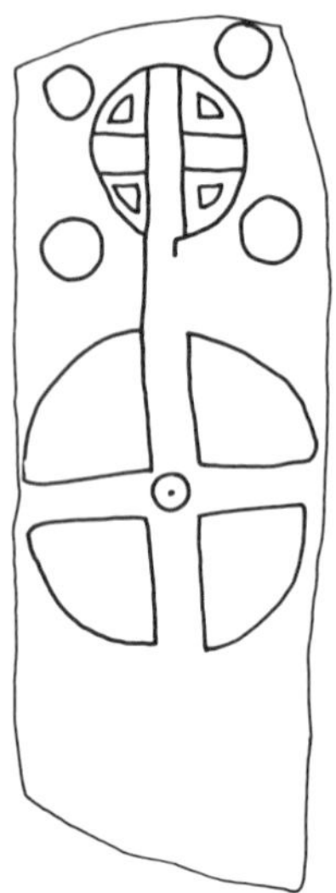

Eastern face of the Llanspyddid pillar-stone

The stone is on the south of the church, away from the road. It is 0.9m high, and stands among a row of gravestones, about halfway along the building, and about 15m from it.

The eastern face of the stone has two lightly carved outline ring-crosses, one above the other, joined by a line on the left of their common central axis. The lower of the two is the larger and the simpler, although it is now very worn; the cross within the circle is indicated by the outlines of the four separated quarters, and has a ring-and-dot at its centre. The upper cross is more complex, with the circle more or less complete except at the base, and the quarters partially infilled. This cross is flanked by four small circles of uneven size. The base of the stone looks damaged.

84
Llanfihangel Cwmdu Stones

Early Christian stones and medieval churchyard cross

6th–7th, 7th–9th/12th–13th and 14th–15th century AD

OS 161 SO 180238 U2

From Crickhowell, take A40 towards Brecon. After 1.8ml (2.9km), fork R on A479. 3ml (4.8km) further on, church is just up R turn by Farmer's Arms. Some parking

Nash-Williams 1950, nos 54, 54a

The oldest of the stones at the church is set into a buttress on the south side, facing the gateway. It sits in a recess, and a brass plate beside it records that it was moved to its present position in 1830 from a field called Tir Gwenlli, about one mile south-south-west of the church. Its existence was noted by Lhuyd in 1699 near Crickhowell, and in 1773, it was recorded lying about a quarter of a mile south-east of the Roman fort at Pen y gaer (appendix); all these sources presumably refer to the same actual position.

The stone itself is 1.8m high, and is inscribed CATACUS HIC IACIT/ FILIUS TEGERNACUS , or: *Catacus lies here, son (of) Tegernacus*. The final s in the second line is reversed. It would originally have been a grave marker, and the lettering suggests a date in the late 6th or early 7th century.

Llanfihangel Cwmdu stones

The second early Christian stone lies in the eastern of the two southern porches. It has been laid flat, so that only one side can now be seen. The earlier work is in fact on the underside, consisting of a Latin cross with splayed ends to its members, outlined in simple incised lines, probably dating to the 7th–9th centuries. Later, probably in the 12th–13th centuries, the other side was carved with the inscription [*H*]IC IACE[*T* ...] , or: *here lies (name)*. Part of this inscription has been cut away by the remodelling of the stone as a grave marker with a raised Latin cross. Another fragment of a slab lying in the porch has an incised linear cross with expanded arm-ends, probably of pre-Norman date.

The third main feature of interest on the site is the base and part of the shaft of the medieval churchyard cross, probably 14th or 15th century. This has been adapted as a sundial, with the addition of a modern capital, but its location, to the south of the church, towards the east end, is probably original. The base consists of two steps, 2.3m square and 0.6m high, with a socket stone above them with chamfered corners and, unusually, a niche in the centre of the north face. The surviving 0.8m of the cross-shaft, which is 0.3m square at the base, is chamfered to an octagonal shape, with stops at the base of the chamfered angles.

85
Maen Huail, Ruthin

Stone with early medieval legendary associations

6th century AD?

OS 116 SJ 124583 U1

In centre of Ruthin, stone stands within railing beside Exmewe Hall (Barclays Bank). Limited parking nearby; other car parks in town

This stone is a large, flat-topped block of rough limestone, 1.2m wide, 0.6m deep and

0.6m high. It was referred to by Lhuyd in 1699 as a 'flat stone in the middle of the street'. It is an unusual shape for a prehistoric standing stone, and, according to the tablet which accompanies it, it was traditionally the stone on which King Arthur beheaded Huail, brother of Gildas the 6th-century writer.

86
Tomen Garmon, Llanarmon Dyffryn Ceiriog

Early medieval preaching mound

5th–7th century AD

OS 125 SJ 158328 U2

From Llangollen, take A5 towards Oswestry. After 5.5ml (8.8km) take B5070 R towards Chirk. 1.5ml (2.4km) further on, take B4500 R towards Glyn Ceiriog and Llanarmon Dyffryn Ceiriog. In Llanarmon (11.6ml, 18.7km), turn L at crossroads; entrance to church on L after c.*50m. Mound on LHS through church gate*

This mound is an irregularly shaped grassed oval, 2.4m high above the churchyard and 18m long. It may originally have been a barrow, but has traditionally been regarded as one of the preaching mounds of the semi-mythical early medieval St Garmon. It would certainly be well placed for such a use, since it overlooks the river valley to the north, as well as an area to the west now occupied by housing; even the churchyard is overlooked to some extent.

There is a small stone on the top of the mound, of unknown date and purpose, the wide sides of which face east and west. There is some suggestion that it may once have held a sundial, but there is no trace of this now.

Tomen Garmon

87
Cwrt Llechryd Moated Site, Builth

Early medieval moated site

8th–10th century AD

OS 147 SO 026533 R3

From Builth, take A470 towards Rhayader. Follow it L at roundabout after 0.2ml (0.3km). 1.7ml (2.7km) further on, turn L towards Builth Road station. Park after c.*150m at bottom of hill. Take track on L before Post Office for Court Farm; earthworks of site visible to L before buildings and on both sides beyond. Public access on track through farmyard only*

Musson and Spurgeon 1988

This extraordinary site consists of a roughly square embanked moat, with sides between 150m and 200m long, within which lies a 7m-high natural mound. It lies in the Wye valley near the mouth of the Dulas brook, with higher ground to the north-east; the name (Llechryd) indicates a nearby paved ford. The moat, and much of the internal bank, survives well, apart from a strip on the west lost beneath a former railway, which has left the western corner isolated; the overall appreciation of the site is however disturbed somewhat by the farm buildings in the centre.

Excavation at the western corner in 1983 showed the bank, 1.25–1.90m high, to be of

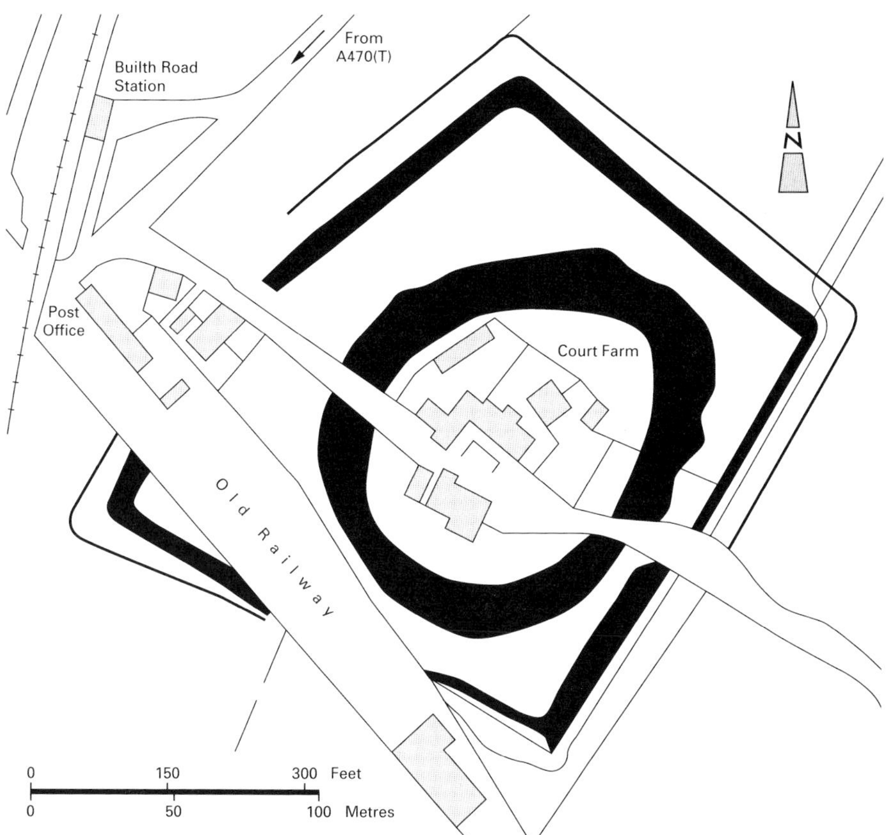

Cwrt Llechryd moated site

simple dump construction, with no sign of revetments, while the ditch was flat-bottomed and relatively shallow. A slight counterscarp bank along the north-west side, and intermittently elsewhere, may be an original feature, since the excavated portion of the moat showed no trace of cleaning out. Beneath the bank lay a layer of charcoal which may have come from undergrowth burnt during initial clearance of the site. This charcoal was radiocarbon dated, after calibration and allowance for the age of the wood, to between AD 750 and AD 1040.

The site was probably founded in the 9th or 10th century AD. It was clearly a fortress capable of housing a substantial garrison. A few similar sites in mid-Wales, mostly commanding fords, may be contemporary. If Cwrt Llechryd was built by a prince of Powys, it would have been before Powys fell to Gwynedd on the death of Cyngen in AD 855. Alternatively, it may be a 10th-century foundation, inspired by the defended *burhs* of Mercia and Wessex.

6

Long Dykes and Short Ditches

Clwyd and Powys adjoin much of the border between Wales and England, along which the linear earthworks of Offa's and Wat's Dykes bear witness to just one stage of a continuing struggle. Other episodes, which may or may not be related, are marked by the short ditches, much more limited earthworks, some of them well to the west of Offa's Dyke, presumably reflecting more local requirements.

For the most part Offa's and Wat's Dykes each consist of a bank of earth and turf, fronted, where it survives, by a ditch to the west, with occasional stretches also having a counterscarp bank in front of the ditch or a quarry ditch to the rear of the bank. The size of the surviving earthworks varies considerably, reflecting differences in preservation and probably also in the original scale of construction.

The western ditch suggests that the earthworks were built by the English as a defence against the Welsh; indeed the longest of them, Offa's Dyke, which runs from Treuddyn in the north to Rushock Hill near Kington, together with some fragments across Herefordshire and a stretch along the Wye valley south of Monmouth, is recorded in Asser's 9th-century *Life of King Alfred* as having been built 'from sea to sea' by Offa, king of Mercia (roughly, the West Midlands), who reigned from AD 757–96; it was most probably built after Offa was fully established in 784. The Dyke does not appear actually to have been constructed for the entire distance; the northern portion is missing, although the Whitford Dyke, a generally slighter earthwork with a ditch to either side, running south-east from Trelawnyd, has been postulated as filling part of this gap. Offa's Dyke is also apparently incomplete through Herefordshire, perhaps in part reflecting the presence of the small British kingdom of Ergyng (Archenfield) which the Mercians may not have seen as a threat.

Wat's Dyke, in contrast, seems to have been confined to the northern part of the border, and runs south from Holywell to the Morda valley near Maesbury. Its historical context is less clear, although it is basically the same type of earthwork as Offa's Dyke and has generally been regarded as of similar date. Equally good arguments have been advanced for its being both earlier and later than Offa's Dyke; an earlier date would be suggested by the apparent absence of Offa's Dyke in the north, which would already be defended by Wat's, while a later date might be indicated by the generally better engineering and siting of Wat's Dyke, suggesting that lessons had been learnt.

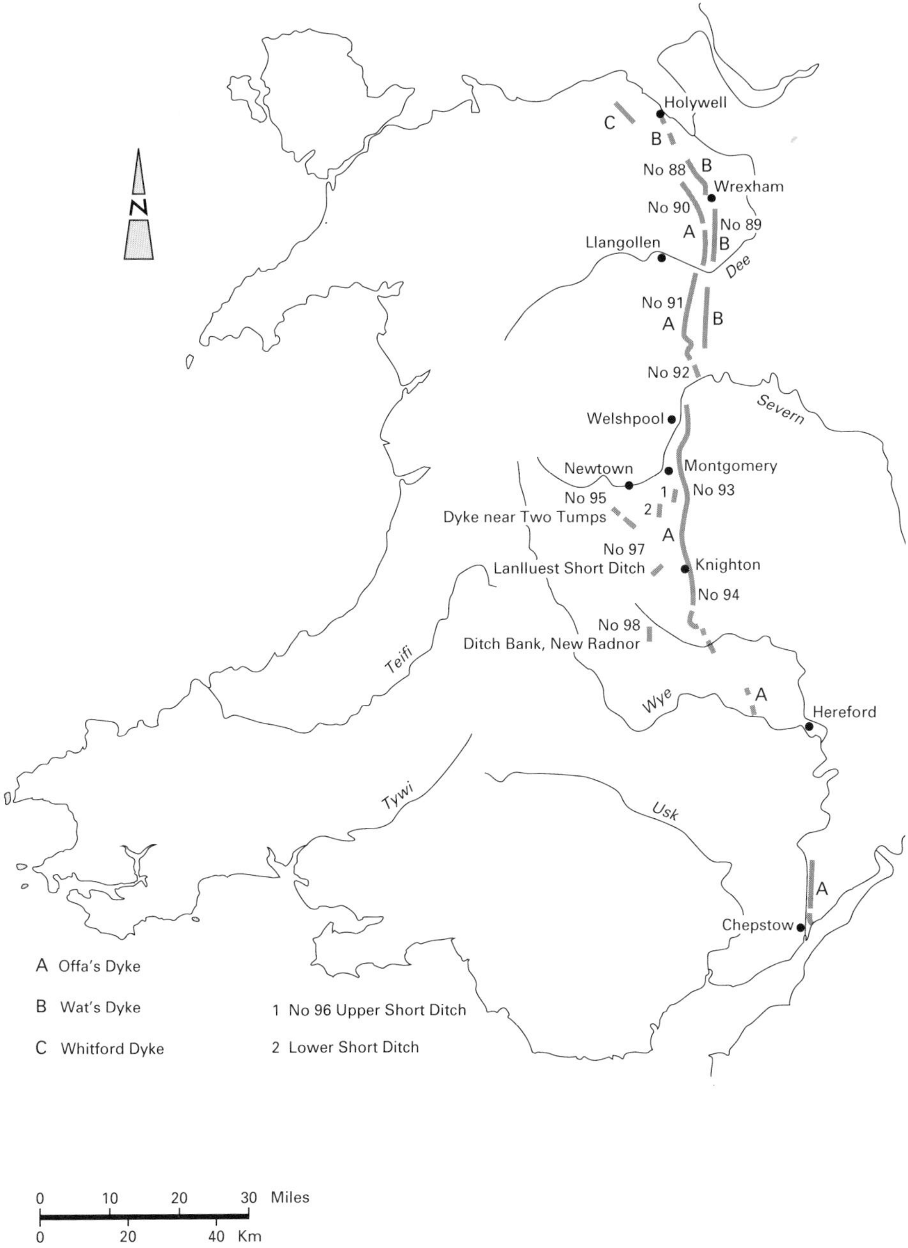

N

Holywell

C

B

No 88

B

Wrexham

No 90

No 89

A

B

Llangollen

Dee

No 91

A

B

No 92

Severn

Welshpool

Newtown

Montgomery

No 95

1

No 93

2

Dyke near Two Tumps

A

No 97

Lanlluest Short Ditch

Knighton

No 94

No 98

Ditch Bank, New Radnor

Teifi

Wye

A

Hereford

Tywi

Usk

A

Chepstow

A Offa's Dyke

B Wat's Dyke

C Whitford Dyke

1 No 96 Upper Short Ditch

2 Lower Short Ditch

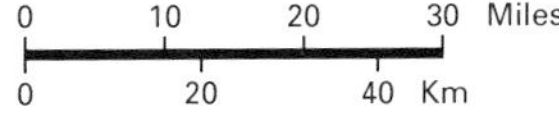

Map showing the location of the dykes described in this chapter

Both these arguments are inconclusive, however, and the Dykes themselves probably reflect only a relatively short-lived situation. South of the Severn, Offa's Dyke divided English communities, but the English inhabitants to its west appear to have remained and flourished, suggesting that, despite archaeological evidence that the ditch was continuous, entrances must have existed through the Dyke, perhaps with drawbridges.

In the north, English penetration into eastern Clwyd apparently continued in the 9th century, making variable progress according to the balance of military power. An Anglo-Saxon defended *burh* was established at Rhuddlan (no. 99) in AD 921, although this tells us little of the overall extent of English settlement, since it may have been built with the consent of Gwynedd as a defence against the Vikings. In 1086, the Domesday assessment for the hundred of Atiscross, west of Wat's Dyke, between Holywell, Prestatyn and St Asaph, is much less complete than that for areas east of the Dyke, suggesting that it was not as firmly under English control.

The short ditches are even less well understood, and were probably built on different occasions over a long period for various purposes. They tend to occupy the tops of ridges, but can be taken in conjunction with streams and other natural features to form longer lines, although these would not be readily defensible. They were regarded by Cyril Fox in his magisterial field survey and analysis of the Dykes, carried out in the late 1920s and early 1930s, as being somewhat earlier than Offa's Dyke, reflecting piecemeal defences built by local Anglo-Saxon communities in the absence of a strong central power. Alternatively, they may reflect the defences needed by later English communities west of Offa's Dyke against continuing Welsh raiding; some may represent boundaries dating as late as the 13th century. A variety of examples is included here (nos 95–98).

Much of Offa's Dyke can be visited on the Offa's Dyke long distance footpath, although the latter takes a more scenic route across the Clwydian Hills north of Llangollen; several stretches of Wat's Dyke are followed by local footpaths. Practical information for those walking the long distance path is available from the Offa's Dyke Centre in Knighton (see How to Use the Book).

88
Wat's Dyke: Soughton Farm, Northop

Early medieval linear earthwork

8th century AD

OS 117 SJ 239674–SJ 235679 U4

From Mold, take A494 towards Queensferry. After 0.6ml (1km), take A5119 L at lights towards Northop and Flint. 1.4ml (2.3km) further on, turn L and continue (along line of Dyke) for 0.4ml (0.6km) to sharp L and R bend by house. Park in lay-by on RH bend; footpath signposted alongside house. Total length 0.3ml (0.5km)

Fox 1955

The footpath initially follows the ditch of Wat's Dyke, with the bank beneath the hedge

Wat's Dyke: Soughton Farm

to the right. The Dyke has been damaged by mining between the next two stiles, but beyond this, the bank and ditch are both well preserved, showing a typical profile, and commanding a good view to the west. Further on, ploughing to either side has tended to isolate the Dyke and it is becoming a little overgrown, although its profile is still impressive. At one point, wire mesh has been laid to combat stock erosion. The path finally leads back into the lane over another stile, permitting a return by either path or lane.

89
Wat's Dyke: Erddig to Wynnstay Park

Early medieval linear earthwork

8th century AD

OS 117 SJ 326481–SJ 310434

U4 NT

From Wrexham, take A5152 towards Rhostyllen (or take Wrexham turn from Croesfoel flyover on bypass). Turn S after about 1ml (1.6km), signposted for NT Erddig. When house open (part week, summer only; tel. 01978 355314 for times), continue for 1.1ml (1.8km) to entrance on L; take drive to main car park. If house closed, turn immediately L into country park car park; take path through kissing gate beyond cottage and across two fields into park proper; turn R at bridge. Follow track past castle (no. 110) and front of house to junction with drive (1ml, 1.6km). Walk starts further S along drive from here. Length of walk from house 3.3ml (5.3km). Second car can be left at various points. Boots advisable; numerous stiles

Fox 1955

This is one of the longest and best preserved surviving stretches of Wat's Dyke, running across generally flatter farmland, unlike the more northerly parts which make considerable use of steep natural scarps. Much of the Dyke immediately to the north of this stretch has been destroyed during the development of Wrexham, although there are some remains further north in Erddig Park, in particular along the path to the castle (no. 110).

Starting in the trees beside the noticeboard, this section follows the natural drop southwards along the first part of the drive, with only slight traces of a bank. Further on, the drop swings away from the drive; well preserved sections survive in the trees on the right and across the field after the first cottage.

At the second cottage, the footpath turns left, rejoining the Dyke a little further on. The bank here is mostly a simple scarp, although the ditch to its west is clearly visible, despite some scrub growth; the stretch is best appreciated from this side. Further on, the bank gains height above the east too. At Middle Sontley farm, the path goes left across the road, then right to join a track which runs on top or just to the east of the scrub-covered bank most of the way to the next road. The ditch has been overdeepened in places by use as a drain. A viewpoint at the end of the second field shows this well.

At One Oak Cottages, the path crosses the busy road and then goes into the bushes on the right of the field beyond (tricky to find). It soon meets the bank of the Dyke, and follows it through some woodland (mind the badger holes!), before emerging into pasture. The Dyke is more spread here, but still visible. A

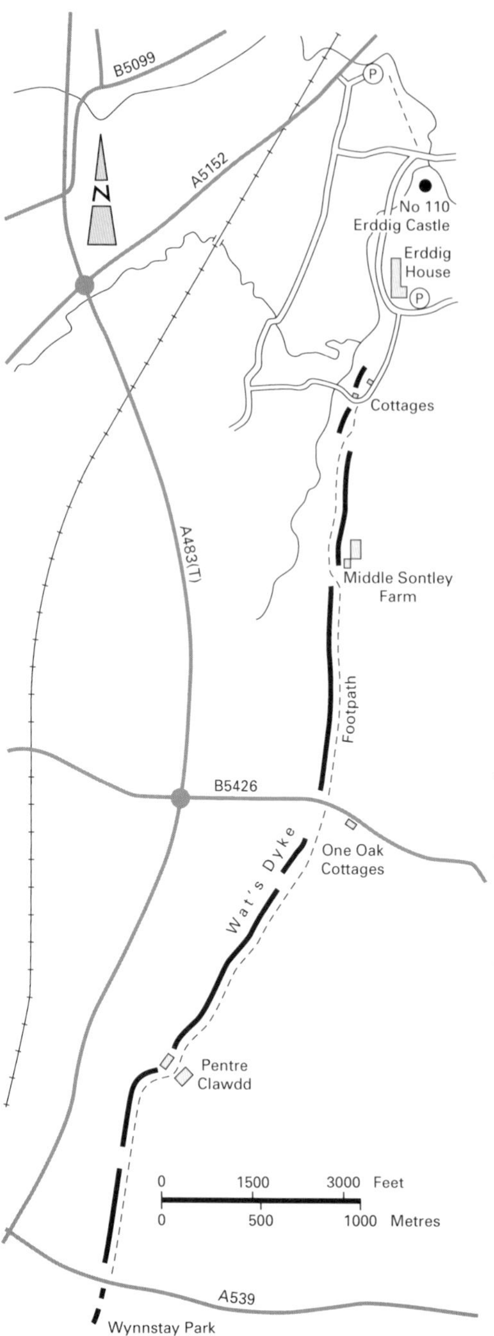

bridge crosses a drain at the next boundary, after which the Dyke is virtually lost for a distance. In the field beyond, the wood widens to cover the bank, and the path enters it to follow a relatively well preserved stretch, which can be clearly seen despite the trees.

At the end of the next field beyond the wood, the effect of cultivation is vividly shown; the Dyke profile preserved in the hedge bank near the stile is noticeably higher than that in the regularly ploughed fields to either side. Further on, the path crosses a lane, returning almost immediately to the east through a stile in the hedge. Although the Dyke here is for the most part reduced to a scarp, and the ditch filled in, the wide views from the bank can be easily appreciated.

The path shortly enters another area of scrub. The scarp is higher here, with the path in the ditch beneath it. The bank and ditch are better preserved beyond this up the hill towards Pentre Clawdd, and can be readily appreciated for some distance, particularly from towards the top of the hill.

Through the farmyard and a short way down the lane, the path rejoins the Dyke through a gate on the left. It skirts the fairly substantial bank around the top of the hill; further on, the ditch reappears and the profile is impressive. The path follows the bank in the bushes beyond this, but returns to the east of the earthwork at the end of the section. After a short stretch of green lane, it again emerges into the fields. The bank has been ploughed down, but shortly reappears; the hedge lies in the ditch. The ditch profile (in the next field) is very fine towards the ravine at the bottom of the hill. Beyond this the Dyke passes into Wynnstay Park, where it has been ploughed and landscaped, surviving as only a very faint trace. This is the most southerly surviving portion of Wat's Dyke in Wales, but in England it has been traced for some distance beyond Oswestry, although its exact end is uncertain.

Wat's Dyke: Erddig to Wynnstay Park

Offa's Dyke in Big Wood, Bersham

90
Offa's Dyke: Big Wood, Bersham–Pentrebychan Crematorium

Early medieval linear earthwork

8th century AD

OS 117 SJ 297498–SJ 299479 U4 WT

From Wrexham, take B5099 towards Bersham (alternatively, B5098 W and N from Rhosllanerchrugog or E and S from Ruthin junction on Wrexham bypass). Turn towards Wern and Minera just E of bypass; continue past Bersham 18th-century iron works for 0.6ml (1km) to parking bay with stone wall. Continue on foot through kissing gate on R a short distance further on. Cross footbridge near weir; turn L at T-junction. Dyke crosses path near notice beyond; path on R gives views along northern stretch. Retrace steps from far end to continue walk along southern stretch. Total length 1.5ml (2.4km). Parking available at crematorium

Fox 1955

This is a fine well preserved stretch of Offa's Dyke across relatively flat farmland, showing a profile of sometimes impressive size. In Big Wood, the ditch has been greatly overdeepened by the stream, to a total of 6m in places uphill from the path crossing; the bank stands about 1m high on the farther side. The Dyke recommences in the trees south of the Clywedog after a gap in the valley bottom; this portion is best seen by returning to the kissing gate and turning right along the road.

South of the road, a hedgerow crowns the Dyke bank, which stands 1m or more high along most of this stretch, as far as Cadwgan Hall; a footpath of sorts follows it. Only one good portion of ditch survives, a little way along, where the path passes through an area fenced out for wildlife interest (mind the drain!). Alternatively, the car can be taken to Cadwgan Hall by turning round and going right at every junction.

At Cadwgan Hall, a stile leads to the ditch of the Dyke, which is well preserved along most of this stretch. Immediately on the left beyond the stile lies the Cadwgan Hall mound. Various commentators have regarded this as a motte (now discounted), a burial mound and even a natural feature, part of a spur dug away by the construction of the farm. The reported discovery of 'more than a cartload of armour' in 1804 might suggest that it was a burial mound, possibly Anglo-Saxon, but the armour has been lost and no certain record of the find can be traced. In 1914 the mound had a hollow in the summit, but this has disappeared following the construction of an air-raid shelter, the entrance to which can be seen near the top facing the stile.

The Dyke here, beneath the hedge, stands 2–2.5m high above the ditch. At the end of this field the path passes through a rough area and then through the gap left by an old railway bridge. In the field beyond, the Dyke is less well preserved; a cross-section was recorded here during work on a gas pipeline in 1990.

Once across the B5097, the Dyke once again becomes impressive, with a holly hedge on the outer margin of the ditch. A stile beyond leads into Pentrebychan Crematorium; skirt the garden wall before returning to the Dyke. On the far side, the ditch can be followed among the rhododendrons before emerging into a grassed area. A new stretch of bank has been built here, across the back of the crematorium, replacing a section destroyed by the 19th-century landscaping of the Pentrebychan Hall gardens. The Dyke continues into the woods beyond this but is very overgrown. The small ditch here is a miniature ha-ha, a boundary, invisible from the house, designed to allow stock (probably sheep) to cross easily in one direction but not the other.

91
Offa's Dyke: Penybryn–Craignant–Orseddwen

Early medieval linear earthwork

8th century AD

OS 126 SJ 261372–SJ 251335 U4

From Llangollen, take A5 towards Oswestry. After 5.5ml (8.8km) take B5070 R towards Chirk. 1.5ml (2.4km) further on, take B4500 R towards Glyn Ceiriog. After 2ml (3.2km), turn L across bridge to T-junction (0.1ml, 0.2km). Parking to L, by limekilns on R c.*75m up hill. Path begins opposite junction, signposted. Limited parking for second car at several points, including far end. Total length 2.7ml (4.3km). Boots advisable*

Fox 1955

This is one of the finest surviving stretches of Offa's Dyke, forming the modern boundary between England and Wales. To reach it, go right by the gate a little way up the path, then cross a track. The hedge-line at the far side of the next field follows the Dyke; the path joins it and follows it up the hill. On this eastern side, the Dyke is about 2m high; it stands about 3m above the ditch on the west. Traces of coursed stone are probably the remains of a later field wall, since the original Dyke is thought not to have incorporated stonework.

There is a good view from the lane at the top of the field down both sides of the Dyke, and across the Ceiriog valley, where the earthwork climbs beneath a hedgerow towards Chirk Castle (see no. 113). Along much of the next stretch, the path runs on top of or east of the Dyke, although there is some view of the western side at the top of the hill.

Across the next lane, the Dyke becomes smaller, and drops away into a wooded dingle, where there is a gap in it. Beyond this it resumes to the right of the path, near the stile, on an impressive scale, although only the eastern side is visible. Across a green lane lies a short portion of good Dyke, under grass, with a few straggling trees; beyond this, it is bracken-covered, and the path follows its crest. The ditch is less pronounced and the view to the west limited, while the bank gradually loses height. Towards the farther end, however, the ditch survives well in a plantation on the right.

Beyond the road, the bank is not especially high, but a slight ditch survives; this is wet in the next field. At the bottom of the next field,

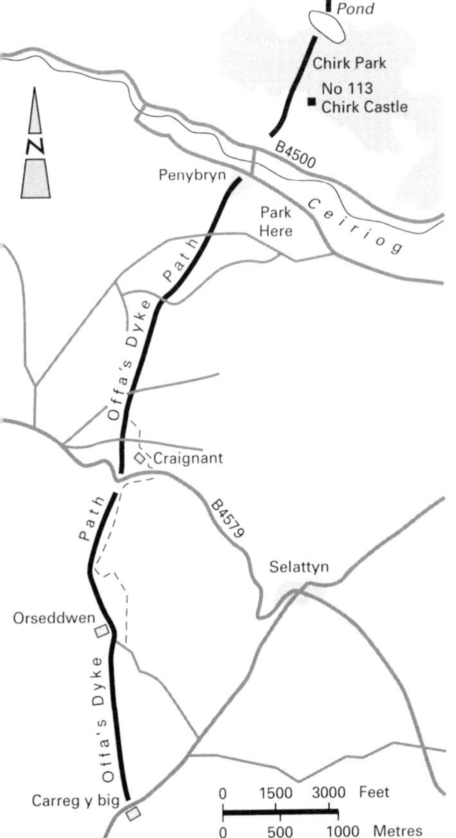

Offa's Dyke: Penybryn–Craignant–Orseddwen

Offa's Dyke south of Craignant

the path leaves the Dyke to negotiate the steep valley at Craignant. Go left along the road, then right down a scratchy green lane, which becomes a tarmac drive to the valley bottom road. Follow this right, then take the track left at a fork, near which the Dyke is visible across the valley. Continue up the hill to the top of the wood.

Beyond this, the bank of the Dyke, to the right across the narrow field, is again imposing. On the west here, there is a steeper drop, but little in the way of a ditch. At the top of the track, follow the path diagonally away from the Dyke at the field corner on the left ahead; from here to Orseddwen, there are only intermittent glimpses of it. The path crosses the fields and follows an old track a short way, before rejoining the farm track. Further on, the path turns right towards the farm. From here, the Dyke, still an imposing bank about 1.5–2m high on the east, can be seen running up the hill behind the buildings.

The road from Selattyn to Carreg y big lies just down the lane to the south. This walk can be extended southwards into Shropshire, where the Dyke remains very fine, and there are further potential pick-up points.

92
Offa's Dyke: Four Crosses to River Severn

Early medieval linear earthwork

8th century AD

OS 126 SJ 270186–SJ 282155 U4

From Welshpool, take A458/A483 towards Oswestry. At Four Crosses, after 8.1ml (13km), turn R, 0.1ml (0.2km) beyond B4393 crossroads. Limited parking down Domgay turning, immediately on L; otherwise continue and take B4393 R; park at creamery 150m on L. Path begins opposite Domgay turning and crosses field between roads; continues through creamery yard to gate at S end. Nearest point for second car some way S of walk described; path continues along Severn, ultimately to Pool Quay (about 3.1ml, 5km further). Walk described is 2.2ml (3.5km). Boots advisable in wet weather

Fox 1955

This portion of Offa's Dyke is of interest because it runs across low-lying and largely flat ground to meet the river Severn, which seems to take over as the border defence for some distance to the south. The next certain stretch of Dyke lies at Buttington, although numerous flood-banks in the area complicate the picture.

The stretch of Dyke between the roads at Four Crosses, despite past ploughing, is a pronounced grassy rise, with traces of a ditch to the west, occupied by a pond towards the southern end. The Dyke is next visible to the right beyond the creamery yard as a slight rise beneath the green lane past the sewage works (note the roses!). Continue beside the hedge; skirt the left-hand side of the farmyard muck heap, returning to the rather muddy track, which follows the line of the flattened Dyke for several more fields, through the gate beyond.

In the field at the far end, the Dyke is better preserved, and clearly visible. It has been ploughed, and little of the ditch survives, but there is a substantial bank about 1–1.5m high. The path continues along this, past some nasty examples of burrowing by badgers or foxes; there are fair views in both directions. Beyond the road, the Dyke is lower, gradually becoming wider and more spread in the pasture beyond the small shelter belt. There are good views ahead of Breidden Hill (see no. 58), particularly of the quarry on its south-west.

Offa's Dyke south of Four Crosses

Beyond the pylon, the Dyke gets mixed up with a flood-bank, recognisable by its steeper and narrower profile, which the path follows round to the right. Looking back from near the next stile, the slight rise of the Dyke is just visible continuing its original alignment to the edge of the field; it is much more pronounced along the hedgerow in the field beyond.

Across the lane, the path continues past the buildings, through two gates and along a stretch of scratchy green lane (avoidable in part by a short diversion to the right), following the line of the Dyke. Further on, the bank reappears as a narrow grassy rise between trees, but soon becomes confused with another flood-bank. This later swings away to the left, while the path drops down to the right to a stile and a plank bridge across a muddy brook.

Offa's Dyke was visible in the next field when Fox visited in 1928, but has since been bulldozed and is now traceable only from the air. It ran from just west of the plank bridge towards the sluices in the middle distance towards the quarry. The path continues across the bridge ahead and along the flood-banks to these; beyond them, a portion of Dyke is just visible on the left, running towards the quarry face and petering out towards the river. The Offa's Dyke path continues south along the flood-bank to make a longer walk if desired.

93
Offa's Dyke: Dudston to the Kerry Ridgeway

Early medieval linear earthwork

8th century AD

OS 137 SO 235974–SO 258896 U4

From Montgomery, take B4386 towards Chirbury. After 1.5ml (2.4km), Dyke visible on RHS; limited parking on LH verge just beyond gate opposite. Second car can be left at Blue Bell, Cwm village or at far end. Walk described 5.6ml (9km). Boots advisable in wet weather

Fox 1955

This is a very fine well preserved stretch of Offa's Dyke, part of it on the present border between Wales and England. It crosses generally undulating country, not all of which affords good views to the west; this may have dictated the impressive scale on which parts of it were originally built.

The Dyke south of the road is one such stretch, the bank standing up to 3m above the base of the ditch, but a little further on the earthworks have been flattened. The path continues along the hedge, then crosses over to skirt Dudston Covert, where the Dyke is very overgrown, but is just visible at the far end. There is a good section just before the tarmac track further on. Beyond this, the bank gradually rises up beneath the hedge, although the ditch does not survive. After the little wood, the Dyke again stands 2–3m high above the base of the ditch, becoming more difficult to see in the next field, where the boundary moves to the outer edge of the ditch.

Beyond the next lane, the Dyke is more readily visible, but becomes slighter further down the field; Fox in his 1928 survey attributed this to a change in geology. At the bottom, the path crosses a brook, which seems to become the Dyke ditch for a distance. Further on, the Dyke consists of a bank up to 3m high, with little trace of a ditch. It is largely lost through 'The Ditches' farm-yard, but the path follows its line and emerges alongside a hedge, through which the bank can be glimpsed a little further along.

Towards the end of the next field, the Dyke is better preserved (and easier to see), with the bank about 3m above the base of a more convincing ditch. The bank reduces in size as it approaches Brompton Hall, where the path follows the roads right and left to the Blue Bell Inn. Beyond the inn, the lane swings round a fine motte and bailey castle, built on the line of the Dyke.

After the bridge, the somewhat damaged Dyke reappears. It lies among the trees to the right of the driveway ahead, and after about 100m the path turns to rejoin it. Across the naturally overdeepened ditch beyond, an additional bank is visible, described by Fox as an 'outwork'. The path continues into a pasture field, where the Dyke bank stands a formidable 2m high on the east, although the ditch fades out. Unfortunately there is some serious damage from burrowing badgers along this stretch.

The path then follows the bank into a large wood, where the ditch, overdeepened in parts, reappears, although it peters out beyond the track (please use the steps here). The remains of a garden wall are visible beside the caravan park. Beyond the woods, the scrub-covered bank and ditch are well preserved; the path follows the bank and the pasture below is rather boggy.

Across the road, a lane occupies the Dyke ditch; some of the bank survives to its left, but is not visible from it. Continue through Cwm village, forking left at Old Drewin Cottage, and up the steep hill beyond. The Dyke lies to the left until the lane joins it near the top of the next field.

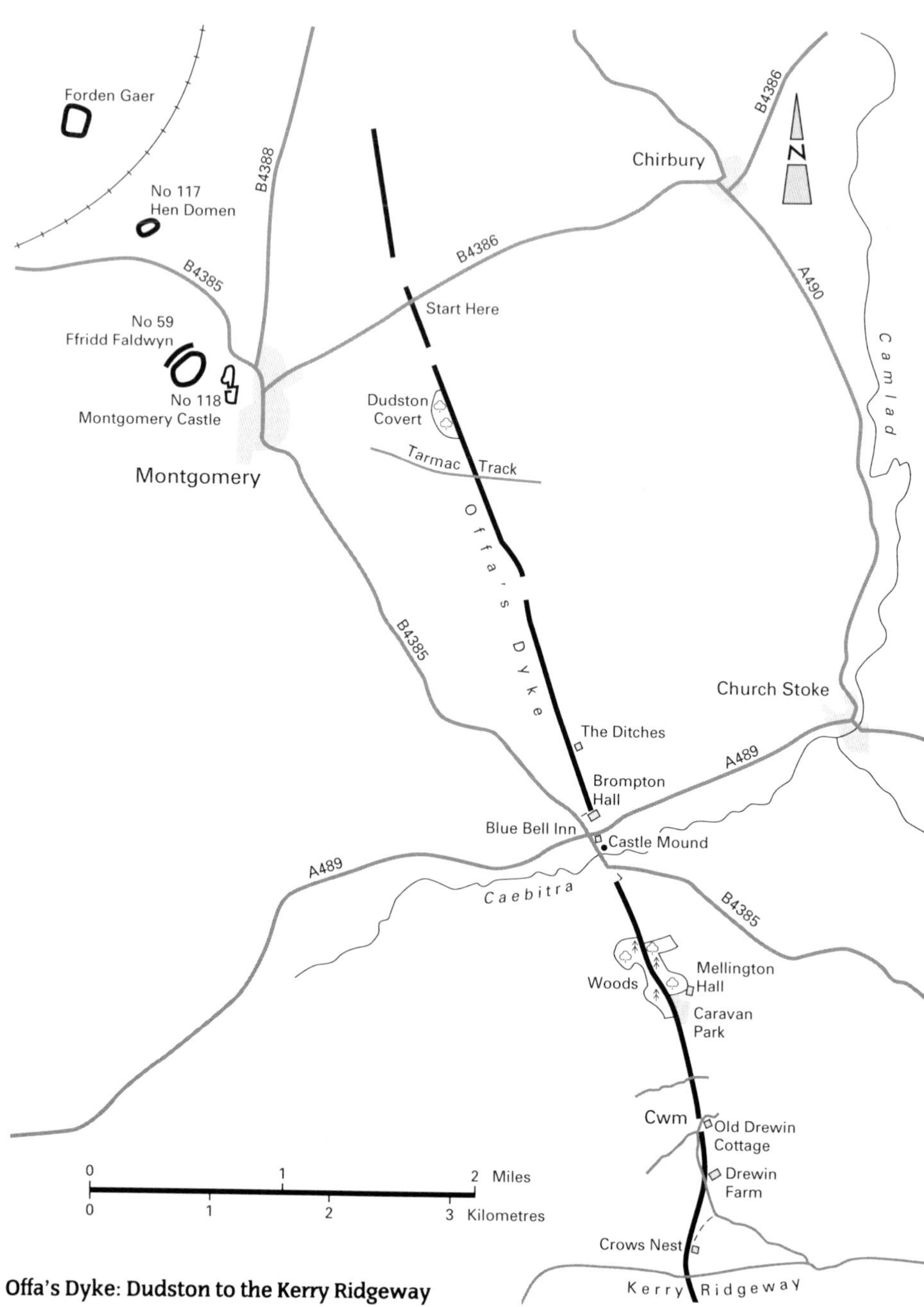

Offa's Dyke: Dudston to the Kerry Ridgeway

Beyond the turn for Drewin Farm, the ditch reappears in the fields on the right, and the path forks right to follow a fine stretch of Dyke up the hill, from which there are wide views back to the north. Towards the top of the hill, the ditch peters out and disappears.

Further on, the path crosses the hedge, and the well preserved Dyke is largely hidden behind it. Beyond a house, the path joins a drive, on the line of the ditch, while the bank becomes increasingly visible on the left. The road beyond is the Kerry Ridgeway, following the Roman line from the West Midlands via Bishop's Castle to (probably) Caersws (no. 68); further fine stretches of Dyke continue into England beyond it.

94
Offa's Dyke: Knighton to Burfa

Early medieval linear earthwork

8th century AD

OS 137 SO 284720–SO 279614 U4

From A4113 through Knighton, take B4355 Frydd Road towards Llandrindod and Rhayader; park among housing at top of hill beyond hospital. Path begins on LHS, signposted through housing. Total walk 8.1ml (13km), best done with two cars (park second car at Hen Burfa, SO 279614). Parking also en route (see text). Boots advisable in wet weather

Fox 1955

This stretch of Offa's Dyke, which, although constructed on a generally less grand scale, is fairly well preserved, makes its way across what Fox in his 1929 survey called 'the mountain region'; as you do the walk you will soon notice why! Views from hill to hill give more opportunity than elsewhere to appreciate the course and siting of the earthwork. Information and maps for those walking the Offa's Dyke path are available from the Offa's Dyke Centre (see How to Use the Book) in Knighton; another fine stretch of Dyke walking (in England) lies north of the town.

The Dyke at the bottom of Ffrydd Wood was removed by the 19th-century aqueduct connecting the Elan Valley reservoirs with Birmingham. Further up, it appears some way right of the path, which turns to meet it at the top of the trees; it is fairly slight here, its ditch barely surviving. Towards the top of the hill, fine views open up to the west. At the top, one of the most impressive stretches anywhere on the Dyke begins. The path crosses to its west, where its scale can be fully appreciated. Further along is a rare stretch of counterscarp bank.

Beyond this, the Dyke has been ploughed out across three fields; slight traces are visible in the second. It resumes on a larger scale, to the right of the path, as far as Dyke House, where the path follows the road left, and left again. The Dyke, long gone here, must have continued across the fields opposite.

After the T-junction, there is parking by the phone box (1.5ml, 2.4km from the start). Go right at the next T-junction, then take the path left about 100m beyond a cottage on the right, following the Dyke again. The remains here are sizeable, but can be bracken-covered. Beyond the brow of the hill, the somewhat lower Dyke continues to a lay-by on the road (2ml, 3.2km); a 19th-century stone here commemorates (probably incorrectly) the construction of Offa's Dyke in AD 757.

Beyond this, the Dyke is fragmented among gorse. The path veers left at the first gate and follows the Dyke right past the plantation after the second gate, from which the monument to Sir Richard Green-Price, 1803–87, responsible for local railway construction and MP 1862–9 and 1880–5, is easily reached.

Past the top of the first plantation, the Dyke is visible as a low mound alongside the second. It then resumes as a moderately sized bank, surmounted by the path. Unusually, the surviving ditch here on Hawthorn Hill lies on the east, perhaps reflecting downhill construction; cultivation may have

Offa's Dyke on Hawthorn Hill

obliterated a western ditch. There are wide views westwards towards Radnor Forest.

After the summit, the fence rejoins a reduced Dyke. At the next stile, beyond which the Dyke has long been ploughed out, the path turns right; after another stile and a left turn past a derelict barn, followed by two more stiles, the bank runs down the hill from the left, beneath a fence, to rejoin the path. The fence then follows the much reduced Dyke, continuing along the edge of the plantation on Furrow Hill, while the path forks left to join a track running down into Dolley Green (parking; 4.7ml, 7.6km).

The path turns right along the road, forking left after 200m along a track and continuing along the hedge beyond to a footbridge. After a small wood, it turns left towards the lane at the edge of the valley. The Dyke on the north-facing slope up the next hill is again extremely impressive. Towards the top, the Dyke is lost for a short distance, but resumes beyond this with the path on its left, running towards another lane (6.3ml, 10.2km). There is some parking by the plantation, where Castle Ring (no. 60) lies.

Beyond this, the Dyke is somewhat broken. Fox suggested an entrance here, although excavation showed the ditch to be continuous. The path follows the Dyke between two fences to the hilltop, where Dyke and path pass separately through a plantation. Although the Dyke has not been planted, scrub makes it difficult to follow.

On the far side, the slight remains of the Dyke underlie the hedge. At Granner Wood, it carries on to be truncated by a quarry, while the path drops steeply to a forestry track, which takes it left to the top of the next rise. Here it goes right, and soon enters the trees as a well-worn track, probably following the line of the Dyke, although no trace of the earthwork is now visible. The bank would have provided a ready-made foundation for an access track to the old quarries at the head of the valley. At the bottom of the plantation, the path, in the Dyke ditch, can be overgrown; the forestry track provides an alternative exit to the lane beyond (some parking; 7.2ml, 11.6km).

The Dyke across the lane (right and left from the forestry track) is again impressive, although the ditch only resumes about halfway down the hill. The path follows the crest of the bank most of the way, giving extensive views over the Walton basin. At the bottom of the hill, the path goes left and right to Hen Burfa (parking). The Dyke continues through the forestry, then crosses the valley and resumes (in England) on the hills opposite for another couple of miles; the Offa's Dyke path follows only some of this.

95
Dyke near Two Tumps, Kerry

Early medieval short dyke

7th–8th century AD?

OS 136 SO 115851 R4

From Newtown, take A483 towards Llandrindod Wells. After 4.5ml (7.2km), take B4355 L towards Knighton. 2.3ml (3.7km) further on, park at entrance to farm on R; take track up hill through gate to L. Dyke a short way beyond second gate; 0.4ml (0.6km). Boots advisable in wet weather

Fox 1955

Dyke near Two Tumps, looking north from the Kerry Ridgeway

This dyke is the most westerly of three short dykes which cross the Kerry Ridgeway, an important east–west ridge-top route south of Newtown. It differs from Upper Short Ditch (no. 96) and the similar Lower Short Ditch, both in construction and in layout; whereas the others consist of a single bank and west-facing ditch, this dyke has a western counterscarp almost as large as the main bank, earning it its alternative name of Double Deyches. It is also longer than most of the other cross-ridge dykes in the area, crossing not only this ridge, but, unusually, resuming beyond the lower-lying ground to both north and south, giving three distinct stretches in all.

The earthwork probably defined a boundary across the ridge-top routes of the area, which concentrate at this point between the headwaters of the Ithon and the Severn; it would also provide a means of controlling traffic. The fact that it appears to face west suggests that it was built by the English to control the Welsh, although its date is by no means certain. Fox argues that most of the relatively numerous short ditches in the area were part of localised efforts by the Mercians to defend themselves against the Welsh of Powys, before Offa's Dyke was built.

The dykes in the Kerry area have, however, been alternatively interpreted as the somewhat later boundaries of historically attested divisions within Ceri, which until the later 13th century was closely associated with Maelienydd to its south; this interpretation sees them as working together with the streams whose headwaters they join, as parts of much longer lines. The variations in construction make it likely, however, that the dykes are of differing dates and purposes; indeed similar earthworks of proven prehistoric date are known in southern Britain.

The 'Two Tumps' of the name are impressive Bronze Age barrows on the hilltop. One is visible just over the fence near the dyke crossing, while the other can be seen in the field to the right of the track some distance further on.

Upper Short Ditch

96
Upper Short Ditch, Kerry

Early medieval short dyke

7th–8th century AD?

OS 136 SO 193871–SO 194872 R3

From A483 in Newtown, take A489 towards Craven Arms and Churchstoke. After 3.7ml (6km), take B4368 R; 0.4ml (0.6km) further on, turn L (opposite turn for sawmills). After 2.5ml (4km), turn L at T-junction; 0.8ml (1.3km) further on, continue ahead up dirt track (Kerry Ridgeway) at crossroads. Site visible ahead on R, parking in lay-by after 0.4ml (0.6km)

Fox 1955

Upper Short Ditch is the middle of three cross-ridge dykes (see no. 95) which cross the line of the ancient Kerry Ridgeway west of Offa's Dyke. It runs across the ridge from dingle to dingle, and consists, like much of Offa's Dyke, of a bank with a western ditch; part of the original 900m length has been ploughed out. The Kerry Ridgeway crosses roughly at its centre, where there may originally have been a simple gateway.

The dyke today appears very different to either side of the ridgeway. The southern section (now in Shropshire) is clearly visible from some distance beneath the field boundary to the right of the track. The northern section, however, now lies in a forestry plantation, although a footpath on its east follows it for much of its length. The dating of this earthwork, like that of others in the area including no. 95, where the problem is discussed further, is uncertain.

97
Lanlluest Short Ditch, Knighton

Early medieval short dyke

7th–8th century AD?

OS 148 SO 191751–SO 187746 U4

From Knighton, take A488 towards Llandrindod Wells. After 4.7ml (7.6km), take B4356 R for Llangunllo; 2.4ml (3.9km) further on, turn R in village for station. Turn L at crossroads after 0.5ml (0.8km), R after 0.3ml (0.5km). Continue past station to L turn beyond (2ml, 3.2km from village), park and continue up lane on foot (waymarked). Go straight on beyond Upper Ferley cottage, and turn R at crossroads; site just beyond next junction in forestry. Total distance to site 2.3ml (3.7km). See map for no. 32, which can be included to make longer walk. Fair conditions recommended; boots advisable in wet weather

Fox 1955

The Lanlluest Short Ditch is a normal cross-ridge dyke, with a bank and western ditch, about 650m long, running north-east to south-west across a saddle of higher ground from dingle to dingle. It is crossed by two ridge-top routes, including the lane now used as part of the Glyndŵr's Way long distance path.

Lanlluest Short Ditch

Ditch Bank, New Radnor, with continuation across valley visible to left

On the north-east, the dyke lies on open moorland, and is unfortunately becoming very damaged by unauthorised motor-cycling, while on the south-west it survives much better, in a field beside a forestry plantation, although it later enters the plantation. Its north-eastern terminal survives well, ending abruptly as the slope steepens, while the south-western end is less clear, extending for only a very short distance beyond the plantation. The dating of this earthwork, like that of others in the area including no. 95, where the problem is discussed further, is uncertain.

98
Ditch Bank, New Radnor

Early medieval short ditch

7th–8th century AD?

OS 148   SO 198600   R3

From B4372 turning at W end of New Radnor, take A44 towards Rhayader. After 0.8ml (1.3km), park in lay-by on L. Site visible over gate on opposite side c.*100m back*

Fox 1955

In contrast to the foregoing three sites, this is not a cross-ridge, but rather a cross-valley, dyke. It lies at the western end of the fertile Walton basin and is a bank between 2m and 3m high, with a slight suggestion of a ditch on the south-west; it was presumably intended to defend the good farmland from some threat beyond. The bank runs across the valley bottom and gives out on the slopes to the north; to the south it is less well preserved, although a rise is just visible. Although Fox considers this work early medieval, a somewhat later date, as for some of the cross-ridge dykes, would be equally plausible.

7
The Age of the Castle

The defeat of Gruffudd ap Llywelyn of Gwynedd by earl Harold of England in 1063 left the Welsh kingdoms weak and fragmented; this was quickly exploited after 1066 by the Normans, who set about the conquest of Wales with gusto. The campaign was entrusted to close companions of the king, who were allowed almost complete autonomy to seize what they could for themselves. They made rapid progress along the southern lowlands and in north-east Wales, partly anglicised areas which were suited to Norman heavy-armoured fighting techniques, and easily held from their new castles. Progress elsewhere was slower, although the Brecon area was fairly readily secured; this enclave was extended northwards to Builth and westwards across the uplands towards Norman-held Ceredigion. The mountainous central parts of the border proved more difficult, as is shown by a higher concentration of castles, including 27 small strongholds in the Vale of Montgomery alone.

The castle was the prime weapon in the Norman conquest of Wales, being not only an effective military base but a potent symbol of power. Its central focus was usually the motte, a mound of earth and stones up to 10m high, normally surrounded by a ditch, and surmounted by a wooden tower serving as both lookout and defensible stronghold. Sometimes a ringwork was constructed instead, a small enclosure surrounded by a palisaded bank and ditch, within which buildings might provide accommodation and storage; sometimes the gatehouse might support a tower. Whether the main stronghold was a motte or a ringwork, it would frequently be adjoined by a bailey, sometimes more than one; these enclosures, usually defended by a palisaded bank and ditch, could hold more stores and provide stabling and accommodation for servants, craft specialists and a garrison. Hen Domen (no. 117), Tomen y Rhodwydd (no. 109) and Twthill, Rhuddlan (see no. 99) are good examples of motte and bailey castles, while The Warden, Presteigne (no. 123) is a fine ringwork and bailey.

Not all castles were built by the Normans. The Welsh dynasties continued to be dogged by internecine strife, both within and between kingdoms. A number of strong native leaders in the 11th and 12th centuries nonetheless proved able to halt or reverse Norman progress, particularly Rhys ap Tewdwr and his grandson the Lord Rhys in Deheubarth (the southern kingdom centred around the Tywi valley and with claims to Ceredigion), and Gruffudd ap Cynan and his son Owain

Reconstruction drawing of a motte and bailey castle

Gwynedd in the north. Cadwgan ap Bleddyn, one of the revived Powys dynasty created in the settlement of 1063, built a castle at 'Trallwng Llywelyn', probably Welshpool (see no. 115 and appendix), while Owain Gwynedd was responsible for the fine site of Tomen y Rhodwydd; Castle Caereinion (no. 114) and Rhayader Castle (no. 122) are also Welsh in origin.

Boroughs, like Roman *vici* around forts, were established alongside the greater castles, to ensure supplies for the garrison and to provide an enforced focus for local economic activity, which could then be taxed. This was done by the English at Rhuddlan, Builth (no. 125), Brecon (no. 128), and elsewhere; the native Welsh were slower to adopt this alien institution, although Welshpool was probably a fairly early foundation.

The territories carved out by the Normans became formalised as virtually autonomous 'Marcher lordships', in which the lords had powers and maintained officials and warbands rather like the native princes. The latter followed the Norman example in exploiting their lands more systematically, essential if they were to survive in the relative absence of the pillage and petty wars by which they had previously lived. Income was raised by levying tributes, both regular and special, in cash or in kind, and by charging fees for services such as the administration of justice, which was the prince's prerogative. Largesse and military success were still seen as the marks of a leader, but the ruler was increasingly seen as responsible for the safety of those he ruled.

A number of castles were refurbished in stone during the later 12th century; in most cases a circular or polygonal wall known as a 'shell keep', was built around the summit of the motte or ringwork, with buildings against it and in some cases integrated into it. The bailey too might be walled. The most complete surviving instance of this treatment is at Tretower (no. 129), but Crickhowell (no. 130) and possibly Tinboeth (no. 121) are also examples.

After 1172, there was a truce between Henry II and the Welsh, and the more rapacious of the Norman barons moved on to try their luck in Ireland. The anarchy of Stephen's reign allowed the Welsh to win back some lost ground, although the weakened and divided kingdom of Powys was by this time virtually an English protectorate. The Lord Rhys of Deheubarth campaigned over a wide area of mid-Wales with considerable success, but his death in 1197 plunged his kingdom into internal dissent, and the initiative passed to Llywelyn ab Iorwerth of Gwynedd. Llywelyn had managed by 1210 to neutralise his rival claimants, and was set to expand his area of control; King John mounted a successful campaign against him in 1211–12, but was prevented from consolidating his gains by problems elsewhere. Llywelyn went on, despite reverses in 1223, when castles were established by the English at Montgomery (no. 118) and Painscastle, to become master of most of native Wales by his death in 1240, and it was with his reign that the Gwynedd dynasty began to formulate their vision of a united princedom of Wales. Despite Llywelyn's best efforts, however, his son Dafydd ap Llywelyn failed to secure the succession against the supporters of his illegitimate half-brother Gruffudd, and after six years of serious Welsh reverses, Llywelyn's mantle fell to his grandson, Llywelyn ap Gruffudd.

It took the new ruler until 1255 to gain primacy over his brothers; even after this his lenient treatment of the perfidious Dafydd was to bring him problems. Meanwhile, the English had regained the initiative, building castles at Dyserth and Deganwy near the north coast, and carrying out further work at Montgomery and Builth, where boroughs were now established.

The castles of the early 13th century again reflect developments in military thinking; much stronger natural sites such as Montgomery now tended to be chosen, and building in stone became the norm. The emphasis in the plan shifted towards the curtain wall, often incorporating towers and providing a support for the internal buildings; the gatehouse was becoming more strongly defended. Devices such as the portcullis and murder holes were introduced, and the round tower was an important development, providing a stronger and more readily defended structure than a square or polygonal keep. At Tretower the round tower clearly supersedes the earlier shell keep and its buildings, which were largely demolished to make room for it, while that at Bronllys (no. 126) surmounts the earlier motte.

The Welsh were also building stone castles by the middle of the century; they took elements from the designs of their English adversaries and adapted them to make a distinctive style of their own. Apsidal towers are particularly characteristic, as is a curtain wall linking separated towers; these can be seen at Ewloe (no. 103), Dinas Brân (no. 112) and Dolforwyn (no. 116).

From 1256, Llywelyn made impressive progress, uniting almost all the Welsh princes behind him, and by 1267 he was able to extract very advantageous terms from the hard-pressed Henry III under the Treaty of Montgomery. The treaty did not last, however, with each side blaming the other for breaches. The new king, Edward I, who succeeded in 1272, set himself with implacable resolution to solve the Welsh question; Llywelyn's defiant construction in the early 1270s of the castle at Dolforwyn and his refusal to do homage until his grievances were settled gave Edward the pretext he needed to mount his devastatingly successful campaign of 1277. He attacked along the north coast, systematically clearing woodland to avoid ambush; a second force on Anglesey meanwhile secured Gwynedd's main source of food. Many of Llywelyn's southern allies deserted him, and in November he sued for peace, having lost all but the heartland of Gwynedd. His brother Dafydd, an English ally since 1274, was granted much of northern Clwyd; Dafydd's castle at Caergwrle (no. 105), and possibly also that at Denbigh (no. 100), was built with royal assistance. Other castles built during or in the wake of the 1277 campaign include Flint (no. 102), Rhuddlan and Aberystwyth (see *Dyfed* volume in this series, no. 126); those at Ruthin (appendix) and Hawarden (appendix) were constructed privately with royal help, while the captured Dolforwyn, Builth and Gruffudd ap Gwenwynwyn's Powis Castle (no. 115) were refurbished to varying degrees.

The plans of these castles vary considerably, depending on their individual sites and circumstances, but the trends of the period are apparent. The main new development was the concentric castle, with two lines of defence, one within the other; this is most clearly seen at Rhuddlan. These developments continue in the castles which were built after the final defeat of the Welsh, which followed a renewed rising in 1282–3, probably precipitated by Dafydd ap Gruffudd. Llywelyn was killed near Builth in December 1282; some claim that he was lured into a trap by the Marcher lords of the area. Dafydd was finally captured in June 1283, by which time Edward was in full control of Wales.

Once again he stamped his supremacy on the area by the construction of further castles, and the refurbishment of some which had seen action previously. Dafydd's castles at Caergwrle and Denbigh were rebuilt, work continued at Rhuddlan, and a new castle was erected with royal aid at Holt (no. 106). Further west, the great castles of Conwy, Caernarfon and Harlech were begun (see *Gwynedd*, nos 118, 128 and 132). Gwynedd was held by the Crown, but many of the captured lands in

Clwyd and in mid- and south Wales were parcelled out to the king's supporters in recognition of their services. This left a pattern of fragmentation in the Marches which was to last until the Tudor settlement in 1536.

The Welsh under English administration suffered many abuses, and endured a system of apartheid which excluded them from, among other things, being burgesses in the now widespread English boroughs, or participating to any great extent in the growing land market. A military career in the entourage of a lord was however open to them, and a number of Welshmen served with distinction in the following century. A widespread rising in the north in 1294–5 led to the construction of Beaumaris on Anglesey (see *Gwynedd*, no. 114), the classic concentric castle, and probably also of Chirk (no. 113).

The 14th century seems to have been one of relative peace; indeed the population had other problems to contend with. The climate had apparently improved during the 13th century, allowing marginal land to be exploited (mainly for oats) and encouraging a population explosion perhaps also partly due to a reduction of the previously endemic raiding and plunder. In the 14th century, however, the climate deteriorated, and, on top of this, the Black Death struck in 1349 and recurred on a number of occasions down to 1420. The consequent massive depopulation precipitated a number of changes, in particular allowing those with the means to amass large private estates. The trend from cattle to sheep-rearing, in which the great Cistercian houses had led the way in the 12th

Reconstruction drawing of a moated site

century, had continued through the 13th; now, with fewer hands to work the land, sheep became still more widespread and were bred selectively to improve their wool. The droving of livestock into England became more common.

Stone buildings had been known from the 13th century, but were rare apart from military and ecclesiastical structures. By the later 14th century, however, hall houses in both timber and stone, such as that at Sycharth (appendix) belonging to Owain Glyndŵr, were being built by those with the means. Moated sites, where a manor house is defended by a square, water-filled ditch, are fairly common in the anglicised areas of north-east Wales and around Brecon; the Croesfoel Farm moated site (no. 134) is a good example.

After 1370, war with France increased the tax burdens on the Welsh, and their growing resentment ultimately found a focus in Owain Glyndŵr, a descendant of the houses of both Powys and Deheubarth, although both his grandmother and his wife were English. Glyndŵr's rising in 1400 was facilitated by the weakness of the English; Henry IV had seized the throne only the previous year, and many of the Marcher lordships had recently changed hands or were effectively vacant. Glyndŵr enjoyed considerable success until 1406, but the tide gradually turned against him and the rising petered out; he died uncaptured in 1415, having achieved little but a renewal of the distrust between Welsh and English.

Many of the castles, including Rhuddlan, Chirk, Builth, New Radnor (no. 124), Tretower and Crickhowell, had seen little action for over a century, but were hastily refurbished against Glyndŵr's forces, who nonetheless captured a number of them. The boroughs were a major target, sustaining considerable damage in north and south alike. Later in the 15th century, the Mortimer castles of Denbigh and Montgomery, which had passed by marriage to the Yorkist royal line, saw action during the Wars of the Roses.

After this, the castles of Wales continued to rot, or to be adapted as, or replaced by, more modern and comfortable manor houses, as at Chirk, Powis Castle and Tretower. They saw a last flurry of activity during the Civil War, when Rhuddlan, Denbigh, Powis Castle and Montgomery were held for the Royalists; Flint and Chirk were held for a time by each side. At the end of the war, the remaining castles were 'slighted' with gunpowder to ensure that they could never again be used in anger. The age of the castle was over.

99
Rhuddlan Castle

Early medieval and medieval defended settlements and castles

10th–13th century AD

OS 116 SJ 024779 R/U1 Cadw

Castle signposted to S of town centre. Car park. Twthill signposted; footpath along part of Saxon defences on E, also visible on S at far end of Abbey Road, past farm (site of Friary); Edwardian town banks at bottom of Gwindy Street, N of main road. Castle, admission charge, standard hours; otherwise free. Disabled access variable

Cadw Guidebook; Edwards 1991

For many years, Rhuddlan was the lowest crossing point and highest point of navigation on the river Clwyd; this became particularly important between the 10th and 13th centuries. It could control traffic running both along and across the northern part of the Vale of Clwyd, and could be supplied by water.

The evidence suggests three main periods of occupation, apart from traces of Mesolithic and Roman activity: an Anglo-Saxon settlement; a Norman motte and bailey castle with a small defended town; and a stone castle and borough constructed under Edward I in the 13th century. Edward had the river straightened and dredged to ensure continued access for his ships; this improved line survives today, in marked contrast with the sinuous course above the town.

The English probably captured Rhuddlan from the Welsh in AD 796, as part of the enclave of Englefield (Tegeingl), although the Anglo-Saxon settlement is unlikely to be this early. The *Anglo-Saxon Chronicle* relates that Edward the Elder built a *burh* at *Cledemutha* in AD 921, the last in a series consolidating West Saxon gains against the Vikings. The name probably means 'Clwyd mouth', although its identification with Rhuddlan has been disputed; nonetheless there is plenty of excavated Anglo-Saxon material here, and the eastern defences seem to belong to this period. The supposed *burh* is large, by comparison with others in the series such as Eddisbury (near Northwich), Runcorn and Manchester. Viking activity is known from the Wirral, while place-names in northern Flintshire, and the carving on Maen Achwyfan (no. 74) suggest a presence here. Gruffudd ap Llywelyn of Gwynedd used Rhuddlan as a base for widespread raids into English lands until his defeat in 1063 by earl Harold, the loser at Hastings in 1066.

Norman rule brought great changes. Much of north Wales was given by the Conqueror to Robert 'of Rhuddlan', who built the new motte and bailey castle now known as Twthill in 1073. The motte stands 18m high above the river, and was protected inland by a natural valley and an artificial ditch; the small bailey can be seen towards the present town from the top of the irregular mound.

Robert, together with earl Hugh of Chester, also founded a small borough, which had a church and a mint by 1086. Archaeology suggests that this Norman borough lay mainly north of the castle, in the area bordered by Hylas Lane and Abbey Road, although it probably did not extend as far as either. To its south-east lies Plas newydd, the site of the Friary, a house of Dominican or Black Friars, founded in or before 1258. The castle and borough probably changed hands several times, but nonetheless survived until 1277, when Edward I used Rhuddlan, presumably the old castle, as a campaign base against Llywelyn ap Gruffudd, who surrendered there later that year.

By this time, work had begun on the new castle north-west of the Norman town, continuing until it was besieged in 1282 during the Welsh rising which precipitated Edward's second campaign. Work resumed in 1283, and continued until at least 1286. The building was begun under Master Bertram, the king's engineer under Henry III, but he soon retired and was succeeded by Master James of St George.

The castle is concentric in design, consisting of a very strongly defended inner ward, of

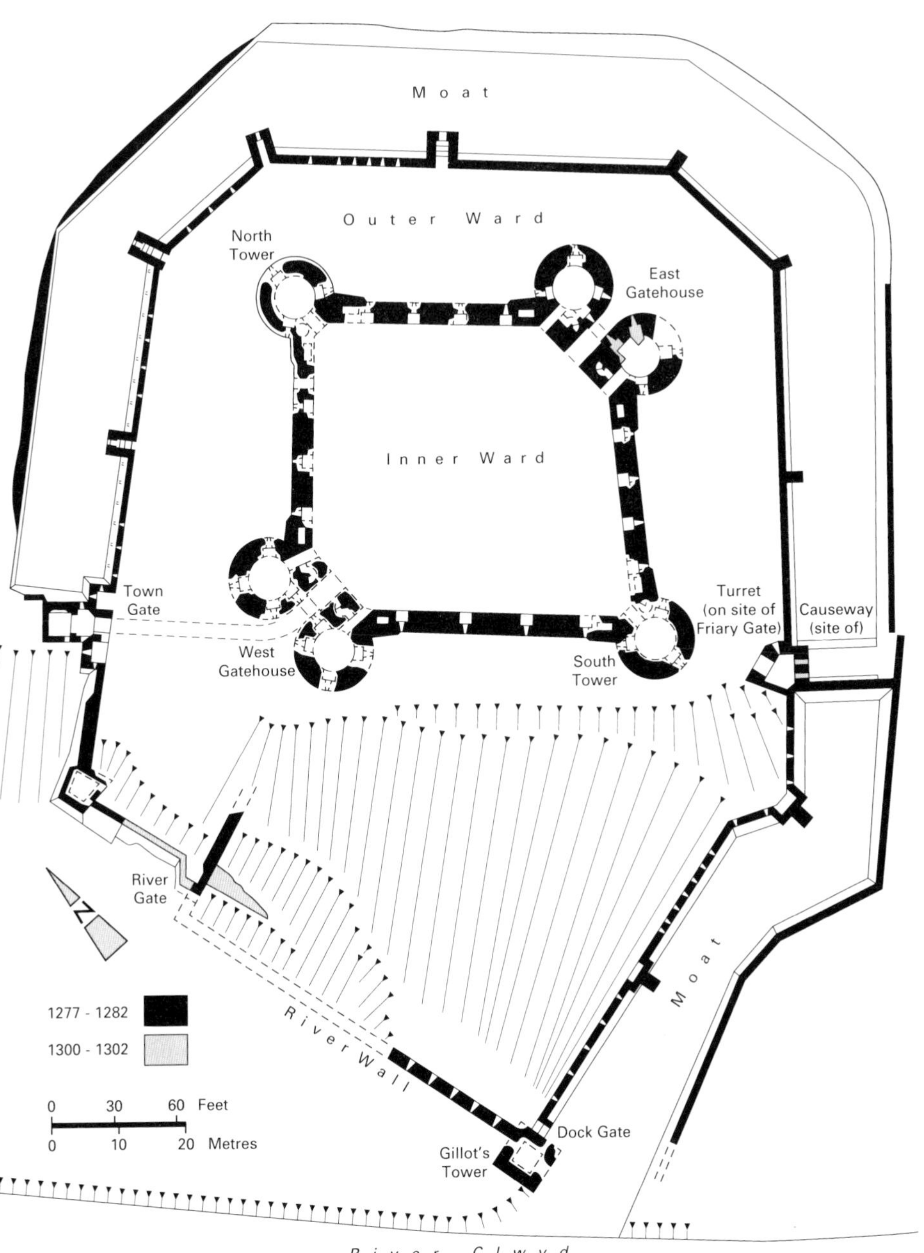

Rhuddlan Castle

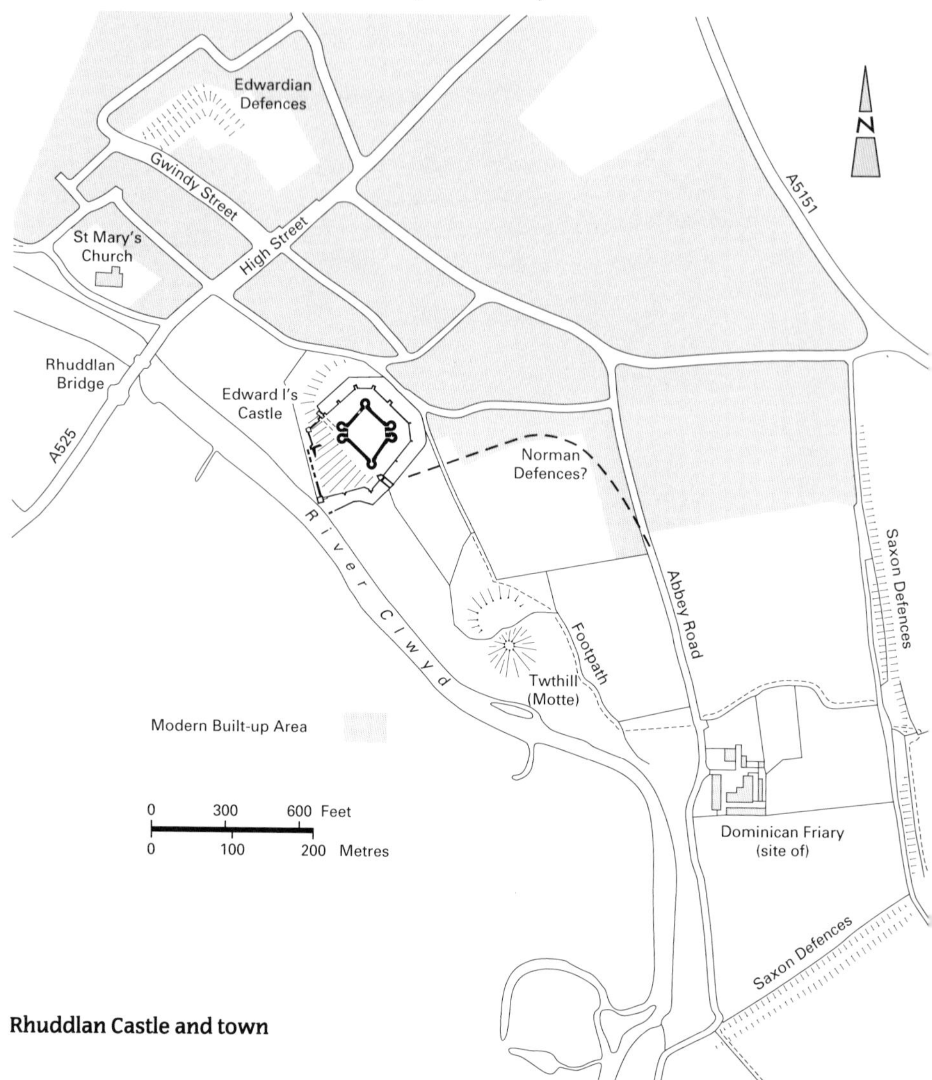

Rhuddlan Castle and town

symmetrical plan, completely surrounded by a slighter outer ward. On the south-west, this fronts the river, but elsewhere, it overlooks an artificial moat, also walled on the outer side, which was dry apart from a short section south of the castle, probably used as a dock. The inner ward is diamond-shaped, with a single tower on each of the sharper angles (north and south), and a gatehouse with double tower on each of the blunter ones (east and west). Various buildings, including a great hall, kitchens, private apartments and a chapel, stood in the inner ward, against the curtain wall; some traces remain of their foundations. The outer ward too included a granary, stables, a smithy, the treasury and a goldsmith's workshop, but little can be seen of these buildings today.

There were four entrances to the castle precinct, later reduced to three. The main entrance, still used today, is at the north-western end of the moat. Another entrance, the Friary Gate, on the south-east, was soon dismantled. Lesser entrances were provided from the river on the west and the dock on the south-west; the latter, like the dock itself, was overlooked by a tower.

Edward I laid out his new borough north of his castle, away from the Norman town and the Friary; the present town largely perpetuates the 13th-century plan. The town defences consisted of a pair of banks with a ditch between, as at Flint (no. 102), supporting a timber palisade; stone walls were never provided and probably never intended. The banks survive well at the northern corner, off Gwindy Street, where they are visible from the footpath. Edward I also replaced the bridge, probably damaged during the Welsh campaign, and made strenuous but unsuccessful efforts to have the episcopal seat of St Asaph removed to Rhuddlan.

The later history of the site was less eventful. It may have been at Rhuddlan, and not Caernarfon, that Edward I, in 1284, cynically offered his infant son to the Welsh nobles as 'a prince born in Wales, who spoke no English and was of blameless character'. The castle came under attack in the Welsh rising of 1294, and again in the Glyndŵr rising of 1400, when the town was badly damaged but the castle held out. Rhuddlan was in Royalist hands during the Civil War, until forced to capitulate in 1646; in 1648 it was partially demolished to prevent its further use.

100
Denbigh Castle

Medieval masonry castle, town walls and associated buildings

13th–16th century AD

OS 116 SJ 052658 R/U1 Cadw

From town centre follow signs to castle; park in car park. Walk down Castle Green to tower of St Hilary's Chapel and Burgess Gate. Leicester's Church and entrance to town walls (key from castle) round to R from Burgess Gate. For Friary, take A543 down hill from market past museum, turn L at lights (0.7ml, 1.1km). Site down Abbey Road, c.*50m further on R. Best parking* c.*50m further on L. Castle and town walls, admission charge, standard hours; otherwise free. Disabled access variable*

Cadw Guidebook

Denbigh Castle and walled town are built on a commanding rock outcrop with wide views across the Vale of Clwyd. The position is known to have been the chief stronghold of Dafydd ap Gruffudd, brother of Llywelyn, between 1277, when he was granted the area by Edward I at the end of his first Welsh campaign, and 1282, when his rebellion precipitated Edward's final conquest of Wales. No trace survives, however, of Dafydd's stronghold; the present remains date from Edward's renewed building effort.

The new fortifications at Denbigh were probably begun soon after 1282. There were two main stages in the development of the castle; the entire circuit of the town wall, probably substantially complete by 1285, appears to have been built first, the castle defences being grafted on inside them once the workforce could be protected. Although Master James of St George, Edward I's chief architect, was probably involved in the design, and other royal assistance was provided, responsibility for construction was delegated to Henry de Lacy, earl of Lincoln, who had been granted a considerable lordship in the area. The added walls were much thicker and of more complex design than those of the original circuit; some areas, including the Great Gatehouse, were probably still incomplete on de Lacy's death in 1311. The weakness of the earlier work on the outer sides was compensated for by providing a 'mantlet', an extra external wall at a lower level, as a second line of defence; this is best preserved on the south of the castle.

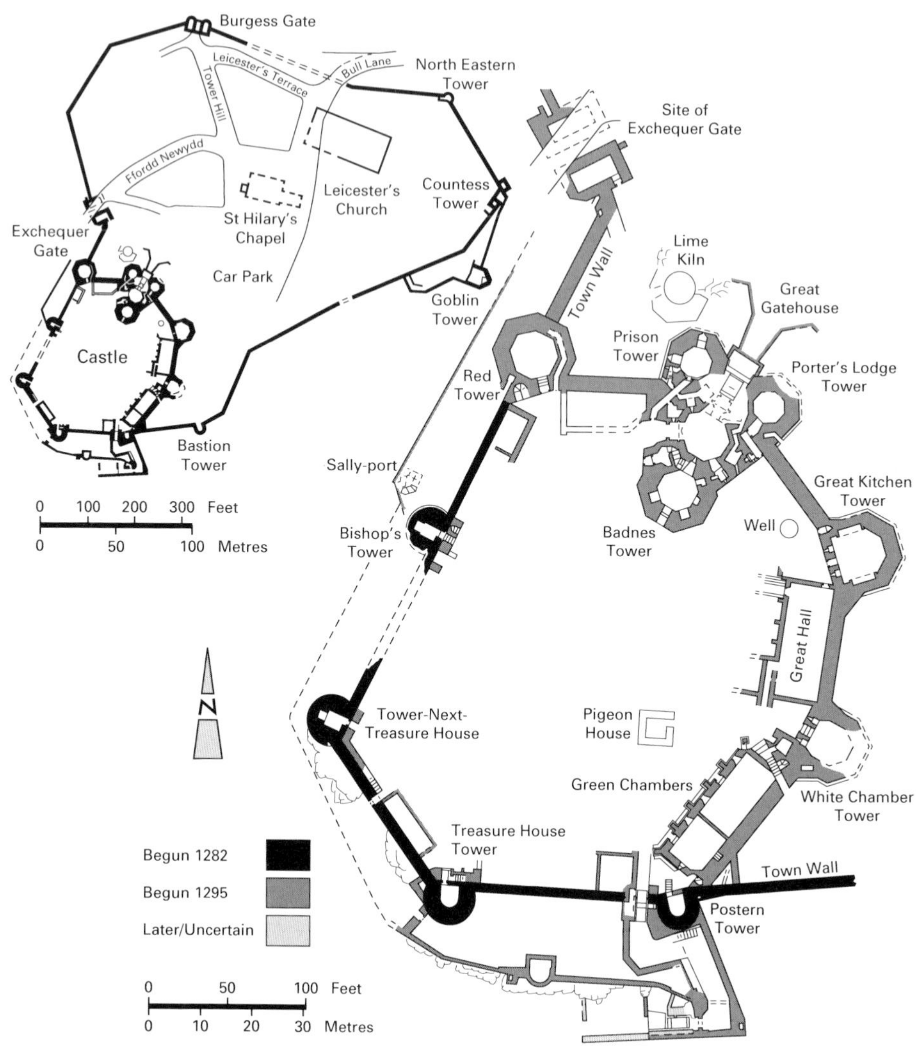

Denbigh Castle and town walls

The town wall had at least two entrances, the Exchequer Gate on the west, beside the castle, now ruinous, and the well-preserved Burgess Gate on the north; there may have been a north-eastern postern. Stretches of the wall, not open to the public, can be seen in the gardens on either side of the Burgess Gate, and running up the hill on the west, but a stretch on the north-east can be visited, including a later salient enclosing a reliable water source; this sector illustrates the breadth of views from the defended town and the complexity of the architecture.

There were four entrances to the castle, two

from the town and two from outside. From the town, the strongly defended Great Gatehouse was the main entrance, while a small gate beside the kitchens probably allowed access to the well in the salient of the town walls. The south postern and the western sally port, through one of the mantlet towers, allowed rapid access to the area outside the walls.

Buildings inside the castle would have included a great hall and kitchens, apartments for the lord, his family and guests, a chapel, and possibly lodgings and workshops for servants and craft specialists. The castle community would have been capable of making and repairing most of its everyday equipment. The remains of the Great Hall and a block of apartments known as the Green Chambers can still be seen alongside the eastern wall.

The castle's history was turbulent. Briefly in Welsh hands in 1294–5, it was threatened at intervals throughout the 14th century, while building continued under several different lords; nonetheless, it is not recorded as falling in the Glyndŵr rising at the beginning of the 15th century. It saw action during the Wars of the Roses, when the Lancastrian Henry VI 'gave' the castle to Jasper Tewdwr, who was obliged to take it by force from its Yorkist Mortimer lords. He succeeded briefly in 1460–1, and in 1468, burnt down the town, although failing to take the castle. The present town began to develop outside the walls at about this time, perhaps as a result of this episode.

By the 16th century, the castle was getting old, and peace had rendered it redundant. Repeated surveys indicated the need for repair, although it found a new use in 1536 as the administrative centre of the new shire of Denbigh. In 1563, it was granted to Queen Elizabeth's favourite, Robert Dudley, earl of Leicester, together with a sizeable lordship in the area, in the hope that he would effect repairs.

Leicester, however, was more interested in constructing a grandiose new church within the old town walls, and may have hoped to capture the episcopal seat from St Asaph. The remains of Leicester's Church stand in the north-east corner of the old town; it was completed to above window level before he was disgraced, but his successors abandoned the work. It is of particular interest as the first large episcopal building designed for the Protestant style of service, although no internal arrangements were completed.

Denbigh Friary

Services continued for many more years in St Hilary's Chapel, the original 14th-century chapel of the walled town; its remains, which had become unsafe, were demolished in 1923, except for the tower. Fortunately old plans and photographs record that it had a nave, a chancel with a crypt beneath, and a north aisle.

Some distance to the east of the town and castle lie the remains of the Friary. This was founded in the 13th century by the Carmelite or White Friars, and apparently enjoyed both clerical and lay patronage. In the early 16th century, two successive friar bishops of St Asaph lived here, although by the dissolution in 1538 there were only four friars left. Only the ruined church survives; the monastic buildings have disappeared apart from a little of the south range, incorporated into the adjoining Abbey Cottage. Friars and laity were separated in the church, by a lobby with a steeple or belfry above. The friars had ornate choir stalls to the east, and the laity their own separate altar and *piscina* to the west.

After Leicester's disgrace, the castle decayed further, although parts were still habitable in 1621. Nevertheless, the Civil War refurbishment by Colonel William Salusbury of Rug for the Royalists after 1643 must have been a daunting task. Charles I stayed at Denbigh for three days in 1645, and the castle was besieged from April to October 1646. Traces of the siegeworks survive in the school playing field. Eventually it capitulated, and for the remainder of the war, was used to house Royalist prisoners. After the restoration of Charles II in 1660, the disused castle and town walls were plundered for building materials. During the 18th century they aroused some interest as a 'romantic' ruin, but only in the mid-19th century was any effort made to tidy up and repair the remains.

101
Prestatyn Castle

Medieval motte and bailey castle

12th century AD

OS 116 SJ 072833 U3

From Prestatyn railway station, go N to join A548 and turn R. After 0.6ml (1km), keep straight on as road turns R; turn immediately R into Warren Drive. Park after LH bend; follow footpath near bend over railway footbridge, across stile, through gate and across field beyond. Site beside footpath just into next field; visible from A548 to E of turn. Vegetation can be high in summer

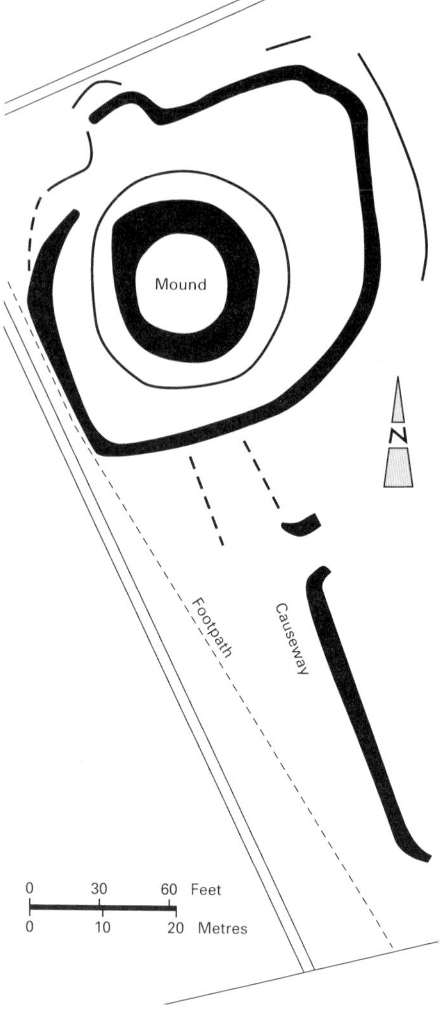

Prestatyn Castle

Prestatyn Castle occupies a low-lying position, but still commands a view across much of the flat coastal plain. It consists of the remains of a motte *c.*20m in diameter with surrounding ditch, and a bailey which, unusually, encloses the whole of the motte. Excavation in about 1913 revealed a substantial stone wall 1.2m thick surrounding the bailey, inside its ditch, but no trace of a structure on the motte. A slightly raised causeway approaches from the south (away from the railway), but no detail is now visible where it meets the bailey; there is no obvious entrance gap in the motte ditch. A rubbing stone for animals on top of the motte is presumably modern.

The castle was probably built by the Norman Robert de Banastre about 1164, and was destroyed by the resurgent Welsh under Owain Gwynedd in 1167. At some point, a Robert de Banastre (the name persisted for several generations) decamped with 'all his people' from Prestatyn to Lancashire. In 1279, when the area was once again under English control, part of the castle remained, but litigation in this period focused on the manor and nothing further is heard of the stronghold.

102
Flint Castle
Medieval masonry castle and borough
13th century AD
OS 117 SJ 247733 U1 Cadw

In centre of Flint, take A548 SE from junction with A5119. Castle up small turning on L after a short distance. Cross railway bridge; car parking on foreshore ahead

Cadw Guidebook

Flint Castle stands on the foreshore of the Dee estuary, dominating both the river and the route along the coastal plain. Construction began in July 1277, during Edward I's first Welsh campaign; the castle was essentially finished by 1284; it was unsuccessfully besieged by the Welsh in 1282. It consists of a four-square ward with one of the angle towers offset and dominant; this plan, originating on the Continent, may have been thought particularly suitable for a waterfront location; Rhuddlan (no. 99) was constructed at a similar date, probably by the same architect, but to a quite different design.

The exceptionally interesting Great Tower on the south-east is divided from the main courtyard by a moat, which probably contained seawater, at least at high tide, and was crossed by a drawbridge. This highly sophisticated separate tower or donjon has a strong barrel-vaulted circular gallery at basement level, surrounding a central space and supporting a ring of small interconnecting

Flint Castle from the north-east

rooms on the floor above. It probably contained all the facilities necessary to withstand a siege (storerooms, well, residential accommodation, chapel), many of them duplicated in the courtyard, and was effectively a castle within the castle and presumably the final refuge under attack; its thick walls made it very strong.

Numerous masons' marks, most consisting of a crossed circle, are visible in the basement, along with the bases of latrine chutes from at least two upper levels; the chute for each level runs down the back of that for the level below; presumably they were boarded in! Fireplaces and windows for the first floor rooms can be seen above; one of these at first-floor level was probably the chapel.

In 1399 Flint was Richard II's last refuge before he conceded the Crown to Henry Bolingbroke (Henry IV). It changed hands several times during the Civil War, before finally falling to Parliament in 1646; shortly afterwards it was substantially destroyed.

Little survives of the curtain walls; only the southern wall and a portion at the north-west still remain on the original scale. The rest, together with the three corner towers, were robbed to varying extents during later reuse of the castle, when the courtyard contained a variety of different buildings, traces of which still remain.

To the south of the castle lies a moated outer ward, similar to that at Rhuddlan, although it does not totally surround the castle. An 18th-century prison building stood here until relatively recently. Part of the stone revetment on the south of the bailey is visible as a free-standing wall west of the castle where industrial activity has lowered the ground level. Beyond this lay the borough, founded by Edward I for English settlers at the same time as the castle. The modern streets still follow its layout, although its double defensive banks, similar to those at Rhuddlan, are largely lost. The borough provided a useful source of rental income for the Crown, business opportunities for the burgesses, and, socially, a base for English colonisation in the area.

Ewloe Castle

103 Ewloe Castle

Medieval masonry castle

13th century AD

OS 117 SJ 288675 U4 Cadw

From Mold, take A494 towards Queensferry. After 3.5ml (5.6km), follow A494 through A55 interchange. At next exit, take B5125 L towards Northop Hall; after 0.8ml (1.3km), castle signposted R through kissing gate. Parking nearby. Entrance to S of castle after c.300m. Pedestrian access also through Wepre Park from Connah's Quay

Cadw Guidebook; Hemp 1928

Ewloe Castle lies in dense woodland which in medieval times was part of the great forest of Ewloe. It commands a north-facing slope above two deep ravines, but is overlooked on the south, where a substantial earthwork has been built outside the moat.

The castle, of typically Welsh design, consists of a walled upper ward on a natural outcrop, surrounding a rectangular keep with an apsidal eastern end; a lower ward encloses a well and incorporates a western round tower. A bridge on the north-east originally led directly to the upper ward, where the corresponding gap in the wall is clearly visible; steps mount the wall-walk just to its south. Part of the outcrop facing the eastern ditch was provided with a glacis, a covering of smooth stone to deter missiles. Wooden steps provide access today through a gap at the eastern end of the outer ward wall.

There are traces of other buildings in the inner ward, particularly around the steps south of the keep. From the wall-walk around the latter's apse, the internal subdivisions of the basement can be seen, as well as the large windows of the principal apartment, at first-floor (entrance) level, with traces of a roof-line above it, some way below the battlements. The outer ward presumably contained further buildings, housing garrison, horses, servants and craft specialists, but no traces remain.

Llywelyn ap Gruffudd is known to have 'built a castle in a corner of the wood' (at Ewloe) in 1257, most probably from scratch, although earlier commentators suggested that he refurbished an existing castle, perhaps built by Llywelyn ab Iorwerth at some time after 1210. The site would have lost its importance following Edward I's conquest of the area in 1277.

104
Trueman's Hill, Hawarden
Medieval motte
12th century AD
OS 117 SJ 313660 U2

From Mold, take A494 towards Queensferry. After 3.5ml (5.6km), follow A494 through A55 interchange. At next exit, take B5125 R to Hawarden; site in small park on L beyond railway bridge after 1ml (1.6km); park nearby or in car park on A550 towards Wrexham beyond

Trueman's Hill is a mound about 40m across at the base and 6.7m high; its summit is flat, about 14m across. Much of it is now covered with trees and scrub, but its outline is still visible. Modern building makes it difficult to appreciate its siting, but it probably covered the valley of the small stream which runs through the grounds of the more recent Hawarden Castle (appendix) to the south-east.

The irregular earthworks to the north of the mound could be the remains of a bailey, but may possibly be dumps from nearby sand extraction. Part of this area has been disturbed by the construction of a reservoir.

105
Caergwrle Castle
Early medieval hillfort/medieval masonry castle
4th–5th century AD/13th century AD
OS 117 SJ 307572 U4

From Wrexham (or Wrexham bypass), take A541 towards Mold. After 4.7ml (7.6km), park in Caergwrle car park (on LHS); walk back to signposted path up hill beside war memorial and Post Office

King 1974; Manley 1994

Caergwrle Castle (Hope Castle in English records) stands on an isolated hilltop above the Alyn valley with wide views except where Hope Mountain rises to the west. It was well placed to monitor movements between the Cheshire plain and the mountains.

The earliest feature on the hill is a large earthwork enclosure, surrounding most of its summit. The slight bank and ditch are best seen on the north and east, and there is probably an entrance on the north-west about 100m north of the later masonry castle. Quarrying has damaged the western side of this circuit, if indeed it was ever built against the precipice here, and the earthworks of the later castle have confused the picture on the south. Radiocarbon dates from burnt timber beneath the bank suggest a late- or post-

Aerial view of Caergwrle Castle from the north-east

Roman date, which might fit in with a general trend towards hilltop strongholds at that time.

The masonry castle, on the highest point of the hill, was probably first built by Dafydd ap Gruffudd, in lands given him by Edward I after the first Welsh campaign in 1277, in recognition of his help in their capture from his brother Llywelyn. Its architecture reflects Dafydd's divided loyalties, with English elements incorporated into a basically Welsh pattern. A single curtain wall, which survives on the east, is fronted by a substantial ditch with an outer counterscarp bank; there are towers, with blunt apses of English pattern, on the north and south-east and a round keep at the south. Openings for latrines at first-floor level can be seen in the curtain to the west of the north tower, and, unusually, two large holes in the west wall of the tower itself contained timber beams supporting the canopy of an internal fireplace. The south-eastern tower, again unusually, apparently had a living chamber at ground level, and its poor defensive position offers inadequate cover to the eastern curtain. There is no evidence of defences on the precipitous west, although this side has probably been damaged by quarrying. It is uncertain where the entrance lay, although one on the north-west seems likely.

The castle, although probably not complete, was sufficiently well defended by 1282 to provide the base for Dafydd's attack on the English garrison at Hawarden, which sparked Edward's second Welsh campaign. When the English reached Caergwrle in June 1282, the retreating Welsh had damaged the castle and filled in the well; expensive refurbishments, apparently largely in timber, were nonetheless put in hand. The following year Edward gave the castle, probably still unfinished, to his queen Eleanor, but it burnt down six months later. The shell, which had outlived its strategic purpose, passed to their son, Edward of Caernarfon. It was granted in 1308 to John of Cromwell on condition that he repair it, but by 1335 it was nonetheless ruinous.

Excavation revealed stone chippings and mortar-mixing areas in the interior which suggest that the construction or refurbishment work was incomplete. The well and a large bread-oven were found, together with traces of some of the timber buildings within the walls which would have provided additional accommodation. It is not clear whether these remains belong to the Welsh or the English occupation.

The castle has suffered extensive later robbing, undermining the curtain wall on the east. Excavation was needed to trace this across a gap previously thought to have been the entrance. The excavated remains have now been consolidated.

106
Holt Castle

Medieval masonry castle

Late 13th/early 14th century AD

OS 117 SJ 412537 U2

From Wrexham, take A534 towards Nantwich. After 4.5ml (7.2km), turn L for Holt. Park in centre of village after 0.6ml (1km). Path to castle (marked) starts on R a short distance further on; total walk about 300m

Palmer 1907; Butler 1987

Holt Castle, known as Chastellion or Castrum Leonis from the lion sculpture above its gateway, was built some time between 1282 and 1311 by John de Warenne, who was granted this area after Edward I's final defeat of the Welsh. He chose this low-lying but strategically important site on the west bank of the Dee in preference to Dinas Brân (no. 112), which he apparently did not maintain. The King's architect may have been responsible for the design of the castle.

The site lies in a quarry, which presumably provided the stone for the building. It was probably intended to guard the river crossing now occupied by the Holt–Farndon bridge (no. 135), a little further downstream. The castle must have been high enough to see to the west, and to the crossing point. The visible remains are difficult to interpret, since almost all the stonework was removed between 1675 and 1683 for the construction of Eaton Hall, about 5 miles (8km)

Holt Castle

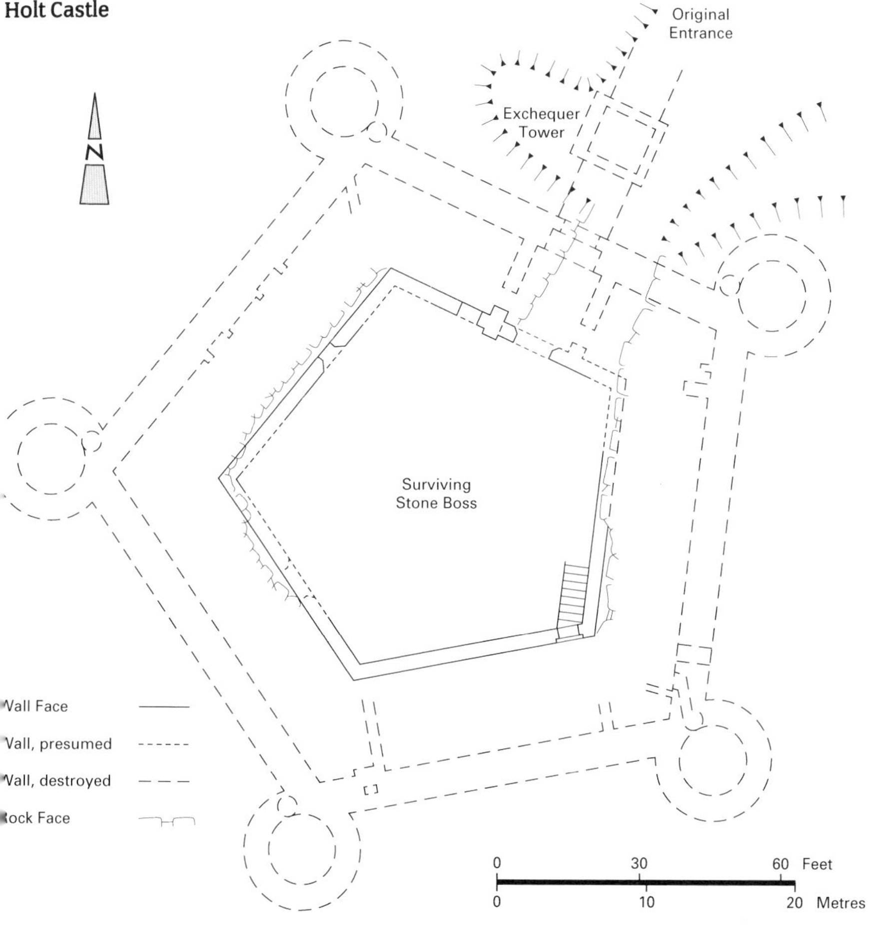

downstream. Written descriptions of the castle survive from the 1540s and 1586, and plans and illustrations from both 1562 and 1620, differing somewhat in detail.

The castle surrounded the eroding boss of stone which remains in the centre of the site; this supported only the inner courtyard. Around this were ranges of rooms, enclosed by a pentagonal outer curtain wall with external corner towers. There was a basement below the courtyard level, and two storeys above it. The towers each had an additional storey, further surmounted by a lookout turret. The entrance was central to the north-east range, approached by a track perpetuated by the modern path. A tower here, on an island in the moat surrounding the castle, could have acted as an additional gatehouse; it was originally the castle's exchequer or accounting office. The 1540s description mentions additional buildings surrounding the castle, and the illustration of 1620 shows a larger enclosure, with barns, stables and cow-houses along the inside of its walls, and a ruined pentagonal dovecote on the east.

The 1562 survey shows all the towers as round, with a rectangular external annexe containing the chapel running the full height of the south-eastern tower, while that of 1620 shows the tower opposite the gate as square or rectangular. Butler suggests that the 'annexe' and the odd square tower may both represent a detached square tower housing a 'water gate' near the river, with a chapel on an upper floor, seen in 18th-century engravings of the remaining ruins.

Discrepancies in the descriptions of rooms between the two plans can be explained if it is assumed that different floors are illustrated, although the 1620 survey appears to have been more cursory, probably because of the poor state of repair. Estimates for renovation were prepared and some work was probably carried out then or later, since the castle held out when the town was taken by the Parliamentarians in 1643, during the Civil War, falling only after a prolonged siege in 1646.

107
Y Foelas, Pentrefoelas

Medieval motte and bailey castle

12th century AD

OS 116 SH 870522 R3

From Denbigh, take A543 to Pentrefoelas (16m, 25.7km). Turn R on to A5 and after 0.3ml (0.5km), R on B5113; after 0.9ml (1.4km), turn R along lane. After 0.3ml (0.5km), park beyond cattle grid. Take footpath through kissing gate to R, across field, keeping hedge on R. View from path only

King 1983

This impressive motte, 7.5m high, readily visible from the footpath, lies at the north-western end of a complex of earthworks, now rather obscured by the woods covering the site, which include a small inner bailey on the south-east, and a larger outer bailey beyond this to the south. The site lies on a largely natural spur, while the stream provides an extra defence on the north and east.

The mound would have commanded a view towards Pentrefoelas and along part of the Merddwr valley where the A5 now runs. The summit probably supported a simple timber tower, although traces of masonry, possibly from a ring-wall, have been reported on the north-east.

Little is known of the site's history, although it may already have been abandoned by 1198, when the area was given to the monks of Aberconwy, north of Llanrwst. The headless body of Llywelyn ap Gruffudd may be buried nearby (but see no. 149).

108
Tomen y Faerdre, Llanarmon yn Iâl

Medieval motte

11th–13th century AD

OS 116 SJ 193561 R3

From Ruthin, take A494 towards Mold. After 4.6ml (7.4km), turn R on B5430 towards Llanarmon yn Iâl; 2.8ml (4.5km) further on, take B5431 on R. Site on L before bridge after 0.2ml (0.3km); parking limited. Some view from road; please ask at large farmhouse in village opposite E end of church before visiting

Tomen y Faerdre is an impressive motte, 6m high on the east and 25m across the summit. It sits on a natural rock outcrop, forming a cliff above the river Alyn on its west. An artificial ditch runs around its remaining sides, tapering down towards the stream on the south, but ending in mid-air above the crag on the north. There is no trace of a bailey.

Presumably the site would have commanded the route along the Alyn valley, but it does not enjoy especially wide views; the valley is, however, narrowed here by cliffs opposite. Possibly 11th-century in origin, the site was a local administrative centre, and, like Tomen y Rhodwydd (no. 109) was refortified by King John in 1212 against Llywelyn ab Iorwerth, when the rock-cut ditch was either dug or enlarged.

109
Tomen y Rhodwydd, Llandegla

Medieval motte and bailey castle

12th century AD

OS 116 SJ 177516 R2

From Ruthin, take A525 towards Wrexham. After 7.5ml (12.1km) take B5431 sharp L for Llanarmon yn Iâl. Continue up lane ahead to top of rise; parking on L in lay-by; access to site across caravan park. Please ask at adjoining farm before visiting

Pratt 1978

Tomen y Rhodwydd, built by Owain Gwynedd in 1149 in conjunction with his annexation of part of Powys, is a very fine motte and bailey castle, commanding wide views except to the north-east. The Nant y Garth Pass (now the A525), connecting the Clwyd and Alyn valleys south of the Clwydian Hills, and the Horseshoe Pass from the Dee valley, meet nearby. The castle was retaken in 1157 by Iorwerth Goch ap Maredudd of Powys and burnt, although, like Tomen y Faerdre (no. 108), it was restored and ditched by the English forces during King John's 1212 campaign.

Aerial view of Tomen y Rhodwydd from the south-west

The remains are mainly grass-covered. The motte, 20m across the top, is surrounded on the north and west by a dramatic ditch and outer bank. It stands 7.8m above the base of the ditch and 4.9m above the bailey to its south-east, with only a slight hollow between the two. The bailey measures about 40m across internally; no visible traces of buildings remain. Its undulating bank stands about 1–1.5m above the interior, and 4–5m above the base of the ditch, which joins the motte ditch on the south and surrounds the bailey except for a causeway at the northernmost corner beside the motte. An outer bank, probably built of spoil from the ditches, survives on the south, although the site has been damaged by the road on this side.

110
Erddig Castle, Wrexham

Medieval motte and bailey castle

12th century AD

OS 117 SJ 327487 U4 NT

Follow directions for no. 89 to Erddig house or country park car park. From house, take path N to kissing gate on R opposite 'cup and saucer' (water feature, signposted); follow old drive up towards house; double back to L at barrier. Where path (which follows Wat's Dyke here) meets landslip, double back to higher level path on R, which continues to castle (outer ditch at next fork). From country park car park, follow path into park (see no. 89); take kissing gate (on L) opposite 'cup and saucer' and continue as above

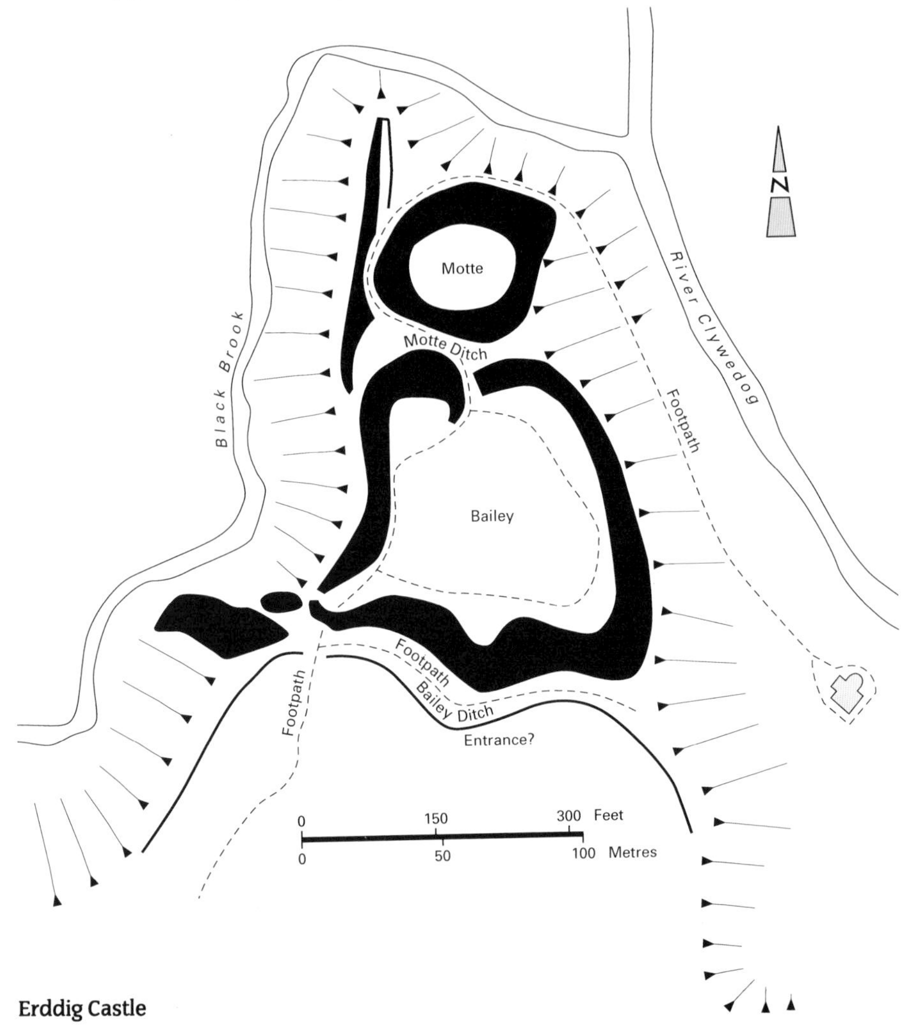

Erddig Castle

Erddig Castle defends a steep north-facing promontory above streams in a manner reminiscent of the Iron Age. Its history is poorly known, although it was probably built before 1161. The area is now wooded, but the earthworks are clearly visible. These include a bank along the western side (left as one approaches), possibly part of the earlier Wat's Dyke (cf. no. 89), or alternatively, constructed as part of the castle's defences to cover dead ground.

A right fork in the path follows the massive bailey ditch, 6m deep, a formidable line of defence across the vulnerable south of the promontory. Further north, on the other side of the bailey, lies another, 4.5m deep, encircling the motte. The interior of the bailey is scrub-covered and difficult to appreciate. The entrance, by drawbridge, probably lay halfway along the outer ditch, where there is a pronounced change in its line; the position of a likely central crossing of the inner ditch on to the motte was damaged during garden landscaping in the 18th century, which included the addition of paths, in particular the spiral walk up the motte.

111
Owain Glyndŵr's Mound, Corwen

Medieval motte

12th century AD

OS 125 SJ 125431 R3

From Llangollen, take A5 towards Corwen. Site visible on RHS after 7.3ml (11.7km). No parking, but safe to stop alongside site. View from road only

Owain Glyndŵr's Mound, which occupies a commanding position overlooking the Dee valley, is 6.5m high, 36m across at the base and 12m at the top, with a ditch 1m deep on its west and south-west, towards the road. It is probably a motte, although no bailey has been traced.

Its active life would have been well before Glyndŵr's rising in the early 15th century; in the same field, however, not visible from the road, is a moated site, destroyed in 1403, with well-attested connections with the hero. It is not known when the property came into his family's hands.

Extensive erosion repair and control works, including the use of various kinds of protective mesh, were carried out on the mound during 1991, to combat damage arising from sheep trampling in soil exposed by the failure of the turf on the mound. This work is experimental, but results so far have been encouraging.

112
Castell Dinas Brân, Llangollen

Iron Age (?) hillfort/medieval masonry castle

Late 1st millennium BC/13th century AD

OS 117 SJ 223431 U4 Clwyd CC

(With car) From Llangollen, take road up hill off A539 just E of N end of bridge; cross canal, turn R, then L after 0.2ml (0.3km). Continue to T-junction past cattle grid (1ml, 1.6km); park on road. Path below grid, waymarked; keep to L above upper stile. Access to castle through centre of bank ahead

(Without car; longer walk) From Llangollen, take footpath beside garage near N end of bridge; cross canal by road bridge; take path up brick steps ahead. Cross drive after gate at top of stretch and continue with hedge on R to next gate. Follow track ahead across crossroads; at far end gate leads on to hill. After short climb, castle visible at top of hill ahead. Please keep to marked paths to minimise erosion

Official Guidebook; King 1974

The spectacular ruin of Castell Dinas Brân, visible for miles along the valley, occupies a steep isolated hill where the Dee valley is joined by the Horseshoe Pass from the north. The medieval castle was built in the north-west corner of a univallate hillfort, probably Iron Age in date; the latter's entrance probably lay on the south-west, beneath the castle defences. A number of possible hut sites are visible in the undulating interior of the hillfort, although the regularly spaced terraces probably reflect the bedding planes of the underlying limestone.

The castle was built by the lords of Powys Fadog, probably during the 1260s; Edward I's campaigning forces found it deserted and burnt down in 1277, but nonetheless placed a garrison there. The site, still probably ruinous, was afterwards restored to its Welsh lords, but after the Welsh rising and subsequent English campaign of 1282 it was transferred to John de Warenne, who made his base at the strategically more useful Holt (no. 106), and apparently did not rebuild it.

A rock-cut ditch, containing a well near the south-east corner, surrounds the castle on the south and east, probably the quarry for its building stone. The bank outside it may be a dump of unusable material. A stretch of rock-cut ditch to the west of the keep, at the eastern end of the castle, separates it from most of the remainder apart from the main gateway.

The south and west sides of the keep survive best. Traces of latrine chutes from the upper floors are visible east of the junction with the curtain on the south, while a passage parallel with the western wall, widening into a room at the north-west corner, would have supported a stair leading to a first-floor entrance. This adjoins a stretch of curtain wall running north to the gatehouse. The latter consists of long parallel chambers, flanking the gate passage, rounded to form towers at the front. The southern chamber survives well, but that on the north is reduced to ground level. There are traces of door-jambs at each end of the passage, and further latrine chutes, serving an upper floor, occupied a buttress at the north-west of the structure. The interior of the gate passage appears from

Aerial view of Castell Dinas Brân from the south-west

fragments to have been elaborately vaulted.

The curtain wall is intermittently preserved, including the remains of a typically Welsh apsidal tower in the middle of the south side, and a postern gate at the south-west, as well as traces of buildings on the west, probably workshops for craft specialists, accommodation, storage and stabling. The arched windows of the great hall (or possibly the chapel) survive to the east of the apsidal tower, and figure prominently in views of the castle from below.

113
Chirk Castle

Medieval castle adapted as house

13th century AD

OS 126 SJ 268381 R1/2 NT

From Llangollen, take A5 towards Oswestry. After 5.5ml (8.8km) take B5070 R for Chirk. 1.4ml (2.3km) further on, turn R for castle and station; drive begins at fine early 18th-century gates after 0.6ml (1km), and is 1.4ml (2.3km) long. Exit N of Park; turn R for 1ml (1.6km) to original gate. Open part week summer only; tel. 01691 777701 for times; admission charge. Limited wheelchair access

Official Guidebook

Chirk Castle, occupied virtually continuously as castle and stately home for almost 700 years, sits on a hilltop with its best views over the Ceiriog valley to the south. The successor to two known mottes in the area, it was probably built by Roger Mortimer, of the powerful Marcher family, who was granted the area by Edward I after the Welsh defeat in 1282. He was almost certainly given royal assistance in its design and construction, and its similarities to Beaumaris suggest that work may have started as late as 1295, perhaps in response to the Welsh rising of 1294.

The castle may originally have been envisaged as a rectangular enclosure with towers at the corners and halfway along each side; if so, only the northern half of the design survives, stopping beyond the central towers on the east and west; the simple gate through the eastern part of the north wall is probably original. Additional outer defences were dismantled during later landscaping.

The spirit of the 14th-century structure is preserved in Adam's Tower (near the well, on the south-west), which has a magnificent dungeon on two levels and a number of upper rooms clearly showing the 5m-thick walls; two of them contain 'murder holes' through which material could be poured on to anyone trying to batter or burn down the doors below. This tower, like the others, was originally at least one storey higher, the upper parts probably being removed after the Civil War bombardment of 1659.

The south curtain was completed on the present line early in the 15th century, under Thomas, earl of Arundel, probably against Glyndŵr's forces, who had strong local support. The chapel in the present south-east corner, possibly begun in the later 14th century, and the adjoining hall are the earliest surviving stone rooms outside the towers; timber structures probably stood against the other walls.

After the Wars of the Roses, the castle settled in royal hands on the execution of Sir William Stanley in 1495. The south range was partially rebuilt in 1529, reusing stone from earlier work; the old hall was subdivided and new living accommodation provided to its west. In 1563, the castle was granted to Elizabeth I's favourite, Robert Dudley, soon created earl of Leicester and Baron Denbigh, who held it as part of his extensive north Wales properties until his death in 1588. He may have reroofed it and added some of the square windows.

The castle was purchased in 1595 for about £5,000 by Sir Thomas Myddelton, a son of the governor of Denbigh Castle and successful London merchant. As a founder of the East India Company, and investor in the expeditions of Drake, Raleigh and Hawkins, he had the means to convert Chirk into a comfortable Tudor residence. His new stone north range contained a hall, buttery and kitchen, with upstairs drawing and dining rooms; this range, with alterations, became the main living quarters of the castle, while the old south range was gradually given over to servants.

Sir Thomas' son, the second Sir Thomas, took up residence on his marriage in 1612, and, as MP for Denbighshire from 1625, found himself on the Parliamentarian side in the Civil War. Royalist supporters seized the castle in 1643, and held it for three years; Sir Thomas' parliamentary forces meanwhile enjoyed some successes including the capture of Powis Castle (no. 115), although he could not bring himself to attack Chirk.

The castle was eventually regained by bribery, and Sir Thomas' son (Sir Thomas III) installed as governor. By 1651, however, the general had changed sides, and further payoffs were needed to dislodge the parliamentary garrison. Chirk was nevertheless besieged and taken by the Parliamentarians in 1659 as punishment for the Myddeltons' support of the Cheshire Rising; at the last moment it sustained the damage they had for so long sought to avoid. Most of the eastern side was demolished, and much of the rest burnt, leaving the family with a huge rebuilding task after the Restoration in 1660.

A new stone range was now added on the east, in conjunction with the reconstruction of the curtain wall and towers. The new towers, although externally similar to their predecessors, had much thinner walls, while the range included a drawing room and long gallery at first-floor level, with an arcaded walkway facing the courtyard beneath it. The old state bedroom in the south-east tower was given a new entrance from the long gallery. Sir Thomas III predeceased his father; his son Sir Thomas IV, who came of age in 1672, supervised the decoration of the newly built rooms, completed, possibly with the help of William Wynde, in 1678. Only the long gallery survives to show the original style of this work.

With the east range, the main structure of the castle was complete, although minor alterations continued to be made. After an abortive episode in 1762–4, when a scheme for a 'gothick' interior was abandoned at an early stage, the north range was extensively refurbished in neo-classical style by Joseph Turner of Chester in the later 1760s and 1770s, the drawing room being completed by John Cooper of Beaumaris in about 1796. In the 1820s, however, gothic vaulting was added, and from 1845 the interior was almost totally reworked in the gothic manner by A W Pugin, architect of the Houses of Parliament; most of these alterations have been undone in recent years, with the exception of the Cromwell Hall, where a collection of Civil War arms is displayed. The castle remained in the hands of the Myddelton family, who still own and work much of the estate, until 1978; it is now in the care of the National Trust.

Offa's Dyke runs through the park; it can be seen from the air beneath the waters of the artificial lake, and is visible as a low bank as far as Home Farm, west of the castle. South of the farm, it is better preserved, running to the west of the track, and out into fields beyond, beside the footpath.

The magnificent wrought iron gate-screen at the entrance to the park was made by

Aerial view of Chirk Castle from the north-west

Robert and John Davies of Bersham between 1712 and 1719. It originally stood a little way in front of the main castle gate, and was moved to its present position in 1770 during the landscaping of the park.

114
Castle Caereinion Castle

Medieval motte and bailey castle

12th century AD

OS 125 SJ 163054 U2

From roundabout on W of Welshpool, take A458 towards Dolgellau. After 4ml (6.4km), take B4385 L; fork L after 100m. Limited parking by church gates, on R just into village after 0.7ml (1.1km). Castle in churchyard

St John O'Neil 1936

The motte is the grassy mound in the northern corner of the churchyard, standing up to 3m high and roughly 20m across; there is a slight depression to the south marking the probable line of the original ditch. The raised north-west and north-east sides of the churchyard may indicate the position of bailey banks, as may the mounds surrounding some of the yews on the south-west where the original entrance probably lay, and south-east where the churchyard has since been extended.

The castle lies at an important watershed, between the Sylfaen Brook and the Banwy valley, on the route west from Welshpool now used by the A458. It was built by Madog ap Maredudd of Powys in 1156, and refurbished in 1166 by Owain Gwynedd and the Lord Rhys, after they had evicted Madog's nephew Owain Cyfeiliog for swearing allegiance to the English. Owain destroyed the castle shortly afterwards with a Norman force, and nothing further is heard of it.

Aerial view of Castle Caereinion Castle, with motte to the left of the church

115
Powis Castle, Welshpool

Medieval castle adapted as house

13th century AD

OS 126 SO 216064 R1/2 NT

From Welshpool, take A490/A483 towards Newtown. After 1ml (1.6km), take signposted turning on R; turn R again up drive after 0.3ml (0.5km); 0.9ml (1.4km) to castle. From exit, turn L for 0.3ml (0.5km) to original gate. Open part week, summer only; tel. 01938 554336 for times; admission charge. Limited wheelchair access

Official Guidebook; Arnold 1985; 1986; 1993

Powis Castle crowns a rocky ridge, with a particularly steep slope to the south-east, now occupied by formal gardens; a similarly steep slope on the north-west may have been partially infilled to support buildings. The easiest access is along the ridge from north-east or south-west. The castle is within easy reach of Welshpool, although, as at

Powis Castle from the south-east

Montgomery (no. 118), direct control of the natural route focus has been sacrificed for strength of siting.

The structural history of the castle is difficult to unravel, largely because of alterations and additions during over 700 years of virtually continuous occupation. Recent work by Chris Arnold, including a detailed study of the masonry of the south-east and south-west faces, suggests that its development may be more complex than previously believed. The historical sources are little help, since it is not always clear whether they refer to the motte near Welshpool station (Domen Castell: appendix), the Lady's Mound, in the park 300m west of Powis Castle, or the present site. Some or all of these may have worked in conjunction in the period before 1277.

The plan visible today consists of an inner ward, surrounding a tiny courtyard little bigger than a light well, with an outer ward on its south-west, through which the visitor now enters. The oldest part of the structure, possibly dating to about 1200, is probably the tower at the north-east end of the inner ward, while the curving masonry at the south end of the south-east wall suggests the presence of a shell keep at a similar date; the north-east tower may have formed a gateway for this. This hypothetical stronghold, which probably had a north-east bailey, seems to have been demolished and replaced by a sub-rectangular structure, containing a hall on the north-west and possibly a second tower on the north-east; later still, probably after 1277, the imposing south-west gateway was built, apparently incorporating some reused stone; the outline of the original crenellations can be seen on the western tower a little below the existing (19th-century) ones. The present outer ward was completed in stone at much the same time.

The historical sources refer to the area as Pool or Pole, from which comes the modern Welshpool. 'Pool' was the stronghold of the Welsh princes of Powys, who held an ambivalent position between the Welsh and the English. Their rivalry with the house of Gwynedd, coupled with a practical appreciation of their situation, tended to drive them towards the English, although expediency could persuade them the other way. In 1196, Gwenwynwyn ab Owain Cyfeiliog was driven out of his castle (Domen Castell?) by a combined force of English and Welsh, but recovered it during the following year. Llywelyn ab Iorwerth of Gwynedd conquered Powys in 1218, forcing Gwenwynwyn into English exile, where he died, but his son Gruffudd returned on Llywelyn's death in 1240. Gruffudd fled when Llywelyn ap Gruffudd recaptured the area for Gwynedd in 1257, but the success of Simon de Montfort, whom Llywelyn supported against Henry III, persuaded him to change his allegiance in 1264. His new loyalty was shortlived, however; he was discovered plotting against Llywelyn in 1274. His castle (probably this one) was reportedly razed to the ground, and Gruffudd again fled.

He returned with Edward I's victorious army in the first Welsh campaign of 1277, and subsequently held his regained lands from the English Crown. He was succeeded in 1286 by his son Owain, better known as Baron de la Pole. The lordship passed via Owain's daughter Hawys to the Cherleton family, and in 1578 came into the hands of Sir Edward Herbert, in whose family it has remained.

The castle Sir Edward took over was probably in serious need of repair and modernisation, and he undertook extensive work between 1587 and 1595, of which only the long gallery survives. His wife Mary brought Catholicism into the family. The Herberts remained staunchly Royalist during the Civil War, but Powis Castle was captured by Parliamentarian forces under Sir Thomas Myddelton in 1644. It seems to have been garrisoned during the remainder of the war, necessitating extensive rebuilding and refurbishment after the Restoration in 1660.

The main surviving features of this work are the grand staircase and the state bedroom (the only one in Britain with a balustrade between the raised bed alcove and the rest of the room), together with the gateway and most of the range in the outer ward. The steps to the main south-west entrance were also added at this time, suggesting that the rise of 1.3m in the level of the courtyard, which excavation showed to be made up of rubble, resulted from damage during the Civil War. The first servants' quarters may have been built in the angle between the old hall and the northern end of the outer ward range at this time; this area was largely gutted by fire in about 1725.

Further extensive building was carried out from 1772 by the young George Herbert, the second earl. A ballroom was built in the outer ward range, and the core of the present servants' quarters constructed, on the earlier site; other rooms were redecorated in the fashionable classical style. George Herbert died in 1801, deeply in debt, but happily for the castle, his sister had married Clive of India's son. Their son (Clive's grandson) was heir to both the castle and the Clive fortune, which allowed it to be properly maintained. A collection of Clive mementoes from India is on display in part of the old ballroom. The castle underwent further extensive refurbishment in 1815-18 (by Smirke), and again from 1902 (by Bodley). Although bequeathed to the National Trust in 1952, it remained in part a private home until 1988.

116
Dolforwyn Castle, Abermule

Medieval masonry castle

13th century AD

OS 136 SO 152950 U4 Cadw

From Newtown, take A483 towards Welshpool. After 4.4ml (7.1km), turn L (just beyond B4386 towards Montgomery). Pass hotel, turn L by farm after 0.2ml (0.3km). Limited parking by gate to driveway on R, 0.5ml (0.8km) further on (don't block it!). Follow driveway up through two gates, round hairpin to R

Butler 1989, 1990

Aerial view of Dolforwyn Castle from the south

Dolforwyn, possibly already a Welsh castle, was fortified by Llywelyn ap Gruffudd in 1273, as a stronghold against both the English and the princes of Powys. The English were sufficiently worried by this, among other things, to order him to cease construction; he did not, and the castle was taken by force in 1277 as part of Edward I's first Welsh campaign. It was given to the Mortimers, a powerful Marcher family, and was kept in repair for some years, but was ruinous by 1398. Llywelyn's fledgling town on the ridge to the west was suppressed under the English, who did not welcome competition with Montgomery (no. 118); Roger Mortimer founded Newtown in 1279 on a more suitable site nearby.

The site occupies the crest of a steep-sided ridge running north-east to south-west above the Severn valley; it enjoys wide views except to the east. The castle stands on a rock platform, up to 6m above the bases of the ditches which define its north-east and south-west ends. The north-east ditch, 30m wide and 3m below the natural ground level, has a bank 1.5m high outside it, while that to the south-west is narrower. A drawbridge led from the town across the south-western ditch to a simple gate in the curtain wall.

The modern track up passes some slight platforms, which may mark the site of buildings in the Welsh town. A temporary entrance ramp has been constructed over the fragmentary northern castle wall to facilitate excavation and consolidation, in progress since 1980. The local building stone is friable, and the rough masonry would originally have been rendered.

The plan of the castle, mostly recovered since 1980, consists of a rectangular curtain wall enclosing, at its western end, a large rectangular keep, and, at its eastern end, a round tower. Both these features are integrated into its circuit, the keep by its south wall, where the latrine shafts are situated. A rock-cut ditch runs across the castle court from north to south, perhaps reflecting a division similar to that suggested at Hen Domen (no. 117). The dating of these features is as yet uncertain.

The excavations showed that repair work had been carried out to the masonry of the keep and it had been divided internally. These may have been the repairs recorded after the castle was captured by the English, since some of the materials used can be traced to sources in English hands. Excavations also indicate that ranges of buildings lay along the southern and northern sides of the courtyard. Stone balls, which may have been fired from English siege engines in 1277, have been found scattered on the site.

117
Hen Domen, Montgomery

Medieval motte and bailey castle

11th–13th century AD

OS 137 SO 213980 U4

From Montgomery, take B4385 towards Newtown. After 1.2ml (1.9km), site signposted down lane to R. Access through farm on L 50m down lane, by courtesy of private owner

Barker and Higham 1982, 1988; Higham and Barker 1992

Hen Domen is a fine motte and bailey castle commanding the important Severn crossing at Rhydwhyman, the focus of natural routes from Shrewsbury, to the north-east, and from Bishop's Castle, to the south-east. Nearby sites indicating the area's continuing strategic importance include Ffridd Faldwyn hillfort (no. 59), Forden Gaer (a Roman fort near the river), and the later castle and town at Montgomery (no. 118).

The castle, called Montgomery in the Domesday survey of 1088, was built sometime between AD 1071 and 1086, by Roger de Montgomery, earl of Shrewsbury, a relative of the Conqueror. In 1102, after earl Roger's son was disgraced, the castle passed to the Crown, and was granted, as the centre of a newly created Marcher lordship, to the de Boulers family, which died out in 1207. In 1216, King John gave the castle to Gwenwynwyn, prince of Powys, as a political gambit, but he quickly conceded it to Llywelyn ab Iorwerth, who was allowed to hold it for Gwenwynwyn's young sons but was evicted in 1223 during the campaign which saw work begin on the castle at New Montgomery nearby. Excavation suggests that limited occupation of Old Montgomery continued to the end of the century, probably as an outpost of the new castle (assuming a tower on the motte, both the river crossing and the new castle would have been visible); after this, peace rendered both sites largely redundant.

Between 1960 and 1992, the motte, part of the motte ditch, parts of the outer defences and the northern half of the bailey were painstakingly excavated by Philip Barker and Robert Higham, revealing evidence of great complexity. Underlying the castle were traces of much earlier, possibly sub-Roman buildings, overlain by ridge and furrow cultivation, which probably dates to a period before constant skirmishing created the 'waste' so widespread hereabouts at the time of the Norman Conquest. Survey suggests that a settlement site possibly associated with these fields may have lain just west of the later castle.

The main feature of the Norman plan is the imposing motte, 8m high and 6.7m across the summit, which supported a wooden tower, frequently repaired up to the 13th century, and may also have had a palisade around its base, above the surrounding ditch. To its east lies the bailey, measuring 39m by 41m, with an entrance at its east end. The bailey rampart

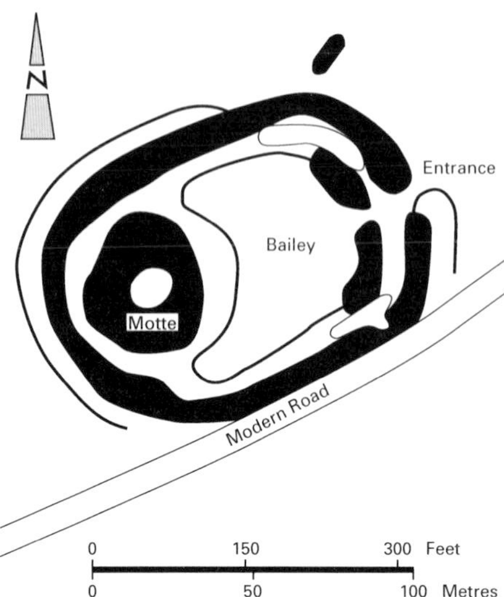

Hen Domen

survives best on the north, where it was at least 1.5m high; excavation showed that it supported a palisade, fighting platform and towers, while the ditch beyond, 3–5m deep, adjoins the motte ditch at its western ends. Both motte and bailey are surrounded by an impressive outer bank, which also carried timber defences at some periods, and which had an outer ditch around at least part of its circuit, now surviving only on the west (towards the farm).

The excavations identified five main phases of building within the bailey, all of timber but using various construction techniques. The best preserved was the third phase, of about 1150, when the bailey was packed with numerous structures, including an upper and lower hall, a possible chapel and a granary, and was apparently separated into an inner and outer courtyard by a range of buildings running north-south. This too may have carried a fighting platform.

No known town is associated with Hen Domen, although several old routes focus on the hamlet at the crossroads to its east. Traders are recorded in the area in around 1200, but it is not clear whether they were resident or itinerant. Any commercial activity focused on the site undoubtedly moved after 1223 to the new town of Montgomery; a small exhibition about the site can be seen in The Bell museum there.

118
Montgomery
Medieval masonry castle and town walls

13th–14th century AD

OS 137 SO 221967 U2 Cadw

For castle, turn S along Kerry Street at Town Hall (W end of Broad Street). Follow road round to R up hill; car park on R just before farm. Entrance through pedestrian gate E of farm. Alternatively, footpath up from garden in Arthur Street, N from Town Hall.
For walls on W, continue past farm by castle to RH bend; stretch of ditch (private) over gate to L, accessible from path opposite car park; path on R of lane follows well-preserved town defences past W of castle. For walls on E and N park in Broad Street; turn R along road towards Bishop's Castle, take 2nd L; fork L into narrow lane following line of ditch around SE corner past backs of houses and garages. Ditch visible beyond far end of lane, in school field (private); continue up hill and turn R past school; good stretch over stile on R beyond, near electricity pole (ditch and counterscarp, adjoins school field). Turn down to L further on, reaching Bricklayer's Arms. To R opposite, take Chirbury Gate into housing estate; turn R and skirt last house to L; rear bank of wall on R here, with modern wall on far side. Turn L, continue to main road. Follow R fork on R to Cottage Inn; scrubby ditch just visible beyond field behind car park. Return to Broad Street by either main road or Arthur Street

Official Guidebook; Knight 1992, 1993

Montgomery Castle and Town Walls

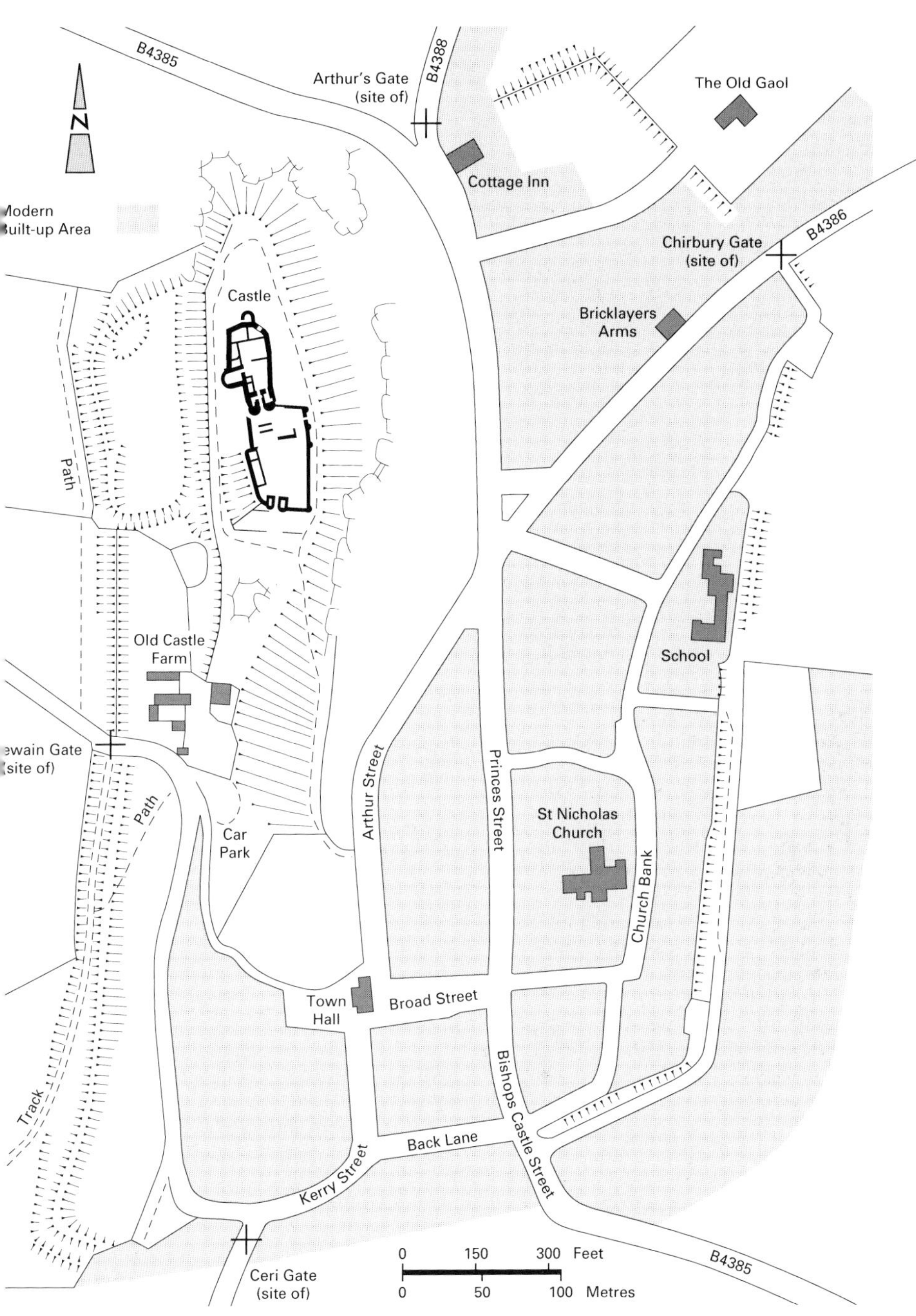
B4385
Arthur's Gate
(site of)
B4388
The Old Gaol
N
Cottage Inn
Modern
Built-up Area
Chirbury Gate
(site of)
B4386
Castle
Bricklayers
Arms
Path
School
Old Castle
Farm
Gate
(site of)
Path
Arthur Street
Princes Street
St Nicholas
Church
Car
Park
Church Bank
Town
Hall
Broad Street
Bishops Castle Street
Track
Back Lane
Kerry Street
0 150 300 Feet
0 50 100 Metres
B4385
Ceri Gate
(site of)

The western (well) tower at Montgomery Castle

The castle at Montgomery succeeded Hen Domen (no. 117), one mile (1.6km) to the north-west, after 1223. It was far more strongly sited, on a steep rocky ridge running north–south, reflecting changing military fashion. The tower at Hen Domen may have been retained to cover the Severn crossing at Rhydwhyman, not visible from the new site. The new castle was built during Henry III's campaign against Llywelyn ab Iorwerth, in whose hands Hen Domen had been left, but whose fidelity had been rendered questionable by his siege, early in 1223, of Builth (no. 125).

The new site consisted originally of the inner ward, at the north end, constructed in stone between 1224 and 1233, and the middle ward to its south, built in wood at this time and converted to stone only in 1251–3. Outworks to the south, the outer ditch of which is occupied by the house left of the path from the car park, were probably added in 1233 and embellished in stone later. A modern wooden bridge, on the site of an earlier drawbridge, crosses the rock-cut ditch into the middle ward, and a further bridge crosses another ditch into the inner ward. This crossing was defended by a gatehouse with two round towers, an early example of the type, much of the ground floor of which survives. Each tower contains a rectangular room, not originally accessible from the gate passage, although a doorway was later provided into that on the west, which may initially have been a prison. The room on the east, from which the drawbar across the gate would have been operated, is entered from the courtyard beyond, and is notable for the number of masons' marks scratched on the stonework. Something of the upper floors can be reconstructed from historical records; a wooden chapel supported on two posts straddled the back of the entrance passage, and both this and the three upper floors of the gatehouse proper were reached via a stair from the courtyard. The two uppermost floors contained private apartments, while the first floor was a single room.

The remaining inner ward defences consisted of a curtain wall with a short-lived tower on the north, and a larger tower, containing the well, on the west. This tower was built out over the precipice along this side of the castle, which, together with seepage from the well, caused repeated structural problems; it was totally rebuilt in the mid 14th century. Buildings nestled against the inside of the curtain wall; the bakehouse (with its large bread-oven) and brewhouse on the north-west appear to be part of an early plan, but almost the entire circuit was later filled with structures on several floors. The middle ward too shows traces of the buildings which would have lined it, although it was later levelled up to support a fine half-timbered mansion with brick infilling built by Sir Edward Herbert in 1622–5.

The town, in the hollow to the east of the castle, was not properly defended for some years after its foundation in 1223. The earthworks and palisade eventually built passed to the west of the castle, providing a further line of defence. The castle survived attacks by Llywelyn ab Iorwerth in 1228, and in 1231, when the town was burnt, and by Dafydd ap Llywelyn in 1245.

Llywelyn ap Gruffudd's work on Dolforwyn (no. 116), four miles (6.4km) to the south-west, begun in 1273, helped to precipitate Edward I's successful 1277 campaign, after which the town walls were rebuilt in stone in

1279–80. Construction at the castle in 1283–8, after the final settlement of 1282, included a new hall, kitchen, chamber, bakehouse and granary.

Peace reduced Montgomery's strategic importance, and by 1343 parts of the castle were already in disrepair. It was refurbished by Roger Mortimer, second earl of March, after 1359, and again under Henry VIII, during the 1530s and 1540s. It last saw action under the Herberts during the Civil War, when it surrendered to the Parliamentarians in 1644; in 1649 it was demolished, along with the recently built mansion in the middle ward.

Simon's Castle during excavation, seen from the 'bailey'

119
Simon's Castle, Churchstoke

Medieval ringwork and bailey

13th century AD

OS 137 SO 286933 R4

From Montgomery, take B4385 towards Bishop's Castle. After 2.8ml (4.5km), take A489 L for Churchstoke. Continue through village for 2.5ml (4km); turn for site on R just after cutting. Parking at end of lane, access gate on R halfway along. Please ask at cottage before visiting

Simon's Castle occupies a natural rocky knoll overlooking the Camlad valley, one of the main routes from England into mid-Wales. The knoll is divided by a partly natural ditch into a main rounded summit and a triangular 'bailey' area to its north. Part of the southern end of the main summit was lost to quarrying before 1950. The approach from the gate runs to the right around the north end of the 'bailey'; access to the main summit is gained by doubling back along the central ditch.

The site was excavated by Chris Arnold and Jeremy Huggett between 1985 and 1994, concentrating initially on the 'bailey' and ditch, and subsequently on the main summit. The 'bailey' appeared to be a defended bridgehead covering the approach to the bridge crossing the ditch. Traces of platforms for timber defences were found around its north-eastern and western sides, flanking a metalled road which entered on the north and turned towards the ditch. There was also evidence of at least one building.

The main summit had been levelled and surrounded by a clay and rubble rampart, lost in the quarry area, forming a ringwork; a gap facing the ditch was probably the entrance. Immediately north-west of this, the footings of a rectangular building, perhaps a guard-chamber, were discovered adjoining the end of the rampart. The only other building revealed on the main summit was a timber structure just south of the centre, constructed without breaking the ground surface, and identified only by the excavators' meticulous recording of the distribution of nails, fragments of burnt daub and droplets of lead from the roof. Both the buildings on the main summit, together with the timber defences of the 'bailey', appear to have been deliberately burnt, although no historical date for this is known.

'Simon's Castle' is first recorded as a place-name in 1327, but the site was probably constructed as part of the same early 13th-century English activity as the new castle at Montgomery (no. 118). The 'Simon' of the name may well be Simon de Parco, who is known to have been in the King's service at the castle of 'Snead' in 1231.

120
Castell y Blaidd, Llanbadarn Fynydd

Medieval ringwork

12th century AD?

OS 136 SO 125798 U4

From Llandrindod Wells, take A483 towards Newtown. Go straight on at roundabout after 3.4ml (5.5km); 11.6ml (18.7km) further on, take first of two turnings after New Inn in Llanbadarn Fynydd, marked as dead end. Site visible to L on knoll in middle distance after 1.8ml (2.9km); park by gate on L before stream. Continue through gate across field, pass to R of trees beyond to site. Boots advisable. Access by courtesy of private owner

Castell y Blaidd (Wolf's Castle) is a strong ringwork, presumably of Norman date, although no reference to it survives. It sits unusually high on the hills near a pass leading eastwards where several tracks still meet, and has wide views apart from to the east and north-east.

The ringwork is horseshoe-shaped, with a gap on the north-west, suggesting that it was unfinished, or has been destroyed, either by enemy action or during agricultural drainage. The bank stands 3–4m high above the base of the external ditch, which has traces of a counterscarp outside it; the site is more strongly defended on the north-east than on the south-west. The very short length of bank and ditch to the north-east may also be unfinished. The interior is domed and undulating, with no obvious sign of structures.

Traces of a settlement with small enclosures are visible on the hillside below the path, looking back towards the parking place. The date of these remains is uncertain, but they are high on the mountain in an area not enclosed until relatively recently. They could be the remains of a medieval shepherding site, or might be still earlier.

Castell y blaidd (left), with settlement (right) from the air

121
Tinboeth, Llanbister

Iron Age hillfort (?)/medieval earthwork and masonry castle

Late 1st millennium BC/12th–14th century AD

OS 136 SO 090755 U4

From Llandrindod Wells, take A483 towards Newtown. Go straight on at roundabout after 3.4ml (5.5km); 8.8ml (14.2km) further on, park on L in lay-by beyond cottages. Path to site runs up steeply opposite; continue to fork, go R. Continue round to R to summit of hill; site across fence at top (0.8ml, 1.3km). Access by courtesy of private owner; please take special care near the masonry

Tinboeth occupies a very prominent steep-sided hilltop with excellent views in all directions, especially over the Ithon valley to the south-west. The easiest approach is from the east; the gatehouse, of which a fragment of standing masonry survives, was on the north-east, forcing anybody approaching against a steeper slope as they neared it. There is fallen masonry nearby and much stone in the ditch here, but surprisingly little elsewhere, despite the plan which strongly suggests that the central area was surrounded by a wall. No trace survives of buildings within this area, but a hollow may mark the position of a well.

The plan is essentially a large, very strongly defended ringwork with no apparent bailey. There is a single deep rock-cut ditch, up to 13m below the crest of the scarp, around the central part of the site, and a substantial counterscarp. The earthworks have some peculiarities suggesting that the site may originally have been an Iron Age hillfort; the wall does not coincide with the ditch on the south; there are possible, if unconvincing, traces of an Iron Age entrance on the south-east; and there is an additional bank and ditch a little way to the west on the same line as the defences. Other ditches in the area are

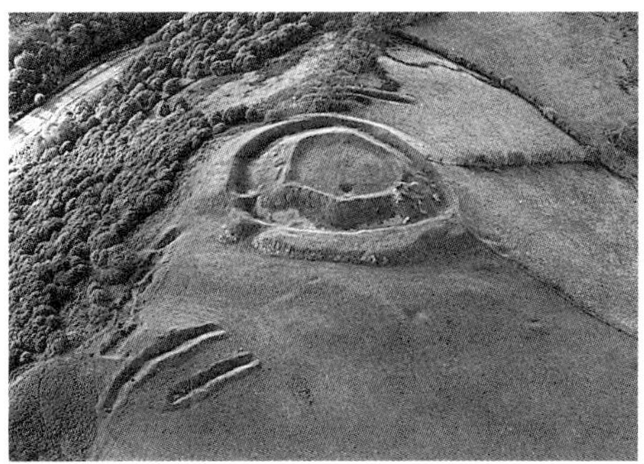

Aerial view of Tinboeth from the east

probably quarries unrelated to the site's defences, perhaps for lead mining.

The history of the site is obscure, and even its correct name is uncertain, although Dinbaud, 'Maud's castle' or Dinboeth, 'hot castle' are two of the more convincing possibilities. It was built by the English, possibly the de Braose family, at an unknown date, perhaps in the 12th century. This early castle belonged to Roger Mortimer by about 1260, when it was taken by Llywelyn ap Gruffudd during a rising of the Mortimers' tenants in the area. It seems to have been rebuilt by the Mortimers after 1282, receiving a licence to crenellate in 1316. Thereafter nothing more is heard of it until Leland mentions it as a ruin in the 16th century.

122
Rhayader Castle

Medieval earthwork castle

12th century AD

OS 147 SN 968680 U2

From clock tower in Rhayader, take A470 towards Llangurig. After c.*200m, turn R for St Harmon; car park on L here. Walk back to A470, cross and take lane opposite past church. After* c.*100m, turn R down alley by Eagles Inn to playground by river; from playground, path up slope to L leads to gateway to top of castle mound*

Rhayader Castle exploits a strong natural crag overlooking the Wye, and is defended on the north and east by rock-cut ditches, with a causeway on the north-east which still provides access today. The northern ditch is the most readily visible, from the riverside path below, while that on the east is partly followed by a footpath. The summit of the site is undulating, and may contain the remains of buildings; a slight bank on the side away from the river may be part of a rampart above the eastern ditch. Any trace of a bailey has been lost below housing.

The castle was built by Lord Rhys of Deheubarth in 1177, at the fringes of his kingdom, and 'rebuilt' by him in 1194. This later work may have been reinforcement in the face of a threat, since shortly afterwards the castle fell to Maelgwn and Hywel, sons of Cadwallon ap Madog of Maelienydd, the adjoining kingdom to the east. They almost immediately lost it to English Mortimer forces, but it was soon regained by Lord Rhys. 'The castle of Gwrtheyrnion' (the Rhayader area) was again regained by the Welsh in 1202, although it is not clear how they had lost it. The site was probably disused by the early 14th century; by the 16th Leland was unaware of any castle here.

There is another motte among the houses at Llansantffraed across the river, although the relationship between the two sites is unknown. They lay in separate administrative areas and may not have been in use at the same time.

123
The Warden, Presteigne

Medieval ringwork and bailey

12th century AD

OS 148   SO 309645   U4

In Presteigne, take B4355 towards Kington. Turn R almost immediately into Warden Road, and take first R. Parking on L opposite stone wall with gate to site

The Warden occupies the summit of an isolated hill south of the Lugg, with wide views across the valley. It was built by the Mortimers of Wigmore between 1160 and 1200, to counterbalance the existing castle across the river at Stapleton. It consists of a ringwork surrounding the highest, western, part of the summit, with an eastern bailey enclosing the remainder of the hilltop; some parts of the valley below are visible only from the bailey, and there is dead ground west of the ringwork. Both ringwork and bailey were fortified in stone at an early stage.

To reach the summit, go right from the gate, and up the diagonal path on the farther side. This enters the bailey through the probable site of the eastern gatehouse, suggested by the forward projection of the defences. The access into the ringwork is less clear, although the bank widens towards the south of the portion adjoining the bailey, again suggesting a gatehouse. There are bumps and hollows but no clear internal features in either ringwork or bailey.

The castle, like many in the Marches, had a chequered history. It fell to Llywelyn ab Iorwerth in 1213, but returned to the English in 1231, only to be recaptured and destroyed by Llywelyn ap Gruffudd in 1262. It was not apparently rebuilt, and by 1337 was hardly defensible. In the 18th century it became a pleasure garden, with promenades, flower beds and a bowling green, and was given to the town in 1805.

124
New Radnor

Medieval castle and town bank

13th century AD

OS 148   SO 212608   U4

In New Radnor, access to castle through gate up hill beyond church; path to church starts at war memorial. Best portion of town bank on SW of village; take footpath beyond last-but-one cottage on L going W below church, follow it behind buildings; bank to R

The extremely impressive earthworks at New Radnor have modified a naturally imposing hill into a strongly defended castle, with views in all directions from the top of the main mound, apart from the north-west, where the bailey lies. The site commands the valley of the Summergil Brook, where the mountains close in at the westernmost end of the Walton basin. The earthwork known as Ditch Bank (no. 98) also covers this valley, a little farther west; the two could have acted together as a defence.

The top of the mound appears now as a ringwork, measuring 50m by 30m, the bank of which may contain the remains of a stone curtain wall; robbed stone buildings lie to the south and north-west of the interior. These appear 'in negative', with trenches representing the lines of the missing walls, and heaps in the middle probably containing mortar and stone too fragmentary to be worth removing. The earthworks suggest that the building on the north-west may have been part of an entrance from the bailey.

The mound is separated from the bailey by two massive ditches, the outermost of which has two possibly original causeways across it, which may relate to the entrance to the mound. The bailey itself lies north-west of the castle, with relatively flat ground beyond it, and is less well defended. A probable later field boundary crosses it on the north, while traces of buildings are visible on the west, against the outer bank. The entrance, giving access to the town, was probably on the south, just above the church.

Aerial view of New Radnor, with town walls in foreground

The western bailey bank is continuous with the town bank, which runs on down the hill to its south; additional earthworks here may be related to a town gate: 'Newgate', judging from present place-names. There was never a stone wall; the earthwork bank and ditch were probably crowned with a palisade. The bank is very clear on the south-west of the town, where it stands to an impressive height beneath a modern boundary, but on the south-east and east it is largely obscured by modern features. The town was laid out on a grid plan, elements of which survive in the present street network, and which can be clearly seen on Speed's map of 1610. Traces of abandoned plots, visible from the air, survive on the south-west.

The town, like the castle, was probably founded in the mid 13th century. Its history is confused, since the sources do not distinguish it clearly from Old Radnor, possibly dating back to the 11th century, which it succeeded as the local administrative centre. A grant of murage (permission to build town defences) was given to Roger Mortimer in 1257, presumably for the construction of these town banks; this was probably the site captured in 1264 by Llywelyn ap Gruffudd and in 1401 during the Glyndŵr rising. The castle was last recorded as defensible in 1405, and seems to have been allowed to decay thereafter.

125
Builth Castle

Medieval earthwork castle

11th–15th century AD

OS 147 SO 044510 U4

In Builth Wells, park in car park W of bridge (round one-way system). On foot, take A470 towards Brecon from S side of bridge; almost immediately, fork right into Castle Street. Continue up lane; stile on R some way up (0.4ml, 0.6km altogether)

Spurgeon 1979

Builth is the least known of Edward I's castles in Wales, and the most unusual. His plan here kept closely to that of the earlier motte and bailey, one of the largest in Wales, possibly prompted by existing stone fortifications. The masonry has been thoroughly removed, probably for rebuilding the town after a disastrous fire in 1691, although some may already have gone to build an Elizabethan manor house nearby.

The site occupies a knoll which overlooks an important crossing of the Wye near its junction with the Irfon. An angled scarp on the east may represent the corner of a Roman fort, otherwise destroyed by the castle earthworks. The first castle was probably built by William de Braose or his son Philip before 1100. A large motte, standing 10m above the base of its ditch, had a crescent-shaped bailey to its south, itself defended by a bank (later removed) and a further ditch. The counterscarp bank of the bailey was carried down the hill on the north to embrace the base of the motte, giving it an effective ditch, even on this steep slope.

The visitor today enters from the east, along a track built to remove robbed stone. The original entrance was obscured by Edward I's work, which also included the division of the bailey into two by a deep cross-ditch; only to the west of this does the smaller original bailey ditch survive. Piles of debris in the motte ditch probably consist of mortar and rubble not worth salvaging. The motte would, like the remainder of the castle, have been originally fortified in wood, and probably carried a tower with accommodation for the lord. The access to this tower was probably on the south-east, an arrangement apparently retained in the Edwardian plan. Service buildings and further accommodation would have been housed in the bailey.

The first de Braose castle was destroyed by Rhys ap Gruffudd of Deheubarth in 1168. Restored, it served the de Braose lords until 1208, when it was seized by King John, for whom it was refortified in 1210. It was obtained by Llywelyn ab Iorwerth in 1230 in a marriage contract between Isabella de Braose

Aerial view of Builth Castle from the south-east

and Llywelyn's son Dafydd. The English recaptured Builth in 1242, after Llywelyn's death, and refortified it yet again, this time probably in stone. It was certainly a stone structure by 1260, when Llywelyn ap Gruffudd besieged it in pursuance of his family claim, gaining it by the garrison's treachery.

It is not known whether Llywelyn rebuilt the castle, but he retained the lordship of Builth under the treaty of Montgomery in 1267. Edward I's forces took the site for the Crown during his first Welsh campaign, and work started on the new castle in 1277. The structure included a great tower on the motte, with an additional wall partway down the mound, the line of which can be traced on the east, incorporating eight lesser towers, two of them flanking a gateway. The eastern bailey ditch was widened as far west as the cut through the old bailey, and a wall built around the resulting reduced area with towers at the northern end, and about halfway round, on the south-east. The stone wall across the motte ditch on the north-east was probably part of this plan. A low platform near the cross-cut may have supported a building of this phase. Unusually, a bank was provided along the inner side of the abandoned portion of the bailey. The new outer ditch was probably not wet until the cart-track obstructed its drainage.

John Giffard, constable of the castle in 1282, may have been involved in the ambush which led to Llywelyn's death near Builth late that year. The castle was besieged but held in the 1294 rising, and further construction and repairs took place early in the 14th century; even so, work was still needed by 1343, when the gatehouse remained unfinished. Repairs recorded in 1409 may have been necessitated by damage during the Glyndŵr rising. A new royal constable was appointed in 1525, but in 1534 the castle was not listed among those regarded as usable. Robbing probably began soon after this.

126
Bronllys Castle

Medieval masonry castle

11th/12th–14th century AD

OS 161   SO 149347   U4   Cadw

From Brecon bypass, take A438 towards Hereford. In Bronllys, after 8ml (12.9km), take A479 R towards Abergavenny. Site signposted on LHS after 0.5ml (0.8km); parking in lay-by opposite

Official Guidebook

Bronllys Castle occupies a commanding position above the confluence of the Dulais and Llynfi, about four miles from the junction of the latter with the Wye. Trees and later enclosure make it difficult to appreciate the full extent of the view from the site today.

The first castle was a motte up to 8m high with inner and outer northern baileys; the inner bailey is today occupied by a large private house and grounds overlooking the river. This castle had wooden defences and buildings, and was probably erected in the late 11th or very early 12th century, soon after the Norman conquest of this part of

Brecknock. It was probably built by Richard fitz Pons, whose son Walter Clifford I inherited it, together with its lordship of Cantref Selyf, in about 1138.

The early layout was retained in the later plan. There was already some work in stone by 1175, but the tower on the motte was probably built by Walter Clifford's grandson, Walter III, who died in 1263. This Walter married Llywelyn ab Iorwerth's daughter, but later transferred his allegiance to Henry III.

The stone tower on the motte is typical of this part of the Marches (cf. no. 129). It was battered at the base, and was entered by a wooden staircase at first-floor level, not unlike that provided today. The interior had a room on each floor.

The first-floor room was probably an entrance hall; steps from one of its window embrasures, perhaps originally concealed by a trapdoor, led to the basement. Wooden steps originally filled the 2.4m drop from the bottom of the stone stair to the basement floor. The basement has no fireplace and little light, and was probably a store or prison. Its ceiling was originally of wood; the corbels for these beams can be seen below the later vault. There are also traces of 'putlog' holes for scaffolding in the walls, and repairs in the masonry where later breaches have been refilled.

The second-floor room, visible from a modern wooden platform, was reached from the other first-floor window embrasure by a stair within the wall. This room had a fireplace as well as two windows and was probably the main living room in the tower as originally designed. Here too, the floor was later rebuilt at a slightly higher level, using new beam holes above the earlier corbels. The windows were replaced by more ornate 14th-century examples, and the fireplace too has clearly been rebuilt.

The stairs from this room originally led only to the roof. A further storey was added, however, probably as part of the 14th-century refurbishment which included the new floors and the improvements on the second floor. The extra storey incorporated a more

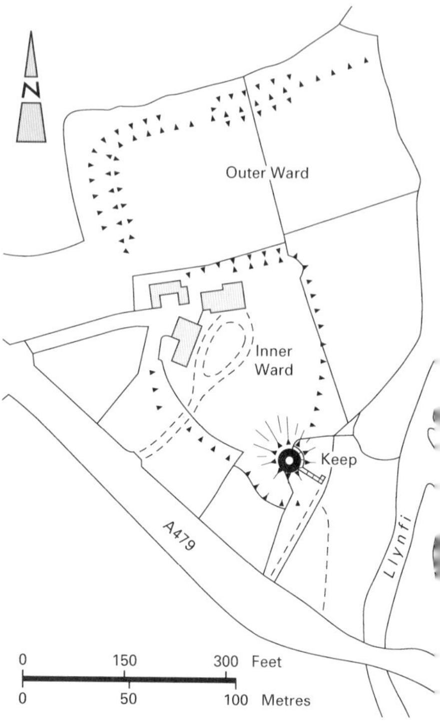

Bronllys Castle

luxurious chamber with three windows, a latrine and a fireplace, which may have superseded that below as the main accommodation.

Walter III had no male heir, and nothing is known of the castle during the later 13th-century wars against Llywelyn ap Gruffudd. By about 1311 it had passed to Rhys ap Hywel, who was succeeded by his son Philip ap Rhys; they were probably responsible for the 14th-century alterations discussed above, and may also have built the detached hall block which stood in the bailey until the 18th century.

The castle subsequently passed through a number of hands, returning to the Crown on several occasions. It was repaired in 1400 and 1409 in response to the Glyndŵr rising, for which there was considerable local support. By 1521 it was said to be beyond repair and fit only for a prison.

127
Castle Tump, Trecastle

Medieval earthwork castle

12th century AD

OS 160 SN 882291 R3

From Brecon, take A40 towards Llandovery. After 11.4ml (18.3km), site on R on E outskirts of Trecastle. Parking at far end of village. View from road only; best from well up hill

King 1961

Castle Tump at Trecastle dominates the watershed between the Usk and Gwydderig. It stands alongside the modern road from Brecon to Llandovery, from which its large oval tree-covered motte can be clearly seen as one approaches from the east. It is overlooked by hills nearby, although the 55m-long bailey to its west enjoys better natural protection.

There is a ditch between the motte and the bailey, and a counterscarp bank runs outside the main ditch around the whole site. The motte, with a ditch in places 4m deep below the crest of its counterscarp bank, is much more strongly defended than the bailey, presumably because its position made it more vulnerable. The bailey has sustained modern damage on the south and south-east.

Little is known of the site's history. It lay close to the border of the lordship of Brecon, probably helping in the early 12th century to secure communications with the short-lived English lordship in Llandovery. Even after this was lost in 1160, Trecastle appears to have continued to flourish as a commercial centre. There is no record of any hostile action at the castle, although the absence of any obvious stonework may suggest that it was abandoned relatively early, before such construction became widespread.

128
Brecon Town Walls

Medieval town walls

13th–15th century AD

OS 160 SO 044284–SO 047285 U2

In Brecon, walls lie along Captain's Walk between museum and river, S of B4601; also traces adjoining cattle market (car park) off Free Street N of B4601

The medieval town walls of Brecon enclosed an area roughly 400m by 300m, between the rivers Honddu and Usk at their confluence. The castle, a motte and bailey with later embellishments, lay to the north-west across the Honddu. This is now cut in two by the modern road, but the 13th-century great hall stands in the grounds of the Castle Hotel while the 12th-century Ely Tower surmounts the motte in the bishop's gardens opposite and is visible from the road below.

The B4601 runs roughly through the middle of the walled town and must have been the main street of medieval Brecon. The area between it and St Mary Street to the south may originally have been a triangular market place beside the church, filled in since with buildings, with Glamorgan Street and Lion Street as back lanes.

The walls ran along the river on the south-west, with a gate serving the bridge, then turned to skirt the Honddu northwards as far as Castle Street, where they turned east; the north or Struet gate lay at the east end of the street. They then followed roughly the southern boundary of the car park and cattle market (which occupy the old town ditch!) round to the B4601, where the east or Watton gate lay. The surviving stretches consist of a small portion on a rise at the south-east corner of the cattle market, running south towards the B4601, and a fine stretch south of the lost Watton gate, running back to the river, where there are the remains of a tower.

The ground is much higher inside the old town than outside along this stretch, probably in part due to repeated demolition

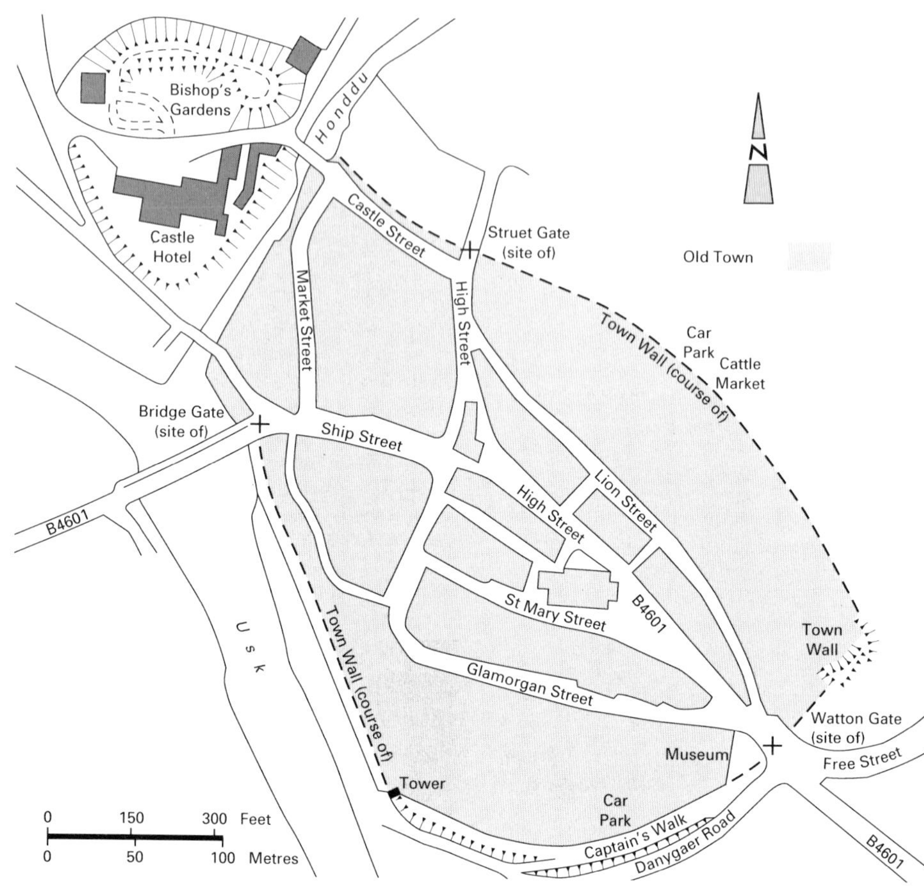

Brecon Town Walls

of timber buildings, which would have been left to rot on site. The wall itself was backed by an earthen bank, which is clearly visible in the car park of the National Park offices and from there looking south towards the grounds of the convent. There would have been a ditch at the foot of the slope, where Danygaer Road now runs. Most of the stonework now visible along this stretch has been frequently repaired, and it is difficult to be certain how much of it, apart from the tower, is original.

129
Tretower Court and Castle

Medieval masonry castle, house and barn

11th–15th, 15th–17th and 16th century AD

OS 161 SO 186212 R1 Cadw

From Crickhowell, take A40 towards Brecon. After 1.8ml (2.9km), fork R on A479. 1.2ml (1.9km) further on, take lane on L. Entrance through doorway in wall on R, beyond junction. Ample parking. Admission charge; standard hours

Cadw Guidebook

The group of medieval buildings at Tretower give, in one small area, a wonderful illustration of the development of a noble residence from an earthwork castle of the early Middle Ages right through to a later medieval house, Tretower Court, close by. The castle, first built in the 11th century, was last refortified in the opening years of the 15th century, in response to the Glyndŵr rising; work on the house may have started soon afterwards. The barn, beside the car park, is 16th century beneath the later adaptations.

The castle is strategically situated in the Rhiangoll valley, near its confluence with the Usk, commanding routes to the north, and, via Bwlch, probably also to the west. The Roman fort of Pen y gaer (appendix) lies about a mile to the north-west.

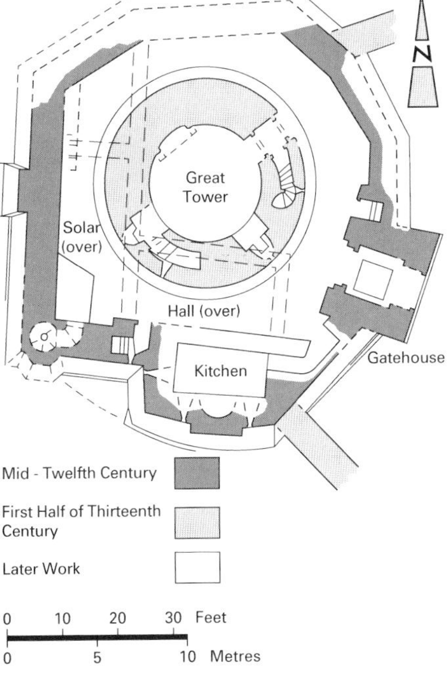

Tretower Castle

The first castle at Tretower was built by Picard, one of the Norman conquerors of the area, in the late 11th century. It was a motte and bailey, presumably mainly of timber, although the marshy ground meant that the motte was revetted in stone. Water diverted from the Rhiangoll provided a moat of sorts. The bailey is now occupied by a private farmyard; it was probably originally defended with a wooden palisade on the line of the later stone walls.

Picard's son Roger provided the motte with a shell keep, a high stone wall incorporating a gatehouse with drawbridge pit, in about 1150. Buildings, including a small hall and solar, together with a kitchen, were constructed against its inner face. Notice the high-quality ornament around the doors and windows of these buildings, a rare example of the secular architecture of the period.

In the second quarter of the 13th century, it was probably Sir Roger's great-grandson, another Sir Roger, who built the stone wall of the bailey, with rounded corner towers, and made radical alterations on the motte. The internal buildings were demolished, and their exterior windows blocked, while the outer wall was raised to provide a stronger curtain with a new wall-walk. A large and very solid round tower similar to that at Bronllys (no. 126) was erected in the centre, in accordance with the latest military thinking. It had three floors and a basement, with one room on each of the levels, although the basement, containing a well, was probably used only for storage. The entrance was on the first floor, and the upper floors provided reasonably comfortable accommodation, although the topmost had no fireplace. Access to the tower today is via a breach just below the original doorway; none of the wooden floors survives.

Residence in the castle, by then considered old-fashioned and cramped, probably ceased during the 14th century, although Sir James Berkeley refortified it for the Crown in 1403, during the emergency caused by the Glyndŵr rising. A four-storey wooden building

Tretower Court

constructed on the north-west between the tower and the curtain may belong to this episode. The castle was still apparently complete at the beginning of the 16th century, although little more is heard of it.

Much of the structure of the court visible today reflects work carried out in the third quarter of the 15th century under the colourful and wealthy Sir Roger Vaughan, who developed it into a fine residence reflecting the aspirations of his day. He was the elder half-brother of the powerful Sir William Herbert, later earl of Pembroke, who gave Tretower Court to Sir Roger but retained the lordship and manor for himself.

Sir Roger may have refurbished an existing north range (on the right as the visitor enters), although the evidence for this is inconclusive. The half-timbered upper wall with its shuttered mullioned windows and balcony, as well as much of the internal flooring, is his work; he also built the west range, at right angles to it, in which some of his pointed windows with high-quality mouldings survive. The west range contained a central hall with a kitchen to its south, both occupying the full height of the building. The northern end of the range had two storeys, and would have contained a private apartment upstairs; the north range likewise would have had apartments for family and visitors (the positions of the partitions have left traces on the timbers) on its upper floor. On the ground floor, another kitchen occupied the corner between the two ranges, and a number of the rooms around it were probably used for storage or servants' accommodation; the apparent duplication of facilities may have been intended to provide Sir William with fitting accommodation should he visit. At the east end of the north range, a direct entrance from the street led into a room adjoined by a small lobby with its own latrine, possibly for the steward.

Sir Roger's staunch Yorkist sympathies led to his execution by Jasper Tewdwr in 1471, and it was probably his son Sir Thomas who built the wall-walk, which was originally open throughout, and the three-storey gatehouse, in about 1480, as the Wars of the Roses continued. 'Murder holes' were provided above the gates, probably in imitation of earlier castle architecture; the presence of the postern immediately beside the main gate suggests, however, that there was no very serious threat. Fragments from a fine oriel window, probably also Sir Thomas's work, formed the basis of the reconstruction near the north-west corner attempted in 1962.

Almost the only 16th-century work is a cellar, probably for cider-making, beneath the west end of the north range. The larger windows on the west range were added in about 1630, during further work, probably by Charles Vaughan. Private upstairs apartments were constructed over the kitchen at the south end of the west range, and covered access to them was provided along the wall-walk on the south and south-east, where matching windows were intended to look like a further range. Two new rooms, possibly a small dining room and an office, were made downstairs from earlier service rooms next to the kitchen. The north range may by this time have been an outbuilding or servants' quarters.

Tretower Court: the west wing from the gatehouse

Beyond the southern wall-walk, traces can be seen of various ancillary buildings, long since demolished. 'Sir Roger Vaughan's garden', a reconstruction based on sound 15th-century evidence (though not from Tretower), now occupies much of this area.

The court was abandoned in the 18th century, when the family moved to another property at Scethrog a few miles to the west. The southern part of the west range became a farmhouse, and the remainder outhouses; the latter were taken into State care in 1929, with the farmhouse following in 1935.

130
Crickhowell Castle

Medieval earthwork and masonry castle

12th–15th century AD

OS 161   SO 218182   U2

In Crickhowell, footpath signposted from A40 opposite car park turn, at SE of town; on-street parking

Crickhowell Castle, also known as Alisby's castle, is a conspicuous feature of the small market town and occupies a vantage point with commanding views along the Usk valley. It began life as a motte and bailey with timber buildings, probably built by the Turberville family in the 12th century. In 1272 (perhaps in response to the growing power of Llywelyn ap Gruffudd) it was rebuilt in stone, still to the same basic plan, by Sir Grimbald Pauncefote, who had married Sybil, a Turberville heiress. The name 'Alisby's castle' comes from a warder of the Tower of London who was custodian of the castle at about this time.

A stone shell keep was provided around the

Reconstruction drawing of Crickhowell Castle

top of the motte, slight traces of which are still visible. The base of the motte and the bailey were also walled and provided with towers and gateways; only two substantial masonry fragments survive. One, to the south-east of the motte, is not a 'keep' as described in some sources, but a strong double tower provided at the eastern corner of the bailey where it adjoined the motte. One side of this survives to a considerable height. More ruinous is the gatehouse, to the south-west of the motte. This originally consisted of a pair of drum-towers, one of which remains to an apparently rather precarious height, while the other is reduced virtually to ground level; its position was recovered by excavation and the remains consolidated. The bailey appears to have occupied roughly the area of the present playing field; the remains of a stone tower were discovered in a service trench at its western corner.

During the 14th century, the castle was in Mortimer hands, but in 1402 it was restored to Sir John Pauncefote, great-grandson of Sir Grimbald, who refortified it by royal command; he was nonetheless unable to resist Owain Glyndŵr's forces, who left it 'in ruins'. Later in the century it was granted to Sir William Herbert, who became earl of Pembroke. It seems unlikely that any further work was done; the keep was uninhabitable by the mid-16th century.

It is uncertain whether there was a walled town associated with the castle. No plausible plan has been suggested, and the evidence for walls consists of one rather dubious tower in Tower Street. To see this, leave the castle by the far gate and follow the lane round to the right; Tower Street is a right turn further on. The tower, which may be a folly built from architectural fragments, is obvious.

131
Llys Euryn, Colwyn Bay

Medieval house

14th–16th century AD

OS 116 SH 832802 U4

Follow directions for Bryn Euryn (no. 44) to parking. Site down path on R near turn from road, not far after short climb

Although the existing remains of Llys Euryn are mainly 15th- or 16th-century, earlier occupation on the site is well-attested. Tradition connects it with Maelgwn of Gwynedd, singled out for censure by Gildas in his 6th-century history, who fortified Deganwy (near Conwy), and supposedly died at Eglwys Rhos in AD 565 or 566; the 'Llys' element in the name suggests an early noble residence. A 13th-century house here belonging to Ednyfed Fychan (Vaughan), steward to Llywelyn ab Iorwerth, was destroyed in 1409 during the Glyndŵr rising, and rebuilt during the 15th century by Robin ap Gruffudd Coch of Graianllyn; poets likened this building, at least part of which probably survives, to a castle.

The remains visible today show further alterations of the Tudor period, when the house was occupied by the Conway family, anglicised descendants of Robin's heir Huw Conwy, who fought for Henry VII at Bosworth in 1485 and was duly rewarded. Edward Conway was High Sheriff in 1565, but by 1592 the family had lost favour, probably due to their Catholic sympathies; the last of them, Rheinallt, went bankrupt early in the 17th century. Some family members remained as tenants until 1654; the house may have been occupied into the 18th century.

The ruins are romantically overgrown, and partially excavated; a shed on the south-east is recent. The plan is difficult to follow on the ground, since the house underwent a number of alterations, probably including division into two separate units. It was basically square around a central courtyard, with its main frontage facing south; the much-restored chimney and fireplace probably belonged to a hall on the west. Remains can be seen of the outer walls to north and south, and of the internal wall on the south; both these ranges must have held apartments. Parts of the walls stand nearly 4m high; on the north, there is a pointed doorway and three long narrow windows, while on the south, four windows were provided. A flight of stone stairs in this overgrown area leads to an upper chamber or latrine. Traces of another range on the east are now completely flattened.

Llys Euryn: the chimney in the west range

132
Hen Ddinbych, Brenig

Medieval enclosed farmstead

14th–15th century AD

OS 116   SH 990563   U4

From Denbigh, follow directions for Brenig Archaeological Trail (no. 14) to car park. Take track S to Hafoty Sion Llwyd (0.6ml, 1km), through farmyard, then SE over shoulder of hill; site in hollow beyond (0.3ml, 0.5km). Can be included in trail. Boots advisable

Allen 1979

Hen Ddinbych is a sub-rectangular farmstead, which nestles in a sheltered hollow near a stream, and is defended by an earthen bank some 6–7m wide and an external ditch. The original entrance was probably at the south-eastern corner, the direction the farm faces, for maximum shelter. A small stream runs down to the north-west corner, and follows the ditch round the north of the site and partway down the east side; it may originally have been channelled along the west side too.

Within the enclosure, towards the south, are the ruined stone footings of a longhouse 34m long and 7m wide, running along the slope. This is best appreciated from the information board overlooking the site. A substantial artificial bank lies to its south. A possible dividing wall, separating domestic accommodation from livestock, has been identified about 10m from the west end, but there is little trace of the doorway, which was presumably on the north. A track from this building leads to the entrance in the south-eastern corner.

Level platforms, which probably supported further buildings, are clearly visible in the north-west corner of the 70m-square enclosure, against both the northern and western banks. The northern platform is small, but has traces of stone towards its east end, and of a possible cross-wall 10m further west. Traces of another possible building platform may lie between these two.

A line of stones running north-south, slightly west of centre, may be the remains of a dividing wall, curving slightly eastwards at its northern end towards an area in which there is a faint suggestion of other structures. Its southern end crosses a levelled area with two parallel shallow indentations running into the centre of the site from just south of the western building platform. This may be a track, though it is not obviously metalled nor apparently associated with any entrance.

There are signs of a larger enclosure adjoining the main one on the south, but this may be part of a relatively recent field pattern and is probably not related to the site. Hen Ddinbych was probably a permanent farm,

Aerial view of Hen Ddinbych from the north-west, with the platform cairn (see no. 14) in the foreground

Llangollen Bridge

rather than a summer pasture outfarm, and would have housed an extended family and a few extra hands. The longhouse would have provided living accommodation for the family and room for cattle, while the other buildings might have contained hay, straw and stored grain; some may also have been pigsties or additional accommodation.

The date of the site, which has few obvious parallels, is not clear, although it is plainly different from the *hafotai* nearby (see no. 14). It was probably a largely self-sufficient mixed farm, perhaps dating to the period of improved climate in the 13th or early 14th century.

133
Llangollen Bridge

Medieval bridge

15th century AD

OS 117 SJ 215422 U1

In centre of Llangollen, linking A5 with A542/539

Jervoise 1936

A bridge spanned the Dee at Llangollen in 1282, although the present structure was attributed by the 18th-century traveller Pennant to Bishop Trevor of St Asaph (1395–1412). It may even be a reconstruction of about 1500, although Leland, writing in the 16th century, does not suggest that it was recent; Lhuyd records its refurbishment in 1656. The upstream side was widened in 1873, when a fourth span was added on the north to accommodate the railway. The arches are pointed, and rather irregular, with the southernmost larger than the two to its north; the parapet has refuges above each of the pointed cutwaters.

134
Croesfoel Farm Moated Site, Rhostyllen

Medieval moated site

14th–15th century AD

OS 117 SJ 304482 U4

From Wrexham, take A5152 towards Rhosllanerchrugog (also accessible from

Croesfoel flyover on Wrexham bypass). Turn R immediately W of bypass, and L at T-junction by bypass bridge after 0.3ml (0.5km). 0.3ml (0.5km) further on, turn L; footpath to site from stile by gate on L after 150m. Keep R of pond, cross second stile, then take stile on R; site in trees beyond. Limited parking in gateway; please check not in use

Croesfoel, also known as Llyntro, is a well preserved moated site lying in a relatively flat area, with a slight rise to the south and south-west. It measures 28m by 24m, and would have contained the medieval farmhouse and probably also ancillary buildings; these were surrounded and defended by a moat, originally water-filled, 3–5m wide and 1.5m deep. The entrance was apparently on the north.

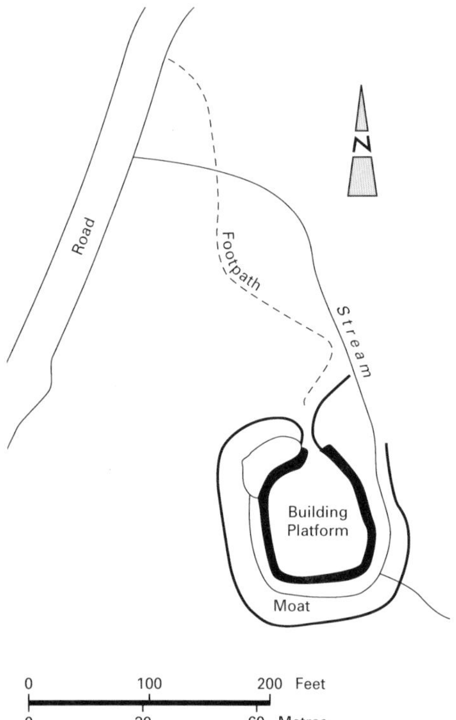

Croesfoel Farm moated site

Timbers said to come from the original buildings survived in later structures on the site as recently as 1914. These have since disappeared, and scrub has taken hold. Parts of the moat remain wet, especially in winter.

135
Holt-Farndon Bridge

Medieval bridge

14th/15th century AD

OS 117 SJ 412545 U3

From Wrexham, take A534 towards Nantwich. After 4.5ml (7.2km), turn L for Holt. Continue through village on B5130 for Farndon. Bridge at bottom of hill after 0.9ml (1.4km). Parking on R at far end (N). Field on SW reached over stile by gate

Jervoise 1936

Holt Bridge today consists of eight spans, two of them dry on the Welsh side and one on the English. The remaining five cross the river Dee, confined to a slight gorge here by the sandstone used to build both the bridge and the nearby castle (no. 106). There is an information panel about the geology on the English side.

The relatively soft sandstone is prone to weathering and erosion by the river, necessitating numerous repairs to the bridge over the years, most recently in 1990. The original construction date is uncertain; a stone bridge at Holt is attested by 15th- and 16th-century writers, and may have been built before the end of the 14th century.

The third span from the Welsh side (the first in the water) has two arches, one above the other. The higher arch is much older than the lower, and originally supported a defensive tower, straddling a drawbridge. Peace on the border under the early 16th-century Tudor settlement would have made this unnecessary, suggesting strongly that what we see today is still basically the medieval bridge. It was recorded in 1778 as having ten

Holt–Farndon Bridge

spans, with the remains of a guard-house in the middle; further spans on the Welsh side may have since silted up.

136 Bangor-is-y-coed Bridge

Medieval bridge

15th/16th century AD

OS 117 SJ 388454 U3

From Wrexham, take A525 towards Whitchurch. After 4.5ml (7.2km), turn L for Bangor-is-y-coed (Bangor on Dee). Best vantage point (limited parking) on R just before bridge; more parking in village beyond. Alternatively, take B5426 from Wrexham bypass; turn R at junction with A525 (4.7ml, 7.6km); take next L (0.4ml, 0.6km); turn L at T-junction in village and continue to church

Jervoise 1936

The charming five-span bridge across the Dee at Bangor is of very distinctive design. The parapet is built of huge sandstone slabs, set on edge, many of which have become very worn, while the cutwaters are squared-off rather than pointed in the more usual manner; this shape is reflected in the refuges to either side of the narrow road above each pier. The abutments, extensively patched and repaired in the past, especially on the west, were refurbished in a sympathetic style as part of an extensive programme of repair in 1993.

A date stone, now illegible, was reported by earlier authors to record repair work in 1636,

Bangor-is-y-coed Bridge

although the bridge itself is probably of 15th- or 16th-century date. In 1876, piles, presumably from a still earlier bridge, were reported in the bed of the channel; these were rediscovered during the 1993 work.

137
Llangynidr Village Earthworks

Medieval village earthworks

13th–14th century AD

OS 161 SO 154192 R3

From Crickhowell, take A40 towards Brecon. After 5.1ml (8.2km), turn L for Llangynidr (7ft/ 2.1m width restriction). At T-junction 1ml (1.6km) further on, take B4558 L; after 0.3ml (0.5km), take Dyffryn Road R into village. Site lies 0.2ml (0.3km) further on, over wall on L beyond church; also visible from Maerdy Lane on SE. Parking opposite churchyard or at junction beyond site. View from road and lane only

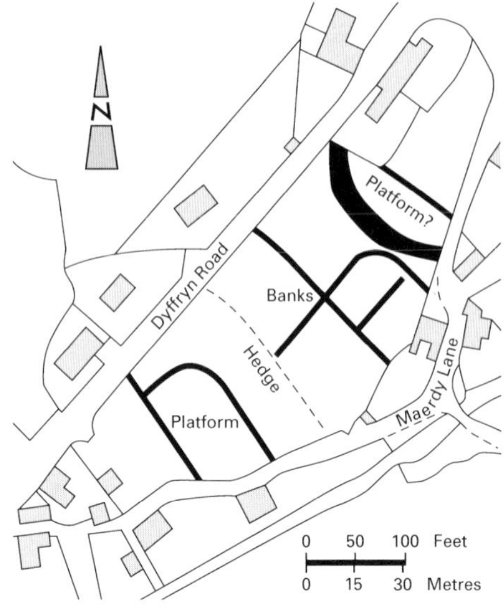

Llangynidr village earthworks

These earthworks represent the remains of a now abandoned part of the medieval village. The pasture field containing them is divided by an old hedge bank, probably part of the pattern of land holdings fossilised in the earthworks. To the south-west of the hedge bank are traces of a level platform where a house once stood, while to the north-east (between the two platform areas marked on the plan) are remains of three adjoining rectangular enclosures, one to the north and two to the south, with a more irregular curved knoll at the northern end of the field. These remains can be interpreted as those of at least two more house platforms and their associated gardens. The next garden to the north is surrounded by a similar bank, quite probably part of the same plan. Pottery from the 13th or early 14th century has been found nearby.

8
The Medieval Church

The Norman conquest brought great changes to the church in Wales. While the native church had been loosely organised, with bishoprics consisting of related foundations, rather than specific territories, the Normans had by 1150 divided the country into the four regional bishoprics of St Davids, Llandaff, Bangor and St Asaph. These powerful posts, in both ecclesiastical and secular terms, were filled almost exclusively by Norman appointees, who were subordinate to the archbishop of Canterbury and owed their fealty directly to the king of England as tenants-in-chief. Beneath the bishops, the dioceses were gradually organised into the pattern still familiar today; cathedral chapters, archdeacons and rural deans provided an administrative hierarchy above the priests in the developing parishes. As well as the cathedrals, many new stone churches were built, perhaps reflecting a greater emphasis on indoor services rather than outdoor preaching, a strong element in the native tradition. Some of these churches probably enjoyed the patronage of the wealthy, but it is likely that many were erected by the enterprise of the local community, reflecting the depth of devotion. Churches also became meeting places at which oaths could be sworn and trade take place.

Many practices of the native ecclesiastical communities, reflecting the wider social order, such as the marriage of clergy and the granting of equal rights to illegitimate offspring, were anathema to the orthodox Normans, who either reorganised the communities as collegiate or family churches or disbanded them and reallocated their lands to the new monastic orders or to the bishoprics. Quite a number of the recipients were based in England or even abroad. The tithes of parish churches could be similarly allocated, and from the late 12th century, measures were needed to ensure that sufficient was left for the vicar to live on; half the English minimum stipend was considered adequate!

The senior churchmen of the 12th and 13th centuries were highly educated, and had often spent much of their lives studying at different centres, both in Britain and abroad, as part of a Europe-wide community of learning. Attempts were made throughout the period to improve the education of the parish clergy; as time went on, the new monasteries, and later the friaries, played an important part in the copying and distribution of suitable textbooks.

Early in the Norman period, the dominant monastic order was that of the Benedictines, and a priory, now the cathedral, was established at Brecon in about

1110 as a cell of Battle Abbey; the order never, however, obtained a strong foothold in Welsh Wales. The Augustinian canons were more successful, but the Cistercians, who first reached Britain in 1128, were the most readily accepted. Their system of rule through related foundations and their ideal of an isolated and self-sufficient community seem to have appealed to a Welsh consciousness already familiar with similar ideas. The need for lay brethren to do many of their more menial tasks was perhaps the decisive factor in the order's successful recruitment; there may originally have been as many as three lay brethren to each choir monk. This option enabled people of limited education who preferred a more active life to offer themselves to God nonetheless. Patronage for the new abbeys was usually forthcoming; indeed, they were a very suitable target for the visible largesse which brought prestige to the nobility, who probably saw such beneficence as a way to save their souls. Monasteries could develop close links with a patron's interests, as did Strata Florida in Dyfed (see *Dyfed*, no. 150) with the royal house of Deheubarth, many of whose princes were buried there.

There were four major Cistercian houses in Clwyd and Powys. Abbey Cwmhir (no. 149) and Strata Marcella, near Welshpool, of which nothing survives above ground, were 'daughter' houses of the great abbey of Whitland in Dyfed, while Basingwerk (no. 139) was originally a Savigniac house, and became Cistercian when the orders merged in 1147; it was allocated to a 'mother' house in England. Valle Crucis (no. 146) was established in the early 13th century, some time after the others, as a 'daughter' of Strata Marcella. The three houses with surviving remains all conform more or less to the standard Cistercian plan, although Abbey Cwmhir was never fully completed.

The most important building in the abbey was naturally the church, where the eight principal services of the monastic day took place. The church was normally in the shape of a cross, with chancel, transepts and an elongated nave. The choir monks, who had their stalls under the crossing, were screened from the lay brethren, who worshipped in the nave, while the eastern side of each transept would be divided into small chapels where the choir monks could say mass in private at other times.

To the south of the nave lay the cloister, a courtyard with a covered walkway around all four sides, and buildings ranged beyond. On its east, continuing the line of the south transept, was the sacristy, where vestments and vessels were kept for services. Next to this was the chapter house, where daily meetings of the choir monks were held, when business was discussed and a chapter from the rule of the order read, and beyond this a parlour, the only room where conversation was allowed. To the south of this again might be accommodation for novices. The choir monks' dormitory would occupy the upper floor of the east range, connected to the church by a night stair, for use during the hours of darkness. The monastic timetable varied with the seasons, but would always start with Matins in the small

Reconstruction drawing of a Cistercian abbey church (Valle Crucis, no. 146)

hours. The monks were, however, free to retire by mid-evening and had other opportunities to rest during the day. Choir monks would be more highly educated than lay brethren, and might spend their spare hours in copying, illustrating, or just studying books.

The infirmary, for sick and elderly monks, was normally isolated from the main buildings. At the east end of the south range lay a warming room, the only room, apart from the kitchen and the infirmary, with a fire. (Note that one might not talk and keep warm at the same time!) Next to this was the refectory; that at Basingwerk has a good example of the pulpit from which a suitable text would have been read to the silent diners. The kitchen, beyond this or constructed separately, was shared with the lay brethren, who had their own dining hall at the south end of the west range. The ground floor of this range would have contained the cellar and the cellarer's office, and other rooms devoted to the lay brethren. The cellarer was responsible for the organisation of the lay brethren, and as their numbers declined, he effectively became a steward, taking responsibility for the management of the abbey's estates and the provision of supplies. The upper floor of the west range normally served as the lay brethren's dormitory, and access to the church was usually provided for them at the south-west corner of the nave.

Competition from the newer orders of friars, from the later 13th century, together with the economic crises and the Black Death of the 14th century, hit recruitment seriously, particularly of lay brethren, and many of the monasteries ceased to work their own lands directly as a result. The monastic ideal was suffering in other ways, and descriptions of the hospitality offered at Valle Crucis in the 15th century hardly suggest an ascetic life. In this case, the accommodation released by the lack of lay brethren was very probably used for the choir monks' dormitory, allowing the old dormitory to be converted into luxurious suites for the abbot and his guests. It was such abuses, as well as the concentration of land and wealth in the hands of the monastic orders, which led ultimately to Henry VIII's dissolution of the monasteries between 1536 and 1540. The monastic assets were sold off to secular entrepreneurs, who often converted the buildings to suit their own needs, or stripped them of anything of saleable value. The whole exercise was, of course, very profitable to Henry's exchequer.

The friars in the later 13th century brought a new ideal of preaching in the vernacular with them, while instead of withdrawal from the world, they advocated engagement with it; friaries tend to be close to towns where they could carry out their mission. Dominican houses were established at Rhuddlan (no. 99) and Brecon, and a Carmelite house at Denbigh (no. 100). Preaching was a practice deeply entrenched in Welsh religious tradition, and the friars attracted many followers; they also played an active part in the drive to educate the parish clergy. Elaborately carved preaching crosses were built or rebuilt in many churchyards in the 14th and 15th centuries (e.g. nos 138, 142, 143, 147 and 150). Most of these crosses belong to a group in the Vale of Clwyd, of which that at Derwen (no. 143) is the best surviving example, although similar examples are known from further south, such as at Llanfihangel Cwmdu (no. 84) and Partrishow (no. 150).

It is easy in this more secular age to underestimate the influence of religious beliefs in medieval life. The twin vagaries of lord and weather must have left many with little feeling of control over their lives. The religion of the age tended to be rather dark in tone, with an emphasis on judgement, and belief in saints and relics was widespread. The Welsh were indeed noted as especially devout. All Cistercian abbeys were dedicated to the Virgin, as was one of Clwyd's two major holy wells (Ffynnon Fair, no. 141); the other, St Winifred's (no. 140) is also dedicated to a woman noted for her purity. Pagan elements also lingered within medieval Christianity; at St Elian's cursing well, south of Colwyn Bay (SH 861768), only recently disused, written curses were thrown into the water in a practice well-attested from Roman times.

138
Trelawnyd Churchyard Cross

Medieval churchyard cross

Later 14th century AD

OS 116 SJ 089796 U2

From Rhuddlan, take A5151 through Dyserth to Trelawnyd. After 4.6ml (7.4km), church visible down lane to R towards W end of village. Limited parking beside gate. Cross beyond church in cemetery

This cross, 3.4m high overall, is a typical example of the Vale of Clwyd group of preaching crosses (see also nos 142, 143 and 147). An octagonal socketed base holds a tapering chamfered shaft carved from a different stone, and decorated with foliage rising from the base of its corner faces. Above this, an octagonal capital supports a rectangular head with tracery surrounding each of its four faces. The narrow sides, to north and south, contain small niches, while the larger eastern panel shows a crucifixion; one mourner, probably the Virgin, survives at the bottom left of the scene, but the figure at the bottom right, usually St John on similar crosses, is damaged, while the western face appears to show a crucifixion without mourners. The head is a poor fit on the column, with flat unworked stone showing at the base of the capital.

Trelawnyd churchyard cross

139
Basingwerk Abbey, Holywell

Medieval abbey

12th–16th century AD

OS 116 SJ 196774 U2 Cadw

From Holywell, take B5121 towards Greenfield. At T-junction after 1.3ml (2.1km), take A548 R; Heritage Park car park not far on R. Path leads up slope past abbey; entrance on far side

Official Guidebook

Basingwerk Abbey was probably founded in 1131 by Ranulf, earl of Chester, as a 'daughter' of Savigny Abbey in western Normandy. In 1147, however, the Savigniac order merged with the Cistercians, and in 1157 Basingwerk was affiliated to Buildwas in Shropshire, also a former Savigniac house. Much of the plan at Basingwerk follows the standard Cistercian layout, similar to that at Valle Crucis (no. 146). The monastery was probably on this site by 1157, but may originally have been founded three miles south along the coast, at a place then known as Basingwerk, and, as often happened, brought its name with it to the present site.

During the 13th-century Welsh wars,

Aerial view of Basingwerk Abbey from the south-east

Basingwerk's sympathies lay with the English; the abbey provided a chaplain for Flint Castle. It apparently suffered little, and by the later 15th century had become quite prosperous, owning extensive estates and entertaining numerous visitors in some style. It was dissolved in 1536, and the remains passed to the Mostyns of Talacre.

Only a little 12th-century walling apparently survives, around the cloister and in the east range. Much of the fabric visible today, including the church, dates from the early 13th century, when the buildings generally were refurbished and extended. The church had seven bays in the nave and two side chapels in each transept. To its south, in the adjoining east range, lay the sacristy, and beyond this the chapter house, which was provided with a vaulted eastward extension which still survives; beside this again lay the parlour. To its south, the novices' lodging or monks' day room was upgraded, and a warming house, extended again in the 15th century, added to the end of the range. The entire upper floor would have contained the monks' dormitory, with direct access to the choir of the church via a night stair.

On the south side of the cloister, the impressive *frater* or dining-hall dates from a little later in the 13th century. It was provided with handsome lancet windows at its south end, a pulpit, from which readings were given during meals, and a serving hatch, connecting it to the kitchens next door.

West of the cloister, little survives of the accommodation for the lay brethren and the cellarer. This range was probably adapted for other uses as lay brethren became harder to recruit. A detached range of buildings south-east of the main complex has been considerably altered by recent use as a farmhouse, but may occupy the site of an original monastic infirmary.

140
St Winifred's Chapel and Well, Holywell

Medieval chapel and well-chamber

15th century AD

OS 116 SJ 185763 R2 Cadw

In Holywell, take B5121 towards Greenfield. Chapel on R beside church. Parking further down, near entrance to well (small charge) through Catholic repository; key to chapel (deposit) also from here: 10am–5pm daily

Guidebooks; Hubbard 1986

The holy spring of St Winifred, an important centre of medieval pilgrimage still venerated today, is said to have risen where St Beuno restored his niece St Winifred to life after her head had been severed by Caradoc, a rejected suitor. While St Beuno is a well-attested 7th-century figure, responsible for bringing Celtic monasticism to much of north Wales, the story of a woman beheaded and restored to life in connection with a holy spring may contain elements of an older pagan Celtic tradition.

The shrine was first mentioned as a place of pilgrimage in 1115, and from 1240 to the dissolution it was part of the possessions of Basingwerk Abbey (no. 139). Henry V made

St Winifred's Well

the pilgrimage in 1416 before his victory at Agincourt, as did Edward IV before Towton Moor in 1461. The future Henry VII, too, is thought to have made a secret visit before winning his crown at Bosworth in 1485.

The present remarkable and architecturally unique building, set into the hillside, dates from the late 15th century. It was probably built for Margaret Beaufort, Henry VII's mother, to replace an earlier structure, and is richly ornamented on the exterior with a frieze of animals, and the badges of Henry VII and Thomas Stanley (Margaret Beaufort's third husband); the quality of the workmanship suggests that royal masons may have been employed.

The building consists of two floors. The well-chamber (managed by the Roman Catholic church) is open on the downhill (northern) side, while there is level access from the south into the chapel above. A copious spring of clear water rises in a central basin in the shape of a truncated eight-pointed star, with steps at the front for access by the sick. The water flows away beneath the surrounding walkway into a more recent swimming pool. The basin is enclosed by a low wall from which columns rise to form part of an elaborately ornamented vault of unusually complex design, matching the form of the pool below. Graffiti attest numerous visitors, including James II and Mary of Modena (on the left of the inner wall of the well basin, just behind the front portion), who came in 1686 to pray for a son; James (the Old Pretender) was born in 1688.

The chapel has a north aisle and an apsidal chancel. The three bays of the aisle mirror the three arcades of the vault in the well-chamber below, although stairs linking the two floors are now blocked.

141
Ffynnon Fair, Trefnant

Medieval holy well and chapel

13th?–15th century AD

OS 116 SJ 029710 R2

From Denbigh, take A525 towards St Asaph. 0.8ml (1.3km) after Trefnant, fork L on B5381. After 0.7ml (1.1km), turn L, and after 0.3ml (0.5km), L again on lane. Parking by building 0.5ml (0.8km) down lane, through gate. Site to R here; gate on far side. Muddy in wet weather
NB *Please apply to Jones Peckover (Agents for Wigfair Estate), 47 Vale Street, Denbigh LL16 3AR or tel. 01745 812127, for permission before visit*

The holy well and chapel at Ffynnon Fair (Mary's Spring) are in many ways similar to those at St Winifred's (no. 140), although more ruined and perhaps never quite as splendid. What the ruins lack in completeness, however, they make up in the charm of their rural setting, to the north of the Elwy, just above the valley bottom, sheltered beneath a wooded slope.

The well would have been suppressed in the 16th century, and religious services in the chapel ceased officially in the 17th century. The site was fenced in the 1840s and laid out as a 'romantic' garden, with rockeries, and thickets of bamboo which still survive. Some repairs and alterations were made to the ruins at this time.

The visible remains consist of a 15th-century well basin, now almost level with the ground, in the form of a truncated eight-pointed star similar to that at St Winifred's, with a small bath to its south-west and an adjoining chapel to its south-east. The chapel is now ruined, although enough remains to gain a good impression; it is unusually of T-shaped plan, resulting from the addition of a 15th-century chancel, forming the stem of the 'T', to an earlier building. The original building faced north-east, with a raised internal platform and external bellcote at the chancel end, while the extension faces south-east.

The spring, and the stream flowing from it, clearly played a crucial part in the design of both the earlier building and the 15th-century version. The stream was channelled across the south-west end of the earlier chapel, just inside the gable wall, from the north-west; anyone entering would have had to cross it, although it is not clear how. The date of this original chapel is obscure, since its windows were altered in the 15th century; traces below the two at the south-west end suggest that the openings were originally taller and narrower. The doorways, not easily dated, may both belong to the original building; that in the chancel probably came from one of the stretches of wall demolished in the 15th-century alterations.

The original treatment of the spring itself is unknown, but the construction of the 15th-century well basin clearly involved the demolition of the earlier north-west wall; the line seen today is probably a 19th-century reconstruction from fragments, one of which, just north-east of the basin, may be the sill from the original window over the outlet of the stream. A clay bank along this wall may also be Victorian. The original water level was probably lower than at present. Investigations in 1963 revealed a lower opening through the front wall of the basin, which would have left about 0.3m of water in it. This opening had been blocked, with a consequent rise in water level, during the Victorian alterations, when the bath was probably added. We cannot be sure of the 15th-century arrangement in this area, but the well basin was almost certainly covered, possibly by a vault.

142
St Meugan's Churchyard Cross, Llanrhydd

Medieval churchyard cross

14th–15th century AD

OS 116 SJ 140577 U2

From Ruthin, take A494 towards Mold. After 1.3ml (2.1km), take B5429 R. After 0.8ml (1.3km), turn R. Church on L after 0.1ml (0.2km). Limited parking by gates. Cross behind church

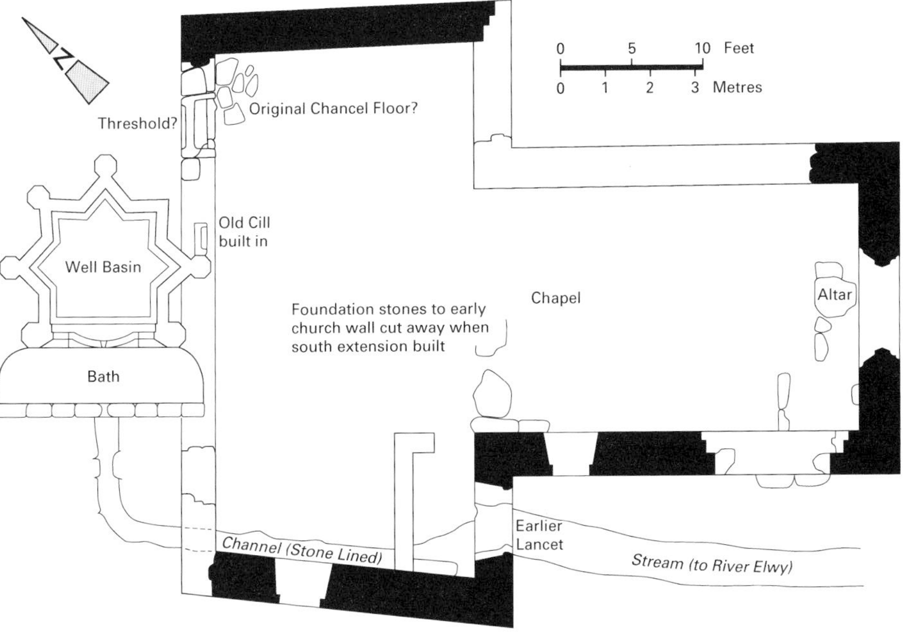

Ffynnon Fair

Only the shaft, chamfered to an octagonal section, and a very worn and cracked octagonal base, survive of this cross, which must have been similar to others of the Vale of Clwyd group (see nos 138, 143 and 147). The shaft has small bosses ornamented with leaves at the bottom of each chamfered surface, and about two-thirds to three-quarters of the way up each one is a mask, possibly a death's head, with a rosette beneath. There are some fairly ancient graffiti. The tenon for attaching the head is clearly visible.

143
Derwen Churchyard Cross

Medieval churchyard cross

15th century AD

OS 116 SJ 070507 U2 Cadw

From Ruthin, take A494 towards Bala. After 7.3ml (11.7km), turn R opposite garage at Bryn Saith Marchog, and R again round LH bend in village. Follow lane 1ml (1.6km) to Derwen. Limited parking immediately below churchyard gate

Derwen churchyard cross

This preaching cross, 2m high (4.3m with its pedestal), is the best preserved of the Vale of Clwyd group (see also nos 138, 142 and 147). The square shaft is chamfered to give eight unequal faces; at intervals, the chamfered areas contain carved bosses, consisting either of foliage or of little faces. The shaft is surmounted by a capital decorated with similar bosses. In the chamfered areas immediately below this capital, longer tongues of stylised foliage point downwards.

The head of the cross is box-shaped, with wider faces to east and west. The faces are outlined, and the top of the block ornamented, with tracery including miniature pinnacles; the very top is missing. The lower part of the head narrows sharply to meet the capital surmounting the shaft, and is ornamented with rosettes. The head portrays a crucifixion on the west, including the Virgin and St John; a Virgin and Child on the east; another possible Virgin and Child on the north; and a figure with scales and a sword, possibly St Michael, on the south.

The plinth consists of a large cube with its top corners broached and chamfered to match the shaft. Below this are two modern steps of rough mortared stone. The church retains its late 15th- or early 16th-century rood screen and loft, and is worth a visit.

144
Corwen Churchyard Cross

Medieval churchyard cross

12th century AD

OS 125 SJ 079433 U2

In Corwen, park in town centre or in car park (toilets) on R just down turning to N. Entrance to churchyard on S of marketplace, between Owain Glyndŵr Hotel and Waterloo House. Cross at SW corner of church

Nash-Williams 1950, no. 276

The Corwen cross is earlier than and rather different from most others in the area. Only its tapering shaft survives, with a socket at the top and rounded corners; deep vertical grooves towards the edges of the faces give the impression of small columns. At its top is a 'capital', reminiscent of Eliseg's pillar (no. 77), made up of four swags or inverted curves containing fields of interlace design.

About two-thirds of the way up the east face is a small Latin cross in relief; a similar cross is cut into the corner moulding to its right, a little lower down. The bottom 0.7m of the north side has faint lines cut into it, which may be the remains of an interlace design, but have also been claimed as a runic inscription. The cross is set in a large round stone, 1.7m across and 0.3m high, with seven or eight possible cup-marks on its upper surface.

The lintel of the south chancel door is a reused 7th–9th-century pillar-stone with a large, coarsely cut linear Latin cross (Nash-Williams no. 273). It is now protected by a 19th-century porch.

Corwen churchyard cross

145
Llangar Church, Corwen

Medieval church

13th?–18th century AD

OS 125 SJ 063424 R3 Cadw

From Llangollen, take A5 to Corwen. Beyond village (11.3ml, 18.2km from Llangollen), take B4401 L towards Cynwyd. Church on R after 0.7ml (1.1km). Park on verge or in lay-by on L beyond, footpath across field through stile and gate. View into church through E window
For interior visit and guidebook, enquire at Rug Chapel, on L 0.2ml (0.3km) up A494 from junction N off A5, 0.5ml (0.8km) W of Corwen. Admission charge; standard hours

Cadw Guidebook; Shoesmith 1980

Llangar Church, which occupies a delightful secluded hillside overlooking the river Dee, is of particular interest for its 18th-century interior and its fine 14th- to 18th-century wall-paintings. This building was superseded by a new church at Cynwyd in the mid 19th century, and has not been used for regular worship since. It passed into Welsh Office guardianship in 1967, and during the subsequent repairs, the church fabric and the graveyard were closely studied and part of the interior excavated.

A parish church is first attested in 1291, but none of the present building is demonstrably this old. The earliest visible work consists of a featureless wall, now heavily buttressed on the north, which clearly predates the 14th- and 15th-century paintings in the nave; the 15th-century paintings lap on to the timber wall-plate, suggesting that the four easternmost trusses of the roof are also medieval. The little window at the east end of the south wall may occupy one of the original medieval lights, while the cupboard opposite it may fill another.

Work dated to about 1615–20 included the insertion of the large east and south windows and the provision of the porch, while the western end, unstable on made-up ground, was substantially rebuilt in or after 1656 and again, though less extensively, in the early 18th century, when the gallery (for singers and musicians) was probably added. The north window of the nave was enlarged at about this time, the west window in the south wall inserted, and the porch reroofed. Further work was carried out in or shortly after 1730–2, including the construction of the fine triple-decker pulpit, partly from existing components, in its present position. Later work, since removed, included the insertion of a plaster ceiling and of wooden partitions in and under the gallery.

Internally, the easternmost roof bay is panelled to form a canopy of honour, a fairly common local feature. Apart from the 14th-century bishop, towards the east of the north wall, much of the wall painting in the nave is 15th-century, consisting of scenes outlined by a grid of red 'timberwork'. These paintings acted as a reminder of the Church's teachings for those unable to read, and their subjects could include Biblical scenes and moral warnings; those on the south wall feature the Seven Deadly Sins, mounted on appropriate animals. After the Reformation, pictures fell into disfavour, but the Ten Commandments and other suitable texts, together with the Royal Arms, were displayed. At Llangar, there seem to be two phases of text paintings from before 1600, two from the 17th century, and two or three from the 18th, including the Royal Arms (now moved to the reception area at Rug) and the figure of Death. The texts were all in Welsh, the language of worship here until at least 1775.

Llangar Church: looking east from the gallery

The internal arrangement focuses on the fine triple-decker pulpit beneath the main south window. Opposite it, along the north wall, lie enclosed pews, belonging to each of the wealthier local houses; several are dated, the earliest to 1711. A similar pew for the Rector's family lies just south of the altar. Elsewhere, benches accommodated the less privileged. The layout demonstrates the emphasis placed upon preaching at this period, rather than Holy Communion, which was only celebrated once a month.

The burials excavated from the nave included quite a few children and teenagers, while many of the adults had clearly suffered serious childhood illnesses, and very few had apparently lived to old age. Outside, the churchyard had clearly expanded from an early focus immediately south of the church; the earliest stones were in English, but the proportion in Welsh gradually increased. South of the church, where a preaching cross might once have stood, is a sundial base.

146
Valle Crucis Abbey, Llangollen

Medieval abbey

13th–15th century AD

OS 117 SJ 205442 R1 Cadw

From Llangollen, take A542 towards Ruthin. After 1.9ml (3km), turn R for Abbey Caravan Park. Parking on LHS at end just before Abbey gate. Admission charge; standard hours

Cadw Guidebook; Price 1952

Valle Crucis (Valley of the Cross) takes its name from Eliseg's Pillar (no. 77) nearby, which would already have stood for nearly four centuries when the abbey was established in 1201. The new foundation was a Cistercian house, a 'daughter' of Strata Marcella, near Welshpool; its patron was Madog ap Gruffudd Maelor, ruler of northern Powys. So that the abbey could enjoy the solitude required by the order, the existing settlement of Llangwestl was removed to Stansty, north-west of Wrexham.

The layout of the abbey largely followed the standard Cistercian plan (note the similarities with Basingwerk, no. 139). The abbey church accommodated both the choir monks, who spent their time in prayer and contemplation, and the lay brethren who undertook more mundane duties, such as agricultural work, enabling the community, at least in its early years, to remain largely self-sufficient. The monks observed their daily offices in the choir, beneath the crossing of the church, separated by a screen from the lay brethren, who worshipped in the nave. The choir monks would also say mass individually in the transept chapels at other times.

The 40 or so lay brethren would have been accommodated in the range to the west of the cloister. This has undergone later alterations (the number of lay brethren declined sharply in the 14th century, partly due to the Black Death in 1349), but would originally have contained a cellar at the north end, a central day room and a refectory on the south, now lost. Upstairs would have been a dormitory similar to the choir monks' in the eastern range opposite. The refectory, which would have shared the adjoining kitchen with the choir monks' refectory beyond it in the south range, was later replaced by an office for the cellarer.

The choir monks' accommodation, built for about 20, lay on the east and south of the cloister. Access from the church would have been by a day stair, later removed, and a night stair, leading directly to the first-floor dormitory. Below this, next to the church, lay the sacristy, housing vestments and plate for the services; alongside this was the chapter house, with a book-cupboard in the thickness of the wall. Daily meetings of the choir monks took place here; a chapter from the rule of the order would be read and business discussed. The normal Cistercian plan would have continued with a parlour, and possibly accommodation for novices, but at Valle Crucis a passage ran south of the chapter house, perhaps to a separate infirmary; beyond it the range finishes with the lower level of the latrine block serving the dormitory above. Traces of a longer range beneath the present later 14th- or early 15th-century plan, however, may suggest that the missing rooms were relocated in the now under-used accommodation on the west.

The abbey suffered a serious fire soon after its founder's death in 1236; traces of burning are visible on the lower stonework of the church and the south range. Substantial rebuilding (distinguished by putlog holes for the ends of the wooden scaffolding) had already taken place when the abbey found itself on the losing side during Edward I's Welsh campaigns in 1276–7 and 1282–3, although subsequent compensation enabled it to flourish for much of the following century. Repairs to the church, notably the reconstruction of the magnificent western gable end, commemorated by the inscription above the rose window, were carried out under Abbot Adam in the early to mid 14th century. Whether this was restoration of

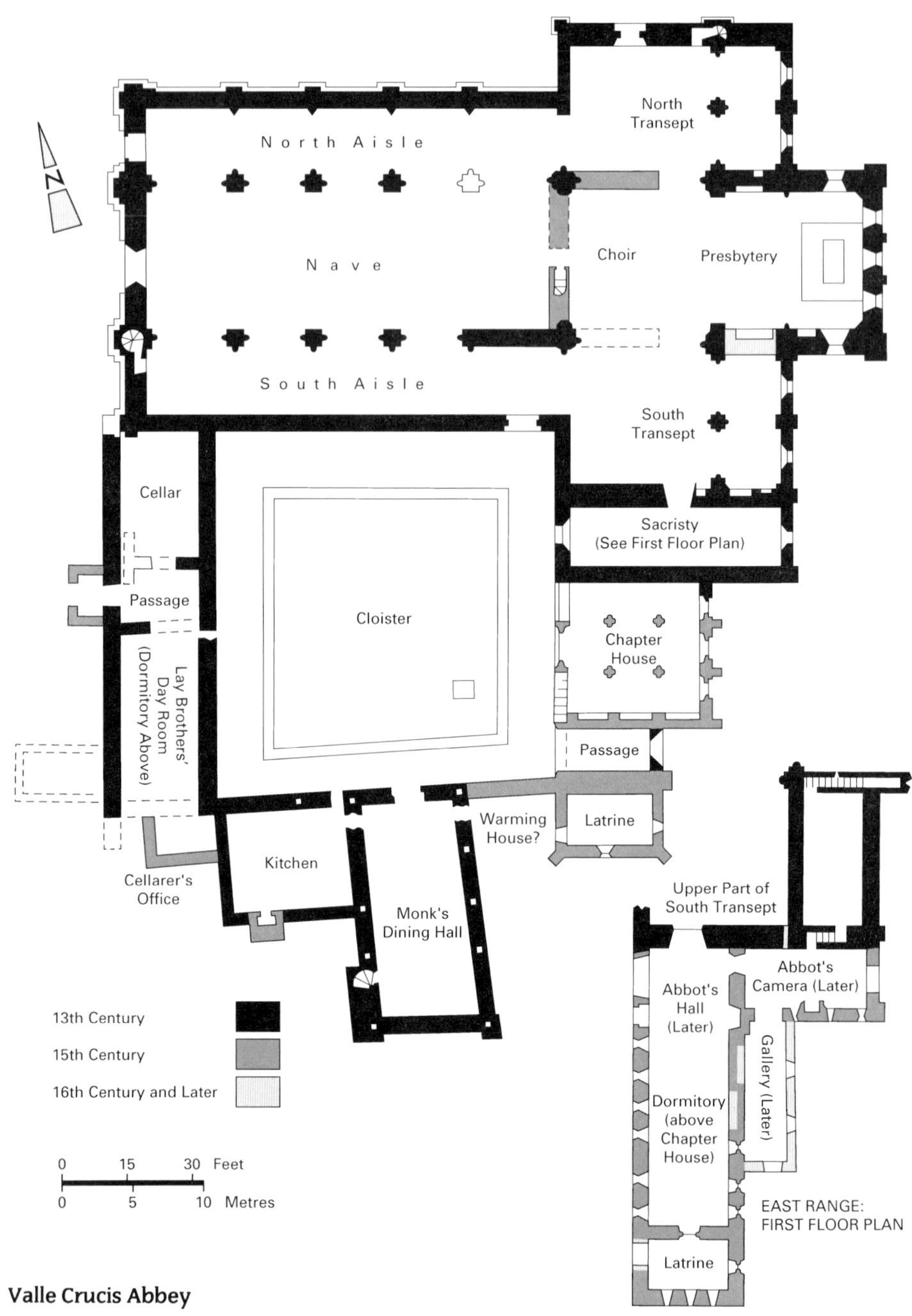

Valle Crucis Abbey

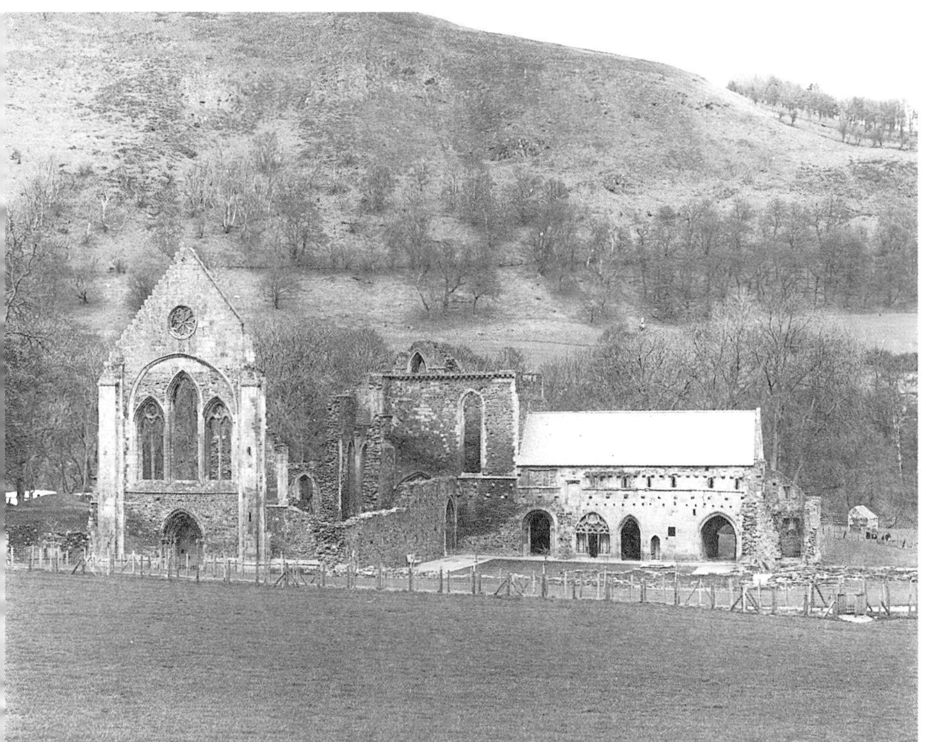

Valle Crucis from the west

damage in the Welsh campaigns or in some later episode is not clear. After the Black Death, numbers declined, not only of lay brethren but probably also of choir monks; late in the century the screen behind the choir stalls was moved eastwards from its original position one bay into the nave to the crossing arch where it can be seen today.

It was perhaps after the alleged damage during the early 15th-century Glyndŵr rising that the east range rebuilding was completed. The superb vaulted chapter house is an especially well preserved feature and dates from this time. The wealth of the abbey certainly increased, and by the end of the century poets praised the hospitality of its abbots. At about this time, part of the first-floor east range dormitory, together with an adjoining room, was made into a comfortable suite for the abbot, while the rest was converted into lodgings for the abbot's guests. The few remaining monks may now have slept in the west range, in accommodation no longer required for lay brethren.

This prosperity was limited by comparison with many English abbeys, however, and Valle Crucis was dissolved in 1537 as one of the lesser houses. After the dissolution, the buildings rapidly fell into disrepair; in the late 16th century the eastern range was converted into a house with a new roof-line, although this roof had gone by the early 18th century. Many of the ruins were again roofed later in that century and used as a farm. Excavations and clearance of the ruins were carried out in the mid to late 19th century.

147
Hanmer Churchyard Cross

Medieval churchyard cross

15th century AD

OS 126 SJ 455397 U2

From Wrexham, take A525 towards Whitchurch. At Marchwiel (2ml, 3.2km), take A528 R; after 3ml (4.8km), join A539 for Whitchurch (also accessible from Wrexham bypass). After 7ml (11.2km), turn R into Hanmer. Church on L 0.2ml (0.3km) further on; parking in front. Cross near church R of path

Hanmer churchyard cross

This cross is an outlying example of the Vale of Clwyd group of preaching crosses (see also nos 138, 142 and 143). The three octagonal steps around the base appear relatively modern; the shaft, broached and chamfered at the base, but otherwise an undecorated octagon, rises directly from the uppermost step, without the solid base block of the classic examples. The head is considerably damaged, but has the usual square form. There are four patterned fields acting as supporters, one beneath each main face, including foliage and stylised faces; some of the tracery on the top of the head also survives. The main faces to east and west are larger than those to north and south; the west face appears to show a crucifixion with the Virgin and St John; the south face contains a figure apparently dressed as a bishop, with mitre and crozier; the eastern face shows either a Virgin and Child or another crucifixion with figures. On the north are two figures, but the right-hand part of the field is damaged; this may originally have been a portrayal of the Holy Family.

148
St Mary's Church, Newtown

Medieval church tower and ruins

13th century AD

OS 136 SO 109918 U2

In Newtown, take footpath R from Broad St just before bridge, through Elephant and Castle car park and alongside river above wall. After c.100m, site on R in small park

Haslam 1979

The remains of St Mary's Church, abandoned because of flooding in the 1840s, are ruinous apart from the tower, but the plan can be clearly seen. It consists of a nave and south aisle of virtually equal size, originally divided by a timber arcade. Each would have had a gabled roof, leaving a valley between. Churches of this plan are relatively common in

:t Mary's Church, Newtown, from the east

he northern Marches, but unusual this far outh. The tower, adjoining the west end of he nave, survives best. It is built of stone lmost to roof level, and was perhaps begun n the 13th century, although the windows re 15th-century; the uppermost portion is of imber, with louvred openings for bells.

The church's south wall stands to roof level, nd the east wall, with the bases of two large vindows, survives to about half its original eight. This work appears to be 14th-century. modern wall and flower border supporting he additional 0.5m of churchyard created by he build-up of burials over time, marks the osition of the original north wall. The isused church is now landscaped as part of a emetery, and gravestones have been ranged round its sides; a mausoleum, for the Price amily of Newtown Hall, lies towards the outh-east corner of the ruin.

149
Abbey Cwmhir

Medieval abbey

12th–16th century AD

OS 147 SO 055711 U4

From Llandrindod Wells, take A483 towards Newtown. Go straight on at roundabout after 3.4ml (5.5km); 1.4ml (2.3km) further on, turn L. Park by iron gates on R after 4.4ml (7.1km). Site down hill through gate on L c.50m further on. Access by courtesy of private owner

Williams 1895; Hermitage Day 1911; Radford 1982

The ruins of Abbey Cwmhir lie in the secluded valley of the Clywedog brook, in a remote and delightfully scenic location typical of those chosen by the Cistercian order. The abbey's early history is somewhat obscure; an apparently unsuccessful attempt to found a 'daughter' house of Whitland was made in 1143, possibly on a site at Ty faenor, about a mile to the east. The permanent foundation, however, dates to 1176, probably under the patronage of Cadwallon ap Madog of Maelienydd, as this area of Powys was then called. The abbey's benefactors inevitably changed in its early years as Welsh and English fortunes in this border area fluctuated, although a period of stability under Llywelyn ab Iorwerth, together with his political ambitions in the area, may have provided the impetus for an ambitious 13th-century building programme which was evidently left incomplete. Cwmhir eventually passed to the powerful Mortimers, who neglected it in favour of Wigmore Abbey; it never fully recovered from damage inflicted in 1402 during the Glyndŵr rising.

The ruined walls of the church, all that now remains visible of the abbey, are tucked into the base of the slope below the road. The church, and other parts of the site, were extensively excavated at intervals during the 19th century, confirming Leland's 16th-century assertion that 'the third part of the

Abbey Cwmhir

work was never finished'. Though the remains are slight, what immediately strikes the eye is the exceptional length of the 14-bay nave, designed, again according to Leland, for 60 monks. The abbey was probably well below this ambitious quota for most of its life, and by the dissolution in 1536, only three monks remained. The nave and side aisles, part of the 13th-century scheme begun, perhaps, under Llywelyn ab Iorwerth, superseded an earlier church which probably occupied only the eastern part of the south aisle, with transepts a little to the west of the later line. The eastern end of the new church was never completed beyond the western wall of the crossing and transepts, the central arch of which was blocked; the high altar, choir and space for lay brethren were all fitted into the nave. After the 1402 attack, it is probable that only the easternmost five bays, containing the choir and high altar, were regularly used. Tradition has it that the fine arcade of five arches in the church at Llanidloes came from the north aisle of the abbey church; there is little reason to doubt the truth of this and it gives a good impression of how the nave might have looked. The architectural standard of the work is very high, and the details indicate clearly that the aisles were vaulted but that the nave probably had a wooden roof.

Doorways towards the east and west ends of the nave were intended for access to the cloister, although that on the west is well outside the extent of the monastic buildings revealed during the 19th-century excavations but now grassed over. These were apparently on a more modest scale, although an enlargement commensurate with the new church was presumably envisaged. The plan can be predicted from other Cistercian sites such as Basingwerk (no. 139) and Valle Crucis (no. 146). The south side of the cloister was traced during the excavations, about halfway across the level area between the church and the fishpond on the south of the valley. A strong bank and ditch, enclosing the whole 4ha monastic complex, was also found.

Even after the dissolution, the site enjoyed a chequered history. In 1565 it passed to the Fowler family, and in 1644, during the Civil War, the occupied monastic buildings were besieged and captured by Parliamentarian forces under Sir Thomas Myddelton. After this they were apparently dismantled or abandoned; the Fowlers moved to Ty faenor. The mound south-west of the church may be a spoil heap from the excavations adapted as a landscape feature.

There is a longstanding tradition, based on the evidence of one chronicle, that the body of Llywelyn ap Gruffudd was buried at the abbey after his death near Builth in 1282; a modern slab has been placed at the east end to commemorate this. The only surviving memorial from the site is a tombstone or coffin lid, now in the churchyard, inscribed HIC IACET MABLI C(*UIUS*) A(*N*)I(*MA*)E P(*ROP*)ICIET(*UR*) DE(*US*), or: *Here lies Mabli to whose soul may God be merciful.*

150 Partrishow

Medieval church, churchyard cross and holy well

6th–7th century AD (?)/14th–15th century AD

OS 161 SO 279224 U2

In Crickhowell, turn N off A40 opposite castle (no. 130). Take Standard Street R at T-junction; go straight on at next junction. Follow main road towards Forest for 3.6ml (5.8km), past several junctions; take L fork signposted Partrishow. Fork L again for church after 0.7ml (1.1km). Continue on main track for 1.2ml (1.9km); park in bottom of dingle by holy well. Church c.*150m further on up steep slope; very limited parking at top for disabled*

Church Guidebook

The charming holy well at Partrishow lies down rough steps inside the sharp bend at the valley bottom. A spring is walled on three sides and roughly roofed, producing a cell about 1m in height. There are two niches in the rear wall, one about halfway up, the other close to water level (although the well can be dry at times). Legend has it that St Issui, an early Christian hermit and preacher, had his cell here and was murdered by a passing traveller, giving the place its original name Merthyr Issui (the Martyr Issui), of which Partrishow is a corruption. The sanctity of the spot may actually date to pre-Christian times. In the verge near the top of the steps is a pilgrim stone, probably not in its original position, engraved with two small crosses datable to the 7th–11th centuries AD.

Further up the hill lies the church, a very interesting building with work from several periods. Although a church is attested here by the late 11th century AD when the font was apparently made, most of the present work is 13th–15th-century. The building stands on made-up ground, and the south wall, which required extensive underpinning in 1908, appears to have had problems during the medieval period too, probably necessitating several episodes of rebuilding. At the west end, perhaps the site of the earliest church, is a separate chapel, while the eastern building contains the font, remains of wall-paintings and a magnificent late 15th-century rood screen and loft, which happily escaped the 17th-century Puritan reformers. The separate small structure west of the main building provided a drying room and stable for the priest and his horse.

Partishow Church

Partrishow was visited in 1188 by Archbishop Baldwin and Giraldus Cambrensis, recruiting for the crusades. They are said to have preached from the churchyard cross, although that visible today is of a later medieval type. Only the base, with three steps, and the chamfered octagonal shaft is original; the head is a modern replacement, showing St Issui (facing west), with (working clockwise) Our Lady, Archbishop Baldwin and the crucifixion. It stands in the classic position for such crosses, south of the east end of the church, although the shelf for seating along the church wall is unusual.

Appendix: Sites of Further Interest

This is a list of fine sites, most of which lie on private land. Permission should be sought before visiting sites marked R. It is often difficult to trace the owners of sites, and it is usually best to seek help and information from the owners of the nearest house to the site in question.

Neolithic Period

Tan y Coed (Rhydyglafes) Burial Chamber, Llandrillo

OS 125 SJ 047396 R2

Damaged round or elongated cairn on local crest, with remains of single chamber with capstone exposed near centre.

Pipton Long Cairn, Three Cocks

OS 161 SO 160373 R4

One of the Black Mountains group, with many similarities to Gwernvale (no. 8). Excavated. False portal, chamber entered by dog-leg passage from north-west side. Another chamber, apparently without passage, further to south, with disarticulated bones; some traces of curved revetment walls within mound. Decommissioned by dumping against outer revetment.

Ffostyll Long Cairns, Talgarth

OS 161 SO 179349 R2

Two long cairns of the Black Mountains group; southern better preserved with single gallery chamber with two displaced capstones at north-east; northern has traces of two or possibly three chambers but is more damaged.

Ty Isaf Chambered Tomb

OS 161 SO 182290 R3

Long cairn of Black Mountains group, with false entrance; chambers reached from each side behind it. Unusual oval element in tail, integral to design, contains further, transepted, chamber. Decommissioned like others in group.

Bronze Age

Capel Hiraethog Earthen Circles

OS 116 SJ 037547 U2

Only one damaged example survives, south of road, of two circles originally visible here. It is surrounded by a bank and ditch about 20m across and contains sockets for about 20 standing stones, very few of which survive; slight rise in centre.

Kerry Hill Stone Circle

OS 136 SO 158860 R4

Circle 24–25m in diameter with nine widely spaced stones of variable cross-section, 0.3–0.5m high, two of them forming a pair; one fallen. Central stone 1.4m long, now prostrate. Higher level of interior probably due to cultivation outside.

Rhos y gelynen Stone Row, Rhayader

OS 147 SN 902629 R4

Row of five stones, running east–west, 9.1m in total length. Third and fifth stones from west fallen. Smallest stone at west 0.47m high, largest at east 2.89m, but fallen; probably stood about 2.3m high; other three graduated between these.

Battle Mound and Standing Stone, Brecon
OS 160 SO 006306 R4
Small stony cairn supporting standing stone 3.7m high. Bernard of Neufmarché defeated Welsh forces and killed Rhys ap Tewdwr of Deheubarth a short way to north, AD 1093.

Iron Age

Pen y corddyn Mawr, Abergele
OS 116 SH 915764 R4
Hillfort, with rubble defences, consisting of main stronghold of 10ha and probable sloping annexe to north-west of 5.3ha. Three elaborate entrances, two to north and one to south, 'sally port' on east; annexe has simple entrance on north-west. Early and late Roman material recovered in excavations.

Castell Cawr, Abergele
OS 116 SH 935767 U4 WT
Hillfort consisting of single large bank on west and south, against natural cliff on east. Simple entrance on west. South-east corner and entrance most readily seen among scrub and woods (paths provided).

Bedd y Cawr, Bontnewydd
OS 116 SJ 013720 R4
Bank and ditch cutting off promontory, later occupied by smallholding. Path crosses original bank at possible entrance; defences best seen on south-west, where bank stands about 3m above base of ditch.

Moel Hiraddug, Dyserth
OS 116 SJ 063785 R4
Hilltop hillfort, 800m long and 80–160m wide. Up to four lines of defence, inner of rubble and outer of soil, concentrated on weaker east and south sides; slight above precipice along west. Main, complex, entrance from south-east, finally entering on east; others on south and north-west. Several hut positions visible in interior; 19th-century find of part of La Tène ceremonial shield of 2nd century BC. Parts of site now lost to quarrying.

Caer Caradog, Cerrigydrudion
OS 116 SH 968479 R4
Univallate hilltop hillfort with rock-cut ditch on west and additional outer bank in places. Some trace on north-west of slighter bank in interior.

Dinas Melin y Wig
OS 116 SJ 049491 R3
Hillfort of 5.3ha, on natural spur jutting into valley from south-east. Defences formed by scarping into hill; very slight above natural precipice on south. Mutilated inturned entrance on north-east. Traces in interior of later farmstead, but no obviously Iron Age hut positions. Visible from road, but trees obscure detail.

Craig Rhiwarth, Llangynog
OS 125 SJ 057270 R4
Hilltop hillfort with stone defence on north and intermittently on south; precipitous natural crags on south and east. Entrances centrally on north and at west end of rampart. Very numerous hut positions, many of stone, in interior and to west, some showing alterations suggesting long occupation; rectangular structures are probably late medieval *hafotai* or sheep folds.

Pen y gaer, Llanidloes
OS 136 SN 908869 U4
Hilltop enclosure with wide views, to west of Clywedog dam. Single tumbled stone bank without ditch encloses 0.3ha, with entrance on south.

Pen y clun, Llanidloes
OS 136 SN 926875 R4
Oval hilltop enclosure of 0.8ha, defended by bank and ditch, possibly with stone revetment, largest towards inturned entrance on west; additional length of bank and ditch a short distance away on this side with central inturn. Damaged on south-east by more recent lead prospecting.

Llanddewi Ystradenni Hillforts

OS 148 SO 114698, SO 121699 R4

Two hilltop hillforts. Western, enclosing 2ha, is multivallate, with widely spaced ramparts; traces of entrance face annexe on north-east. Eastern fort of 4ha has single stone defence with pronounced inturned entrance on north-west.

Y Gaer, Defynnog

OS 160 SN 923263 R4

Univallate ridge-top enclosure of 0.7ha with scarped defence; bank and ditch only on north, entrance probably at south-east. Some later quarrying in interior. Subrectangular annexe of 0.35ha on south, approached by embanked hollow way from south-east, apparently predating old ridgeway running past site.

Twyn y Gaer, Garthbrengy

OS 160 SO 054353 R3

Oval hilltop enclosure of 0.38ha, defended by bank surviving as scarp up to 1.8m above base of ditch, which is reduced on north to shelf. One internal platform to south-east, for hut or later sheepfold. Straight bank with ditches either side (only surviving on south), possibly a later pillow mound, runs north-east from entrance on this side for about 50m. Traces to north-east of ridge and furrow or lazy-bed cultivation.

Roman Period

Pen y gaer, Bwlch

OS 161 SO 168219 R3

Small fort 128m by 90m, 1.15ha. Lane roughly follows *via principalis*, with main buildings to its west. Defences survive best on east; three phases, two with stone revetment walls, identified in excavation, spanning period AD 70 to AD 130–40. Traces of internal buildings visible on air photographs.

Roman Road NE of Coelbren

OS 160 SN 865109–SN 925165 U4

Sarn Helen, Roman road linking forts at Neath and Brecon Gaer (no. 73), followed by track for much of 6.3 miles (10km) north-east of fort at Coelbren (West Glamorgan); some original paving survives towards south-west end. Doubtful in bottom of Neath valley. A temporary camp lies at north end of stretch, just beyond Maen Madoc (no. 82).

Early Medieval Period

Llanrhaeadr ym Mochnant Cross

OS 125 SJ 123260 R2

9th–10th-century cross-slab, inside church on south wall of south chancel aisle. Plait to left and fretwork to right of wheel-cross shaft, spirals above head. Inscription on crossbar, +XR[*I*] CO(?)N FILIUS L(?)/TO(?)N , or: *The Cross of Christ. Co(?)n son of L(?)to(?)n, (? set it up).*

Llanerfyl Inscribed Stone

OS 125 SJ 034097 R2

Late 5th–6th-century inscribed memorial stone, inside church against west wall of nave. Reads, HIC[*IN*]/TUM[*V*]LO IA/CIT R[*O*]STE/ECE FILIA PA/TERNINI /AN(*N*)I(*S*) XIII IN/PA(*CE*), or: *Here in the tomb lies Rosteece, daughter of Paterninus, (aged) 13 years. In peace.* Shows Roman Christian, possibly Gaulish, influence; mention of age unusual.

Meifod Cross

OS 125 SJ 155132 R2

9th- or 10th-century cross-slab, inside church, with ring-cross showing figure of Christ above Latin cross; numerous small areas of various designs. Possibly based on an 8th-century Merovingian type from France; also shows Irish and Viking influences.

Trallong Inscribed Stone

OS 160 SN 966296 R2

5th–6th-century memorial stone, with added 7th–9th-century ring-cross, on nave wall near door, inscribed in both Latin and Ogam. Latin reads: CVNOCENNI FILIV[S]/CVNOGENI HIC IACIT, or: *(The stone) of Cunocennius, son of Cunogenus. He lies here.* Ogam reads: CVNACENNIVI ILVVETO, or: *(The stone) of Cunacennivus Ilvveto(s).*

Llangorse Crannog

OS 161 SO 128268 R3

NB *Landing not permitted*

Only crannog in Wales: settlement built on artificial platform of timbers, brushwood and stones. Buildings probably lay towards lake, while rubbish dumped towards shore. Traces of posts beneath water may have supported access causeway to main entrance at north and 4m-wide artificial beach on south-east. Timbers dated to very late 9th or early 10th century AD using tree rings. Site probably royal centre of Brycheiniog dynasty, who originated in Ireland where such sites fairly common. Attacked in AD 916 by Aethelflaed Lady of the Mercians, who captured king's wife and 33 others. Logboats found nearby may be same date or much earlier.

Medieval Period

Hawarden Castle

OS 117 SJ 319654 R2

Open summer Sundays only; admission charge

Motte and bailey with fine earthworks. Motte (originally about 12m high); stone tower, curtain around bailey and remains of buildings all probably added 1297–1329; elaborate gatehouse and barbican later. First mentioned 1205 when retained by Crown. Chequered history during reign of Llywelyn ap Gruffudd; taken 1282 by Dafydd ap Gruffudd, precipitating Edward I's second Welsh campaign. Fell again briefly in 1294 rising. Rebuilt in masonry soon after. Also saw action in 1640s during Civil War. Restored in 19th century and laid out as pleasure garden.

Ruthin Castle

OS 116 SJ 123580 R2

Modern hotel (1853) occupies south-west end of single-phase castle with pentagonal main ward on ridge and small outer ward at lower level on north-west. Original curtain lost beneath hotel, but survives, with semicircular towers, around remainder of circuit in grounds, with double-towered gatehouse on east. Begun by Edward I in 1277; granted to Dafydd ap Gruffudd, and later to Reginald de Grey. Taken in Welsh rising 1294, also in 1646 during Civil War.

Coed Henblas Moated Site, Llanfair Dyffryn Clwyd

OS 116 SJ 147552 U2

Reached over stone stile in wall, site 50m to right of footpath through wood. Roughly square platform surrounded by wet ditch draining to west, cut in shallow 'U' shape, 8–10m wide at top, about 4m at base.

Sycharth, Llansilin

OS 126 SJ 204258 R2

Impressive motte, based on glacial mound, with large partly wet ditch, and bailey to south-west with slighter ditch. Overlooked by crags to east. Probably first built in 11th or 12th century, but noted as residence of Owain Glyndŵr, described in poem of Iolo Goch *c.*1390. Used at this time like moated site, with complex of buildings on summit; excavation of north-east quarter revealed traces of hall and of possible latrine block, on very edge of mound. Destroyed 1403 during Glyndŵr's rising. Fishponds at foot of hill may be related.

Mathrafal, Meifod

OS 125 SJ 132107 R3

Enclosure about 100m square, on spur above confluence of Banwy and Vyrnwy. Bank and ditch on three sides; river along east. Motte at north-east with levelled bailey *c.*40m by 40m to its south and west, built for King John's 1212 campaign, soon burnt. Excavation suggests enclosure constructed post-1200, after bailey levelled. Foremost manor of medieval Powys, but status may date only from 13th century, under princes of Gwynedd, who may have manufactured association with early medieval princes of Powys. Early medieval site likely somewhere in area, however; church at Meifod important. Recent house platform at north-west may perpetuate earlier position; clay pit confuses south-west.

Domen Castell, Welshpool

OS 126 SJ 230074 R3

Motte, with bowling green occupying bailey, of which outer bank survives to height of about 2m. Probably built by Welsh princes of Powys some time before 1196, when captured and briefly held by joint force of English and Welsh.

Lower Luggy Motte, Berriew

OS 136 SJ 198022 R3

Impressive motte, suffering erosion from stream on north, where banded structure visible. Bailey platform on east, with low surrounding bank in parts. No history known.

Cefnllys Castle, Llandrindod Wells

OS 147 SO 088614 R4

Oval hillfort in commanding position on spur above bend in Ithon, reused as bailey of two successive mottes, first at north-east (damaged), then south-west. Built by Roger Mortimer *c.*1242, taken and destroyed by Llywelyn ap Gruffudd 1262. Repaired by English 1273-4, when second motte at south-west possibly built. Taken by Welsh rebels 1295. Made ready by Crown during Glyndŵr rising 1403; probably survived.

Castell Dinas, Talgarth

OS 161 SO 179301 R4

Multivallate hilltop hillfort with annexe to west, 6.5ha in total, commanding pass between Rhiangoll and Llynfi valleys. Reused as medieval castle, when innermost enclosure subdivided and hilltop defences generally strengthened. Remains of well and rectangular stone keep visible in northern part of site; traces of other buildings. Castle gateways on north-east and south-west; possible Iron Age entrance at north-east. Castle probably built by de Braose family before 1180; destroyed in Glyndŵr rising (early 15th century).

Summary of Dates

The prehistoric monuments in this book are ascribed to archaeological periods based on the conventional three-age system of Stone Age, Bronze Age and Iron Age. This system of classification has served archaeology well through the years, but has recently been criticised for giving too great an emphasis to the materials with which implements were made. Our study of settlements and burial places now makes us realise that the periods of greatest change and upheaval in society did not necessarily coincide with the adoption of technological innovations.

Accordingly, archaeologists now tend, when they can, to use absolute chronology for descriptive purposes. This has been made possible by the use of radiocarbon dating. Every living thing contains carbon 14, which, after death, decomposes at a known rate. This dating technique measures the amount of carbon 14 remaining in an organic substance, such as charcoal from a burial mound, in order to give a date for its death – the felling of the tree, for instance. Unfortunately, we now know that radiocarbon dating gives results that are too recent; these dates are expressed as dates 'bc', and can be corrected or 'calibrated' according to a published table to give a 'calendar' reading rather than a 'radiocarbon' date.

There are a number of problems involved both in the dating process itself and in the calibration, so that the dates produced cannot be regarded as more than a rough guide. For this reason, it was decided to retain the conventional three-age system for the basic classification of the monuments in the book; the time brackets given in the site headings are broad estimates only. Most of the specific dates given for prehistoric sites are calibrated radiocarbon dates (BC), unless otherwise indicated; uncalibrated dates are shown as 'bc'. From the Roman period onward, radiocarbon dating is not normally appropriate, and calendar years are always given.

The following table is designed to outline the basic chronology of the time span covered by the book, and may help to explain some of the terms used in the text.

Approximate Date	Archaeological Period	Characteristic Features
220,000 BC	Lower Palaeolithic (Old Stone Age)	Warm interglacial within Pleistocene Ice Age. First human evidence in Wales at Pontnewydd Cave (no. 1).
100,000 BC	Middle Palaeolithic	Mousterian hand-axes deposited in Coygan Cave, Dyfed.
26,000 BC	Early Upper Palaeolithic	Neanderthals replaced by modern humans; Aurignacian tool-types as at Ffynnon Beuno Cave (no. 2). Onset of final glaciation.
15,000 BC	Late Upper Palaeolithic	Ice retreating. Increasing evidence for human activity in S Wales caves; Creswellian tool types appear.
10,000 BC	Early Mesolithic (Middle Stone Age)	Nomadic hunter-gatherers use finely worked microlithic flints to tip arrows and spears for hunting.
6000 BC	Late Mesolithic	Seasonal settlements established, especially in coastal areas, by regional groups of peoples. Some evidence for manipulation of environment.
3500 bc (4500 BC)	Early Neolithic (New Stone Age)	First farmers arrive. Megalithic tombs built, especially in Black Mountains area. Pottery first used, polished stone axes traded. Much forest clearance.
2500 bc (3200 BC)	Late Neolithic	Communal tombs decline in importance. Ceremonial henges, cursus and round mounds built. Farming activity spreading to marginal uplands.
2000 bc (2400 BC)	Early Bronze Age	Beaker pottery and first metal objects appear. Burial mounds and cairns, stone circles and standing stones erected in upland and lowland areas of Clwyd and Powys.
1300 BC	Late Bronze Age	Population pressures, deterioration of climate and soil degradation lead to abandonment of uplands. Defensive settlements first appear in Clwyd and Powys.

Summary of Dates

Approximate Date	Archaeological Period	Characteristic Features
600 BC	Iron Age	Hillforts and small, circular defended farms built in increasing numbers. Iron tools first appear. Regional political groupings emerge.
AD 43	Roman Period	Wales conquered by Romans. Auxiliary forts established. Roads built. Clwyd and much of Powys not strongly Romanised; probably remained largely under military rule.
AD 410	Early Medieval Period	Roman withdrawal. Spread of Christianity. Development of Welsh kingdoms. Offa's and Wat's Dykes built by English. Viking raids, and settlement in NE Clwyd. Hywel Dda and, later, Gruffudd ap Llywelyn establish short-lived unity over parts of Wales.
AD 1066	Medieval Period	Normans invade Wales and establish lordships in E Clwyd, S Powys and along border. Welsh princes, especially of Gwynedd dynasty, gradually win back much lost ground, subject to overlordship of English king. Continental-style monasteries founded.
1276–83		Edward I conquers independent Wales.
1400–10		Owain Glyndŵr leads Welsh rising.
1485	Post-Medieval Period	Henry VII becomes first Tudor monarch.
1536–40		Dissolution of the monasteries by Henry VIII.
1536–43		Acts of Union, whereby a unified Wales merges politically with England.
1642–8		Civil War between Royalists and Parliamentarians brings many medieval castles back into use for the last time.

Glossary

Aisle Lateral division of nave or chancel of church, usually separated off by columns, and lying to one or both sides.

Antonine Roman dynasty in power AD 138–92.

Apse Semicircular or polygonal end to building or part thereof.

Apsidal Apse-shaped.

Arcade A row of arches usually supported on columns.

Augustinian Communities of clerics, often known as 'regular canons', following Rule of St Augustine.

Bailey Defended area, usually adjoining a motte or ringwork. Could contain additional accommodation, garrison, craft specialists, supplies and animals.

Barbican Outer defence protecting a gateway.

Barrow Mound of earth or earth and stones used, most often during Bronze Age, to cover burials.

Batter Sloping face near base of a defensive wall.

Bay (of church). Portion, usually of nave or chancel, between one pair of columns supporting a roof truss or vault and the next.

Beaker Type of pot characteristic of transitional period between Neolithic and Bronze Age; also name of this period.

Bellcote Structure to hold bells, usually built on to gable end or roof junctions of churches.

Benedictine Oldest monastic order. Monks followed Rule of St Benedict and wore black habits.

Berm Strip of ground between base of a wall or bank, and ditch.

Boss Decorative knob, often on vaulting ribs or sculptured crosses.

Burgess Property owner in medieval borough who usually held rights in that town.

Burh Anglo-Saxon defended settlement.

Buttery Store-room for wine and other beverages.

Buttress Projecting mass of masonry giving additional support to wall.

Cairn Mound of stones. Used to cover burials in Neolithic and Bronze Age; often had additional ceremonial functions. Clearance cairns are mounds created by clearing agricultural fields of stones.

Camera Private chamber.

Capital Top or head of a column, often decorated.

Carmelite Order of mendicant friars founded on Mount Carmel in 12th century, known as White Friars from colour of habit.

Cellarer Officer in charge of lay brethren in Cistercian monastery. Later effectively steward.

Chamfer Cut-away corner angle of square block or pillar.

Chancel Eastern part of church, which usually housed high altar and was reserved for clergy.

Chapter house Room where monks met daily to discuss business and to hear a chapter of the monastic rule.

Choir Part of church where services were sung, containing choir stalls.

Cist Stone-lined or slab-built grave.

Cistercian Movement of reformed Benedictine monks, established at Cîteaux in 1098. Known as White Monks from colour of habit; especially successful in Wales.

Cistern Storage tank for water.

Civitas, pl. ***Civitates*** Area of territory, similar to modern county, based on major town, used as main Roman administrative unit in lowland Britain. Often reflected earlier tribal areas.

Clavicula, pl. ***Claviculae*** Roman method of defending entrance, with curved extension of one side of bank to rear of gap, often used to force anyone entering to turn their unshielded right side towards the defenders; would frustrate a charge.

Cloister Four-sided enclosure, usually at centre of monastery, with covered walk along each side, used for study.

Constable Governor of castle.

Corbel Projecting stone used for support, often for floor or roof timbers.

Corduroy Logs laid side by side across width of Roman turf/clay rampart to form foundation at base.

Counterscarp Slope, bank or wall on outer side of ditch.

Crenellations Also known as battlements. Parapet of wall or tower equipped with openings ('crenelles') and solid walling ('merlons'); used for defence by archers.

Cropmarks Differential colour of crop reflecting uneven growth due to presence of buried features. Raised features show as parched areas, ripening early, pits and ditches support lusher growth ripening later. Reveals plan seen from air. In grass, same effect often called parch-marks.

Cross potent Cross with T-bars across ends of its limbs.

Crossing Central space at intersection of east–west axis and north–south transepts of church. Tower often stands above.

Crosslet Miniature cross, sometimes incised across arm-end of larger cross.

Cross-slab Shaped stone slab on which is carved, in relief, a cross and often other ornament.

Cruciform Cross-shaped.

Crypt Chamber beneath main floor of church, used for burial or as chapel.

Cup-mark Small hollow cut into stone. Probably prehistoric, and of ritual significance, but not well understood.

Cursus, pl. **Cursus** Two parallel ditches, perhaps originally with banks; possibly a ceremonial way.

Curtain Wall, often strengthened with towers, enclosing courtyard of castle.

Dominican Order of preaching friars and nuns founded by St Dominic, known as Black Friars from colour of habit.

Dormitory Sleeping quarters of monastery.

Drawbridge Wooden bridge which could be raised if necessary at entrance across defensive ditch.

Drystone wall Stone wall built without mortar or clay.

Embrasure Splayed opening, either in parapet for defensive use by archers, or in walls for windows.

Exchequer Finance office of castle.

False-crest Position often used for barrows or standing stones; appears on skyline from certain angles.

Flavian Roman dynasty in power AD 69–96.

Folly Building constructed as landscape feature, often to look like ruin.

Four-poster Commonly found Iron Age building plan, usually slightly rectangular. Six-posters also known. Usually assumed to be for storage, probably granaries, but many other possibilities.

Fretwork Celtic motif of classical derivation, used in decoration of Celtic crosses.

Gildas Moral commentator writing in early 6th century AD. Includes useful historical details.

Hafod, pl ***hafodau*** Summer grazing base on upland pastures.

Hafoty pl ***hafotai*** Summer dwelling attached to the *hafod*.

Haft Handle to which stone or metal tool is attached; also act of attaching.

Hall Room in castle used for administration of estates and justice, and for entertainment on important occasions. Many castles would also have smaller hall for less formal use.

Hall house House consisting of large main

hall, with ancillary rooms on two floors at either end.

Henge Non-defensive circular earthwork with bank and ditch and one or more entrances, apparently used for ceremonial purposes during late Neolithic period.

Hillfort Characteristic defended site of Iron Age.

Hollow way Roadway, often of some antiquity, worn into a cutting by passage of traffic. Unmetalled, at least in early stages.

Hundred English medieval administrative division.

Inhumation Burial of uncremated body.

Interlace Celtic decorative motif derived from late classical art. Patterns used on crosses include plaitwork and knotwork.

Jamb Straight side of doorway or window.

Keep Main, strong, usually free-standing, tower of castle.

Kissing gate Gate for pedestrians only, with C-shaped fenced refuge around free end to allow passage; swing limited to within fence of refuge. Difficult for pushchairs (evict occupant!) and impossible for wheelchairs.

Lancet Plain slender window with pointed arch.

Latin cross Upright cross with lower arm longer than the others, distinguished from equal-armed Greek cross.

Leland (John; 1506?–52) King's Antiquary under Henry VIII. Travelled widely in England and Wales recording features of antiquarian interest.

Levallois technique Method of producing stone flake tool by preparing tortoise-shaped core such that finished tool is produced by single further blow.

Lhuyd (Edward; 1660–1709) Curator of Ashmolean Museum (Oxford). Carried out extensive field survey in Wales for revision of Camden's *Britannia* (first published 1586).

Lintel Supporting wooden beam or stone over opening in wall.

Lordship Area ruled by lord under supremacy of king.

Marches Border or frontier, especially used for the south and east areas of Wales under Norman control.

Marching camp *See* temporary camp.

Metalled (of road or track). Firmly surfaced with closely packed chippings or tarmac.

Monolith Single standing stone.

Motte Mound of earth constructed to support tower and palisade.

Mullion Vertical bar between window openings.

Multivallate Of hillfort, having multiple defensive lines.

Murder hole Openings above and immediately in front of castle gate, to enable liquids to be poured on to any fire lit there and on to attackers; could also be used for missiles.

Nave Portion of church extending from crossing to west end.

Northumbria Early medieval kingdom extending from Ouse to Tweed in north-east England.

Ogam Alphabet composed of strokes across angle(s) of a stone, probably originating in Ireland before 5th century AD.

Oriel window Projecting, curved or polygonal window.

Orthostat Upright stone.

Palisade Strong timber fence.

Parlour Only room in monastery in which conversation was permitted.

Permissive path Path opened to the public by courtesy of landowner, not legally a public right of way.

Pillow mound Specially constructed, often supervised, area for rabbits, bred for food and fur, to burrow in. Usually rectangular, with surrounding ditch (artificial burrows sometimes provided). Usually 14th or 15th century.

Piscina Basin with drain, usually set into church wall by altar, for washing vessels used for Mass.

Portcullis Strong wood or iron grille which could be lowered in grooves in wall of castle gate passage for additional defence.

Postern Small gateway, subsidiary to the main entrance.

Promontory fort Hillfort formed by defending neck of natural promontory, inland or coastal.

Rampart Defensive bank or structure giving protection and height to defenders.

Refectory Dining-hall of monastery, also known as *frater*.

Relief Of carving: design rising out of flat surface. Low relief involves quite shallow carving, high relief stands out much further.

Revetment Timber or stonework built to give support to side of bank or ditch.

Ringwork Early castle type consisting of defensive enclosure, usually circular, with surrounding bank and external ditch.

Rule Code followed by religious order. Most important in medieval Europe were those of St Benedict and St Augustine.

Runic Inscription consisting of runes, an alphabet used by Vikings.

Sacristy Room for storage of vestments and sacred vessels.

Sally port Small entrance in castle wall allowing force out to outflank attackers.

Severan Roman dynasty in power AD 193–235.

Shell-keep Defensive stone wall built around perimeter of motte.

Solar Lord's private chamber in castle.

Temporary camp Fort, quite large but with very slight defences, used by Roman army on campaign.

Tenon Boss or lump in stone or wood construction, made to fit into a hollow or mortice.

Tithes Tax payable to church; one tenth of agricultural produce.

Torc Ornamental neck-ring with gap between ends. Means of wealth storage in later Bronze Age and Iron Age.

Tracery Decorative stonework in upper parts of windows or on walls.

Transept Short transverse arms of cruciform church, orientated north-south.

Transhumance Seasonal removal of livestock to upland pasture some distance from winter base.

Truss A-shaped timber roof support; several needed to complete roof.

Univallate Of hillfort; having single defensive line.

Vault Arched stone roof. A barrel-vault is a vault of semicircular section.

Vicus, pl. ***Vici*** Trading settlement outside Roman fort, providing entertainment and goods for purchase. Could also house soldiers' families (illicit in early part of period).

Wall-plate Timber or stone at top of wall to provide seating for roof.

Wall-walk Passage behind parapet of castle or town wall, used for defence.

Ward A courtyard within walls of castle.

Wattle Infill of woven twigs between main timbers of building, often covered with daub to produce smooth finish.

Bibliography

Guidebooks

The monuments in the care of Cadw and other conservation bodies often have guidebooks which give a more detailed history and tour of the site. Monuments marked with an asterisk should have the guides for sale at the reception areas.

*Basingwerk Abbey D M Robinson, Official Guidebook (Cardiff 1996).
Bronllys Castle J B Smith and J K Knight, Official Guidebook (Cardiff 1981).
Castell Dinas Brân Official Guidebook, Clwyd County Council (Mold 1990).
*Chirk Castle Official Guidebook, National Trust (London 1992).
*Denbigh Castle L A S Butler, Cadw Guidebook (Cardiff 1990).
Flint Castle and Ewloe Castle D F Renn and R Avent, Cadw Guidebook (Cardiff 1995).
Montgomery Castle J D K Lloyd and J K Knight, Official Guidebook (Cardiff 1973).
*The Church of Merthyr Issui at Patricio (Partrishow) A Reed, Church Guidebook (Brecon 1991)
National Trail Guide: Offa's Dyke Path South, Chepstow to Knighton Ernie and Kathy Kay and Mark Richards, rev. edn (London 1994).
National Trail Guide: Offa's Dyke Path North, Knighton to Prestatyn Ernie and Kathy Kay and Mark Richards (London 1995).
*Powis Castle Official Guidebook, National Trust (London 1991).
*Rhuddlan Castle A J Taylor, Cadw Guidebook (Cardiff 1987).
*Rug Chapel, Llangar Church and Gwydir Uchaf Chapel W N Yates, Cadw Guidebook (Cardiff 1993).
*Saint Winefride and Her Well T Charles-Edwards (Holywell n d)
*Tretower Court and Castle D M Robinson, Cadw Guidebook (Cardiff 1996).
*Valle Crucis Abbey and The Pillar of Eliseg D H Evans and J K Knight, Cadw Guidebook, 2nd edition (Cardiff 1995).

Further Reading

This is a very selective list of general books which give further information about aspects of Welsh archaeology and history.

General

Arnold, C J, *The Archaeology of Montgomeryshire to AD 1300* (Welshpool 1990).
Caseldine, A, *Environmental Archaeology in Wales*, (Lampeter 1990).
Lloyd Jones, M, *Society and Settlement in Wales and the Marches, 500 BC to AD 1100* (2 vols, British Archaeological Reports 121, Oxford 1984).
Manley, J, Grenter, S and Gale, F (eds), *The Archaeology of Clwyd* (Mold 1991).
Stanford, S C, *The Archaeology of the Welsh Marches* (London 1980).

'rehistory

radley, R, *The Social Foundations of Prehistoric Britain* (London 1984).
url, A, *The Stone Circles of the British Isles* (London 1976).
unliffe, B W, *Iron Age Communities in Britain* 3rd edn (London 1991).
aniel, G E, *The Prehistoric Chamber Tombs of England and Wales* (Cambridge 1950).
arvill, T, *Prehistoric Britain* (London 1987).
orde-Johnston, J, *Hillforts of the Iron Age in England and Wales* (Liverpool 1976).
owler, P J, *The Farming of Prehistoric Britain* (Cambridge 1983).
logg, A H A, *A Guide to the Hill-forts of Britain* (London 1975).
immons, I and Tooley, M (eds), *The Environment in British Prehistory* (London 1981).
aylor, J A (ed.), *Culture and Environment in Prehistoric Wales*, (British Archaeological Reports 76, Oxford 1980).

?oman

urnham, B C and Davies, J L (eds), *Conquest, Co-existence and Change: Recent Work in Roman Wales* (*Trivium* 25, Lampeter 1990).
avies, J L, 'Roman military deployment in Wales and the Marches from Claudius to the Antonines', in Hanson, W S and Keppie, L J F (eds), *Roman Frontier Studies 1979* (British Archaeological Reports S71, Oxford 1980), part i, pp 255–77.
avies, J L, 'Roman military deployment in Wales and the Marches from Pius to Theodosius I', in Maxfield, V A and Dobson, M J (eds), *Roman Frontier Studies 1989* (Exeter 1991), pp 52–7.
rere, S S, *Britannia: A History of Roman Britain* 3rd edn (London 1987).
›hnson, A, *Roman Forts* (London 1983).
1argary, I D, *Roman Roads in Britain* 3rd edn (London 1973).
Aillett, M, *The Romanization of Britain* (Cambridge 1990).
alway, P, *The Oxford Illustrated History of Roman Britain* (Oxford 1993).
odd, M, *Roman Britain 55 BC – AD 400* (London 1981).
Vebster, G, *The Cornovii* 2nd edn (Stroud 1991).

:arly Medieval

)avies, W, *Wales in the Early Middle Ages* (Leicester 1982).
:dwards, N and Lane, A (eds), *Early Medieval Settlements in Wales AD 400–1100* (Bangor and Cardiff 1988).
'ox, C, *Offa's Dyke* (London 1955).
ones, G R J, 'Post-Roman Wales', in Finberg, H P R (ed), *The Agrarian History of England and Wales, Volume I ii, AD 43–1042* (Cambridge 1972), 283–382.
Jash-Williams, V E, *Early Christian Monuments of Wales* (Cardiff 1950).

Medieval

vent, J R, *Cestyll Tywysogion Gwynedd: Castles of the Princes of Gwynedd* (Cardiff 1988).
Butler, L and Given-Wilson, C, *Medieval Monasteries of Great Britain* (London 1979).
)avies, R R, *Conquest, Coexistence and Change: Wales 1063–1415* (in 1991 paperback as *The Age of Conquest: Wales 1063–1415*) (Oxford 1987).
)avis, P R, *Castles of the Welsh Princes* (Swansea 1988).
Gilchrist, R and Mytum, H (eds), *The Archaeology of Rural Monasteries* British Archaeological Reports 203 (Oxford 1989).
Kenyon, J R, *Medieval Fortifications* (Leicester 1990).

King, D J C, *The Castle in England and Wales* (London 1988).
Knowles, D and Hadcock, R N, *Medieval Religious Houses: England and Wales* 2nd edn (London 1971).
Norton, C and Park, D, *Cistercian Art and Architecture in the British Isles* (Cambridge 1986).
Owen, E, *Old Stone Crosses of the Vale of Clwyd and Neighbouring Parishes* (London and Oswestry 1886).
Renn, D F, *Norman Castles in Britain* 2nd edn (London 1973).
Smith, P, *Houses of the Welsh Countryside: A Study in Historical Geography* 2nd edn (London 1988).
Taylor, A J, *The Welsh Castles of Edward I* (London 1986).
Williams, G, *The Welsh Church from Conquest to Reformation* 2nd edn (Cardiff 1976).

General Reference

The Royal Commission on Ancient and Historical Monuments in Wales (RCAHMW publishes county volumes or 'inventories' which give detailed descriptions of al monuments known at the time of publication. Ellis Davies' volumes on Flintshire and Denbighshire follow a similar format, and provide a useful supplement to the somewhat dated inventories for these counties; Bowen and Gresham do much the same for Merioneth. The *Buildings of Wales* series provides additional architectura material. All these volumes may be found in good reference libraries.

Bowen, E G and Gresham, C A, 1967, *History of Merioneth, Vol I*, Dolgellau.
Davies, E, 1929, *The Prehistoric and Roman Remains of Denbighshire*, Cardiff.
Davies, E, 1949, *The Prehistoric and Roman Remains of Flintshire*, Cardiff.
Haslam, R, 1979, *The Buildings of Wales: Powys (Montgomeryshire, Radnorshire, Breconshire)*, London.
Hubbard, E, 1986, *The Buildings of Wales: Clwyd (Denbighshire and Flintshire)*, London.
RCAHMW, *An Inventory of the Ancient Monuments of Wales and Monmouthshire*:
I – County of Montgomery (London 1911)
II – County of Flint (London 1912)
III – County of Radnor (London 1913)
IV – County of Denbigh (London 1914)
VI – County of Merioneth (London 1921)
RCAHMW, *An Inventory of the Ancient Monuments in Brecknock (Brycheiniog): The Prehistoric and Roman Remains Part ii: Hill-forts and Roman Remains* (London 1986).

Gazetteer References

These are the references from the site entries in the gazetteer. They are intended to help the interested visitor find out more about specific monuments. A few of the gazetteer references are to works of more general interest which will be found in the 'Further Reading' or 'General Reference' sections above, and are not repeated here.

Bibliography

Alcock, L, 1964, 'The defences and gates of Castell Collen auxiliary fort', *Archaeologia Cambrensis*, 113, pp 64–96.

Aldhouse Green, S, 1991, 'The Palaeolithic and its quaternary context', in Manley, Grenter and Gale 1991, pp 26–46.

Allen, D, 1979, 'Excavations at Hafod y Nant Criafolen, Brenig Valley, Clwyd, 1973–74', *Post-Medieval Archaeology*, 13, pp 1–60, for no. 132, Hen Ddinbych.

Arnold, C J, 1985, 'Powis Castle: recent excavations and observations', *Montgomeryshire Collections*, 73, pp 30–7.

Arnold, C J, 1986, 'Powis Castle: the outer bailey', *Montgomeryshire Collections*, 74, pp 70–2.

Arnold, C J, 1993, 'Powis Castle: the development of the structure', *Montgomeryshire Collections*, 81, pp 97–109.

Barker, P A and Higham, R, 1982, *Hen Domen, Montgomery, Volume One*, London.

Barker, P A and Higham, R, 1988, 'Hen Domen', *Current Archaeology*, 10, pp 137–42.

Blockley, K, 1989, *Prestatyn 1984–5*, British Archaeological Reports 210, Oxford.

Boyd Dawkins, W, 1901, 'On the cairn and sepulchral cave at Gop, near Prestatyn', *Archaeological Journal*, 58, pp 322–41.

Britnell, J, 1989, *Caersws Vicus, Powys*, British Archaeological Reports 205, Oxford.

Britnell, W J and Savory, H N, 1984, *Gwernvale and Penywyrlod: Two Neolithic Long Cairns in the Black Mountains of Brecknock*, Cambrian Archaeological Association Monographs 2, Bangor.

Burl, A, 1976, *The Stone Circles of the British Isles*, London.

Butler, L A, 1987, 'Holt Castle, John de Warenne and Chastellion', in Kenyon, J R and Avent J R (eds), *Castles in Wales and the Marches*, Cardiff, pp 105–24.

Butler, L A, 1989, 'Dolforwyn Castle, Montgomery, Powys: First Report, the Excavations 1981–1986', *Archaeologia Cambrensis*, 138, pp 78–98.

Butler, L A, 1990, 'Dolforwyn Castle, Powys', *Current Archaeology*, 10, pp 418–23.

Corcoran, J X W P, 1969, 'The Cotswold-Severn Group, 1 and 2', chapters in Powell, T G E *et al.*, *Megalithic Enquiries in the West of Britain*, Liverpool.

Crampton, C B and Webley, D, 1966, 'A Section through the Mynydd Troed long barrow, Brecknock', *Bulletin of the Board of Celtic Studies*, 22, pp 71–7.

Edwards, N, 1991, 'The Dark Ages', in Manley, Grenter and Gale 1991, pp 129–41.

Evelyn-White, H G, 1914, 'Excavations at Castell Collen, Llandrindod Wells', *Archaeologia Cambrensis*, 69 (6th ser vol 14), pp 1–58.

Fox, C, 1926, 'The Ysceifiog Circle and Barrow, Flintshire', *Archaeologia Cambrensis*, 81 (7th ser vol 6), pp 48–85.

Frere, S S and St Joseph, J K S, 1983, *Roman Britain from the Air*, Cambridge.

Grimes, W F, 1963, 'The Stone Circles and Related Monuments of Wales', in Foster, I Ll and Alcock, L (eds), *Culture and Environment*, London, pp 93–152.

Grinsell, L V, 1981, 'The later history of Ty Illtud', *Archaeologia Cambrensis*, 130, pp 131–9.

Guilbert, G C, 1975, 'Moel y Gaer 1973: an area excavation on the defences', *Antiquity*, 49, pp 109–17.

Guilbert, G C, 1976, 'Moel y Gaer (Rhosesmor) 1972–1973: An Area Excavation on the Interior', in Harding, D W (ed), *Hillforts*, London, pp 303–17.

Guilbert, G C, 1981, 'Ffridd Faldwyn', *Archaeological Journal*, 138, pp 20–2.

Hemp, W J, 1928, 'The Castle of Ewloe and the Welsh Castle Plan', *Y Cymmrodor*, 39, pp 4–19.

Hermitage Day, E, 1911, 'The Cistercian Abbey of Cwm Hir', *Archaeologia Cambrensis*, 66 (6th ser vol 11), pp 9–25.

Higham, R A and Barker, P A, 1992, *Timber Castles*, London.

Hogg, A H A, 1975, *A Guide to the Hill-forts of Britain*, London.

Hogg, A H A and Jones, G D B, 1968, 'The Roman Marching Camp at Esgairperfedd (Radnor)', *Bulletin of the Board of Celtic Studies*, 22, pp 274–6.
Jarrett, M J, and Nash-Williams, V E, 1969, *The Roman Frontier in Wales*, Cardiff.
Jervoise, E, 1936, *The Ancient Bridges of Wales and Western England*, London.
Jones, N W, 1993, 'Caersws Roman Fort and Vicus, Montgomeryshire, Powys, 1984–92', *Montgomeryshire Collections*, 81, pp 15–96.
King, D J C, 1961, 'The Castles of Breconshire', *Brycheiniog*, 7, pp 92–3.
King, D J C, 1974, 'Two Castles in Northern Powys: Dinas Brân and Caergwrle', *Archaeologia Cambrensis*, 123, pp 113–39.
King, D J C, 1983, *Castellarium Anglicanum*, London.
Knight, J K, 1992, 'Excavations at Montgomery Castle, Part I', *Archaeologia Cambrensis*, 141, pp 97–180.
Knight, J K, 1993, 'Excavations at Montgomery Castle, Part II: The Finds (Metalwork)', *Archaeologia Cambrensis*, 142, pp 182–242.
Lewis, D P and Longueville Jones, S, 1857, 'Tumulus at Berriew, Montgomeryshire' and 'Maen Beuno', *Archaeologia Cambrensis*, 12 (3rd ser vol 3), pp 296–9 and 299–301.
Lynch, F, 1993, *Excavations in the Brenig Valley*, Cambrian Archaeological Monographs 5, Bangor.
Manley, J, 1994, 'Excavations at Caergwrle Castle, Clwyd, North Wales: 1988–1990', *Medieval Archaeology*, XXXVIII, pp 83–133.
Morgan, W E T and Marshall, G, 1921, 'Excavation of a long barrow at Llanigon, Co Brecon', *Archaeologia Cambrensis*, 76 (7th ser vol 1), pp 296–9.
Musson, C R and Spurgeon, C J, 1988, 'Cwrt Llechryd, Llanelwedd: an Unusual Moated Site in Central Powys', *Medieval Archaeology*, 32, pp 97–109.
Musson, C R, Britnell, W J and Smith, A G, 1991, *The Breiddin Hillfort*, Council for British Archaeology Research Report 76, London.
Nash-Williams, V E, 1950, *The Early Christian Monuments of Wales*, Cardiff.
Newman, C W, 1981, 'Castell Collen Roman Fort, near Llandrindod Wells: a Summary of Present Information', *Transactions of the Radnorshire Society*, 51, pp 64–7.
Palmer, A N, 1907, 'The Town of Holt in County Denbigh: its Castle, Church, Franchise and Demesne. Chapter III – Norden's survey of 1620', *Archaeologia Cambrensis*, 62 (6th ser vol 7), pp 389–434.
Pratt, D, 1978, 'Tomen y Rhodwydd', *Archaeologia Cambrensis*, 127, pp 130–2.
Price, G V, 1952, *Valle Crucis Abbey*, Liverpool.
Pryce, F N, 1914, 'Excavations at Cae Gaer, Llangurig', *Archaeologia Cambrensis*, 69 (6th ser vol 14), pp 205–20.
Putnam, W G, 1962, 'Excavations at Pen y crocbren', *Montgomeryshire Collections*, 57, pp 33–41.
Radford, C A R, 1982, 'The Cistercian Abbey of Cwmhir, Radnorshire', *Archaeologia Cambrensis*, 131, pp 58–76.
St John O'Neil, B H, 1936, 'The Castle of Caereinion', *Montgomeryshire Collections*, 44, pp 39–45.
St John O'Neil, B H, 1937, 'Excavations at Breiddin Hill Camp, Montgomeryshire, 1933–35', *Archaeologia Cambrensis*, 92, pp 86–128.
St John O'Neil, B H, 1942, 'Excavations at Ffridd Faldwyn Camp, Montgomery, 1937–39', *Archaeologia Cambrensis*, 97, pp 1–57.
Shoesmith, R, 1980, 'Llangar Church', *Archaeologia Cambrensis*, 129, pp 64–132.
Spurgeon, C J, 1961, 'An Early Christian Stone from Carno (Mont.)', *Archaeologia Cambrensis*, 110, pp 155–6.

Spurgeon, C J, 1979, 'Builth Castle', *Brycheiniog*, 18, pp 47–59.

Thom, A, Thom, A S and Burl, A, 1980, *Megalithic Rings*, British Archaeological Reports 81, Oxford.

Thomas, J E, 1872, 'An Account of the Opening of a Tumulus known as 'Twyn y Beddau' near Hay', *Archaeologia Cambrensis*, 33 (4th ser vol 9), pp 1–4.

Wheeler, R E M, 1926, *The Roman Fort near Brecon*, *Y Cymmrodor*, 37, whole volume.

Williams, S W, 1895, 'The Cistercian Abbey of Cwmhir, Radnorshire', *Transactions of the Honourable Society of Cymmrodorion*, 1894–5, pp 61–9

Acknowledgements

This book would never have come into being without the help of numerous other people. Chief among them must be the series editor Sian Rees, who persuaded me to write it in the first place and who has given useful feedback and moral support at intervals throughout its gestation; Cadw's detailed records of scheduled ancient monuments, largely her brainchild, provided an invaluable starting point in the pursuit of references for the sites. David Robinson and Diane Williams of Cadw's publications department willingly gave up their time at a moment's notice on several occasions to advise and assist with both text and illustrations. Peter Lawrence of the Welsh Office cartographic drawing office skilfully produced the line drawings from a variety of rather sketchy originals. Numerous friends were kind enough to read and provide valuable comment upon either individual site entries or entire chapters: Stephen Aldhouse Green, Chris Arnold, Richard Avent, Philip Barker, Bill Britnell, Lawrence Butler, Jeff Davies, Graeme Guilbert, Bob Higham, Jeremy Huggett, Nigel Jones, Frances Lynch, John Manley, Chris Musson, David Robinson, Jack Spurgeon and Gwyn Thomas. Needless to say, any remaining mistakes are my responsibility.

Chris Musson of the Royal Commission on Ancient and Historical Monuments in Wales gave considerable assistance in the selection of air photographs, while numerous others also assisted in drawing the illustrations together: Bill Britnell, Caroline Earwood and Chris Martin at the Clwyd–Powys Archaeological Trust; Chris Kenyon, Peter Humphries and Edward Holland at Cadw; Hilary Malaws, Siân Spink and Gareth Edwards at the National Monuments Record for Wales; Elizabeth Walker at the National Museum of Wales; André Berry at the Clwyd Archaeology Service and David Wilson and his staff at the Cambridge University Committee for Aerial Photography; Peter Dorling, Kathleen Pople, Louis Hurley and Paul Stefford all helped in locating the reconstruction drawing of Crickhowell Castle (no. 130). Thanks must also go to Ruth Bowden at HMSO for her work during the editorial stages of the volume. Many sites could not have been included without the co-operation of the farmers or agents involved, and I should like to express my heartfelt thanks to all of them. One of the pleasures of such a project as this is the practical side, and the friendly hospitality of Lygan-y-wern, Pentre Halkyn, Gales of Llangollen and Greenfields, Kerry rendered my fieldwork all the more enjoyable.

Finally, and perhaps most of all, I must express my gratitude to my husband, Barry Burnham, for putting up with my absences and preoccupation with such patience and understanding. Without his unfailing support, the book would undoubtedly never have been completed.

Sources of Illustrations

Most of the line drawings were produced by staff of Cartographic Services, Welsh Office. Several were redrawn with amendments using plans, published and unpublished, from elsewhere: nos 99, 100, 118, 126, 129 and 146 (Crown copyright plans from Welsh Office or Cadw guidebooks); nos 33 and 35 (Grimes 1963); nos 42 and 65 (Royal Commission on Ancient and Historical Monuments in Wales); no. 68 (Jones 1993); no. 106 (Butler 1987); and no. 141 (Liverpool School of Building).

I am most grateful to the National Museum of Wales and the University of Wales Press for permission to reproduce from Nash-Williams 1950: nos 75, 80, 81, 83 and 84; to Jack Spurgeon and the editor of *Archaeologia Cambrensis* for permission to reproduce no. 78; to the National Museum of Wales for permission to reproduce the reconstruction drawings in the introductory sections to chapters 1 (Casseli), 3 (first drawing, Jenkins) and 4 (Sorrell); to Clwyd Archaeology Service, Clwyd County Council, for permission to reproduce those in the introductory sections to chapters 3 (second drawing), 5 and 7 (second drawing) (all drawn by Timothy Morgan); the reconstruction drawings in chapters 7 (first drawing, Ball) and 8 (Jones-Jenkins) are the copyright of Cadw, Welsh Historic Monuments. The reconstruction drawing of no. 130 is reproduced by kind permission of the artist, Louis Hurley, and the drawing of no. 150 comes from a collection in the National Monuments Record in the Royal Commission on Ancient and Historical Monuments in Wales.

Copyright acknowledgements are due to the following photographic sources: National Monuments Record (as above): nos 48*, 54*, 61*, 64*, 72*, 113*, 115, 116*, 121*, 124*, 132 and 140 (* indicates photographs from the Aerial Photography section of the NMR). Clwyd–Powys Archaeological Trust: nos 8 (film 40 neg. 32), 11 (86-MB-539), 21 (85-6-13), 23 (90-MB-0251), 27 (86-MB-858), 29 (92-MB-0249), 45 (89-MB-514), 49 (88-MB-357), 50 (84-MB-315), 55 (89-MB-275), 56 (90-MB-0848), 58 (87-15-6), 69 (92-MB-0259), 70 (86-7-22), 71 (89-MB-154), 105 (90-MB-0850), 109 (84-32-25), 112 (87-MB-155), 114 (90-MB-0356), 120 (86-MB-150), 125 (92-MB-0199), 139 (87-MB-886) and the back cover (83-C-0244). Cadw, Welsh Historic Monuments: nos 74, 77, 100, 102, 103, 118, 129, 133, 145, 146. National Museum of Wales: no. 1, introductory section to chapter 2 (second picture) and no. 76. Cambridge University Committee for Aerial Photography: nos 63 and 67. British Museum: the Mold Cape (introductory section to chapter 2, first picture).

Index

Note: gazetteer entries are listed in bold, by their **page** numbers. Date ranges in brackets indicate the reign of the individual concerned. In most cases only a date of death is given. In some cases '*fl.*' (*floruit*) indicates a date or dates when the person is known to have been active. Most figures from the 19th and 20th centuries are not dated.

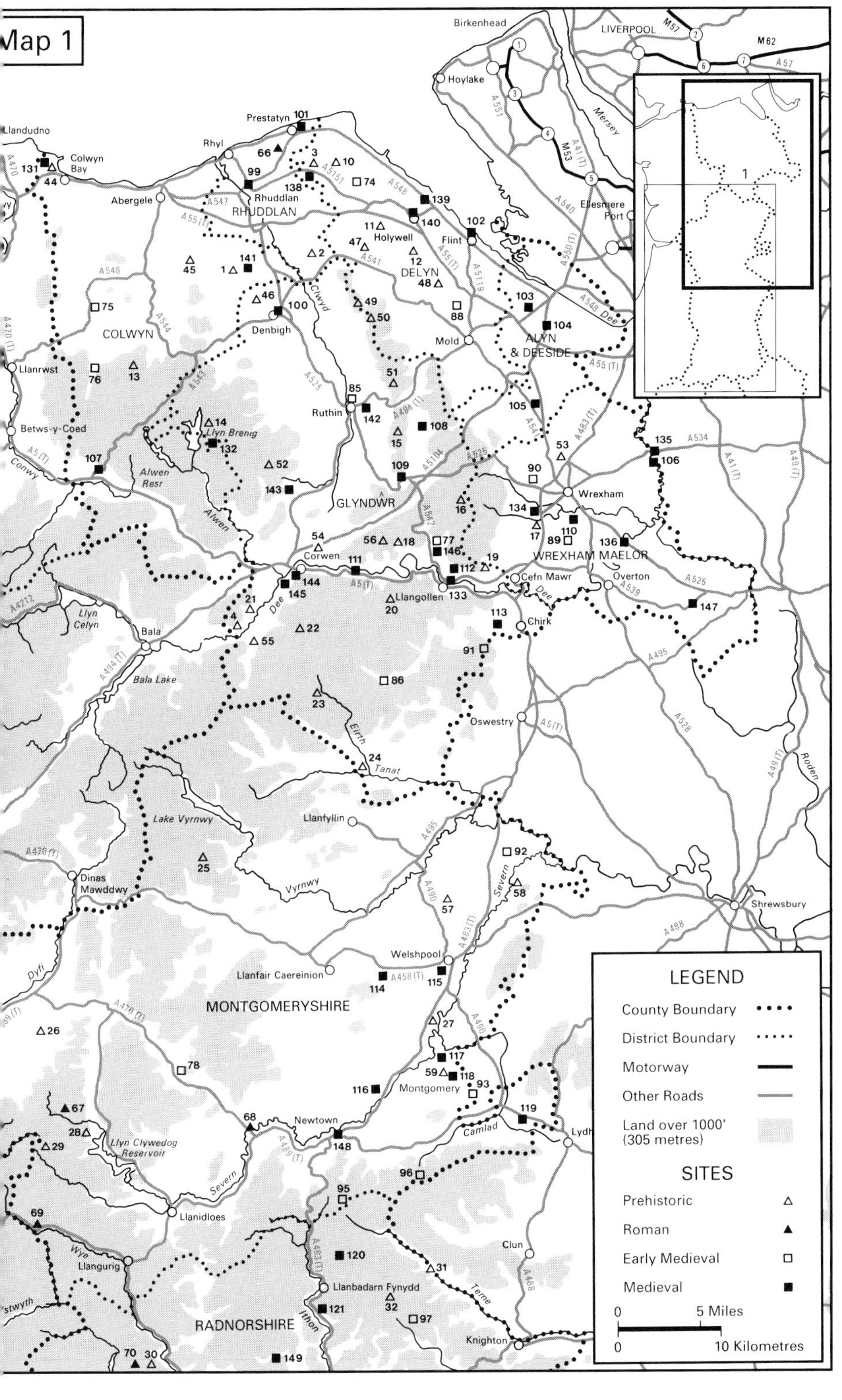

Map 1
LEGEND
County Boundary
District Boundary
Motorway
Other Roads
Land over 1000' (305 metres)
SITES
Prehistoric
Roman
Early Medieval
Medieval
0 5 Miles
0 10 Kilometres
RHUDDLAN
DELYN
COLWYN
ALYN & DEESIDE
GLYNDWR
WREXHAM MAELOR
MONTGOMERYSHIRE
RADNORSHIRE
Birkenhead
LIVERPOOL
Hoylake
Ellesmere Port
Llandudno
Colwyn Bay
Prestatyn
Rhyl
Abergele
Rhuddlan
Holywell
Flint
Mold
Denbigh
Llanrwst
Betws-y-Coed
Ruthin
Wrexham
Corwen
Llangollen
Cefn Mawr
Overton
Chirk
Bala
Oswestry
Llanfyllin
Dinas Mawddwy
Welshpool
Llanfair Caereinion
Montgomery
Newtown
Llanidloes
Llangurig
Clun
Llanbadarn Fynydd
Knighton
Shrewsbury
Lake Vyrnwy
Llyn Brenig
Alwen Resr
Llyn Celyn
Bala Lake
Llyn Clywedog Reservoir
Mersey
Dee
Clwyd
Conwy
Alwen
Eirth
Tanat
Vyrnwy
Severn
Dyfi
Camlad
Wye
Teme
Ithon
Roden

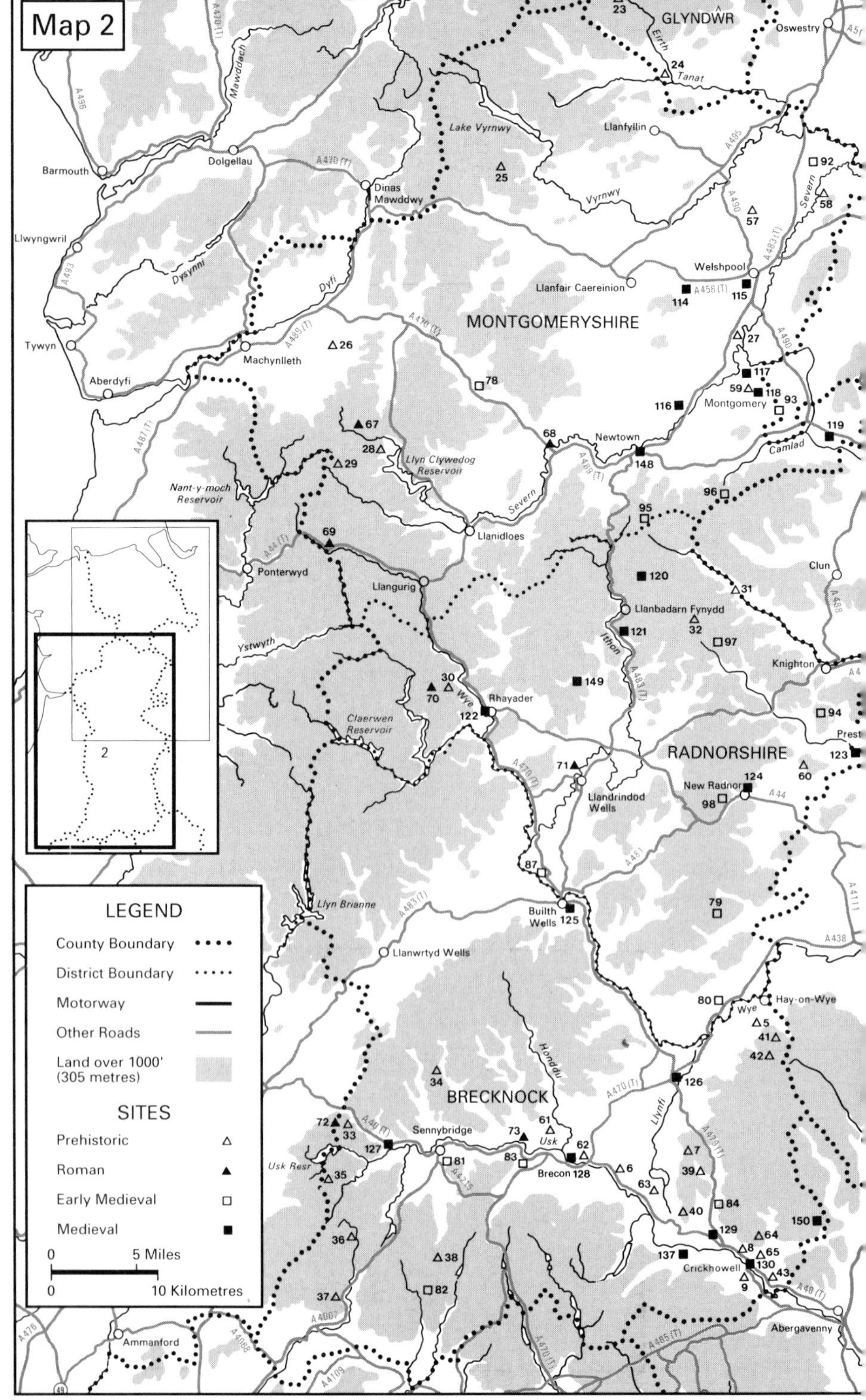
Map 2
LEGEND
County Boundary
District Boundary
Motorway
Other Roads
Land over 1000' (305 metres)
SITES
Prehistoric
Roman
Early Medieval
Medieval
0 5 Miles
0 10 Kilometres
GLYNDŴR
MONTGOMERYSHIRE
RADNORSHIRE
BRECKNOCK
Oswestry
Llanfyllin
Barmouth
Dolgellau
Dinas Mawddwy
Llwyngwril
Lake Vyrnwy
Welshpool
Llanfair Caereinion
Tywyn
Machynlleth
Aberdyfi
Montgomery
Newtown
Llyn Clywedog Reservoir
Nant-y-moch Reservoir
Llanidloes
Ponterwyd
Llangurig
Clun
Llanbadarn Fynydd
Knighton
Rhayader
Claerwen Reservoir
New Radnor
Llandrindod Wells
Builth Wells
Llyn Brianne
Llanwrtyd Wells
Hay-on-Wye
Sennybridge
Usk Resr
Brecon
Crickhowell
Abergavenny
Ammanford
Mawddach
Dysynni
Dyfi
Vyrnwy
Tanat
Eirth
Severn
Camlad
Ystwyth
Wye
Ithon
Hondu
Llynfi
Usk